Free Society and Moral Crisis

Free Society
& Moral Crisis

by ROBERT COOLEY ANGELL

Foreword by
Reinhold Niebuhr

ANN ARBOR

THE UNIVERSITY OF MICHIGAN PRESS

To

Jim and Peggie
Sally and Don

Foreword

This great study is the fruit of wisdom, and of a vast erudition. It deals with moral and social integration in a free society. What is more, it deals with the peculiar problems of a technical society such as ours—its rapid social change, the anonymity of its urban community, the peculiar hazards to which disintegrated sections of its cities expose the life of youth. For these problems of technical civilization the ingenuity and resiliency of a free society are in part the cure—but in part a free society aggravates the moral difficulties of technical civilization.

Angell takes a hard look at the moral problems of our pluralistic society which has not one but many value systems. These, whether religious or secular, are not entirely incompatible. For they are overarched by the ultimate values of a free society, which stresses the dignity of the individual and the uncoerced harmony of the community. On these values, the three great religious traditions and secular idealism of modern culture are all in general agreement. Yet the pluralism of our culture prevents the simple integration of individual life which more homogeneous societies achieve.

However, this is not a political study, analyzing the forces and factors that make for justice and order. It is a study in social dynamics, tracing the various self-righting tendencies in a free society by which pressures from without and within and catastrophies of external and internal origin may be met, and the harmony and creativity of society restored.

But the book is more than this. That Angell is studying not merely social integration but also moral discipline becomes apparent when he traces the social sources of individual discipline, and gives his diagnosis of individual and group "deviants" and particularly of child delinquents. He never loses sight of the full dimension of moral life— its individual no less than its social extension.

The book offers many a fresh insight into the right use of the instruments of education and communication, and into ways to overcome the hazards inherent in a rapidly changing technical society. It presents an invaluable analysis of the roles that institutions—religious, educational, and economic—play in the integration of society, and of the perils of formalism that beset all institutions and threaten to destroy their creative relation to the culture. His chapters on "The Anatomy of the Moral Order" and "The Problems of the Moral Web" give an enlightening account of the complexities of moral consensus in a pluralistic society. There are those who will question why this order should be called "Moral"—whether "The Social Order" would not be adequate. But the reader who understands Angell's analysis fully will see that the author is justified in giving a moral connotation to the communal adjustments he is describing. For these adjustments insure more than just the social health of the community—they insure the moral health of individuals.

Although the book analyzes all free societies, it naturally gives special attention to the peculiar conditions of American life. The high mobility of our class structure, the extent of our technical advances and, above all, our absorption of vast numbers of immigrants create problems unique to American life.

But Angell is no determinist. He recognizes that a healthy society is both the fruit of planning and foresight and the consequence of fateful developments beyond the contrivance of even the most foresighted. Nowhere does he suggest that we should attempt what is beyond our powers—but he does show the extent of our powers and therewith of our responsibility. Thus this book is a precious resource both to the general reader and to the specialist who are concerned with the problems of social and moral integration.

REINHOLD NIEBUHR

Contents

chapter

1. Men Astray **3**

2. The Anatomy of the Moral Order **16**

3. The Problems of the Moral Web **46**

4. The Transmission of Values and Norms **61**

5. The Maintenance of Institutions **85**

6. Reorienting Deviant Groups **105**

7. Punishment and Retraining of Individual Deviants **117**

8. Societal Resistance to External Pressure **137**

9. The Process of Readjustment **149**

10. Changes in Conditions and the Moral Order **171**

11. Incompatibility in the Moral Order **192**

12. The Integration of Democratic Societies **220**

Notes **233**

Author's Note **245**

Index **247**

Free Society and Moral Crisis

CHAPTER 1

Men Astray

Mankind is suffering. Suffering from physical want, yes, but man has always been hungry and sick. This kind of suffering is in fact declining. Rising now is man's moral suffering. Whether in Bombay or Brussels, Sydney or Chicago, Lima or Liverpool, the daily newspapers have headlines like "Husband Murders Wife and Baby," "Race Tension at Public Pool," "Tax Scandals Rock Capital," "Violence Flares on Picket Line," "Atomic Control Vetoed in U.N.," "Can't Enforce Gambling Laws Says Police Chief," "Child Crime Puzzles Psychiatrists."

Such headlines give a vivid and almost overpowering sense of the tensions and conflicts of our times. Man today seems at odds with himself. Serenity is a vanishing quality of life. The world presses in upon us, insistent, confusing, often tragic. Although there is basic social order in most places and most of the time, it is an order continually strained, frequently violated, occasionally disrupted. Some men form aggressive groups to fight for what they conceive to be their rights. Others, uprooted and drifting on a sea of social change, are buffeted by moral storms, often sinking into crime or vice or trying to save themselves by clutching at flotsam in the form of exotic social movements.

The grave condition of man in our times is rendered more hopeful, however, by the extent of concern over moral problems. On every side are signs that people are aware of the seriousness of affairs, and trying to do something about them. The viewers-with-alarm are ex-

All bibliographical references and commentary are to be found in the Notes following Chapter 12.

ceeded only by the do-gooders. Men are aroused on many fronts, battling with evil according to their lights and with whatever weapons are at hand. That their efforts are so little effective only shows that the contest is an unequal one. They are attacking an armored monster with bows and arrows.

The public is aware that things were not always thus. They have heard about the "good old days" before the advent of the large factory, the automobile, the airplane and television, the days when communities were largely self-sufficient and life moved at a leisurely pace. They may know that in isolated places, even as close as parts of French Canada and Mexico, those times still go on. Where life has not been subject to dislocating social change, the web is firmer and moral disorganization is less. It is paradoxical but true that the places of highest technical civilization are little civilized when it comes to a working moral order. Just as an adult can learn from a child, so a metropolis might profit from the example of a village.

The state of affairs would be less alarming if it were not that the whole world is rapidly urbanizing. The number of large cities is growing steadily, and the influence of these aggregates upon smaller communities and the rural hinterland constantly increasing. Modern communication is spreading a way of life of which moral disorganization is an integral part.

All civilized societies are faced with this tremendous problem, which is strongly reminiscent of the late Roman Empire. Demoralization in the literal sense is again an ominous possibility.

The problem is not a recent one. For more than a hundred years some perceptive men have seen the handwriting on the wall. Many men of good will have devoted their thought, their energies, and their resources to the task of reversing the trend. Plans have been laid, laws passed, organizations formed. No one knows how much worse matters might now be if it had not been for these efforts; still we cannot congratulate ourselves on the present situation. Crime rates go on rising, moral confusion does not abate. Obviously the common sense with which we have heretofore attacked the problem is not enough. It has not checked our descent toward the moral depths. We must look elsewhere.

When we face a problem in the physical and biological worlds we seek the help of science. If we want a speedier airplane we look to experts in aerodynamics and the chemistry of fuels. If afflicted with a new disease, we call in medical investigators. We have learned from experience that this produces results. But we have not yet gained an equal faith in the social sciences. They have not in fact given anything like equal grounds for confidence. Only economics has proved its worth to the general public—the other social sciences are less mature, less able to give definitive answers to practical problems. Yet if one believes that human social life exhibits uniformities of cause and effect, these sciences constitute a potentially indispensable resource.

What this study aims to foster is the discovery of laws or principles of social organization that can be applied by human effort to reduce moral dislocations. Since on the surface there seems to be an inconsistency between the idea of laws of human behavior and the choice that is implied in the application of human effort, it may be helpful to digress on this point.

As social scientists see social reality it is not a clockwork running smoothly according to laws of its own being. It is rather a confused intertwining of units and processes, a hodge-podge of acts and relationships. We have learned to make some sense out of what is going on only by applying to this jumble what are called frames of reference. These are like colored glasses which screen out many wavelengths, admitting only a few colors. If a frame of reference has been well chosen, what appears within it will have some homogeneity. The homogeneous data can then be scrutinized for regular relationships. It is thus that the economist has obtained his generalizations about wealth, and the political scientist his about power. The uniformities discovered and reduced to scientific law are, then, the work of the investigator as well as of nature. They are propositions about reality, not reality itself.

What we call choice or will or effort is part of reality. It is an inseparable aspect of the human drama. Together with other aspects it furnishes the data which the social scientist tries to understand and out of which he tries to bring a rational order. Choices sometimes form the heart of the process which a principle embodies. Thus, according to economics, an excess of demand over supply at a given price in a perfect market makes the price rise. Here buyers and sellers are making decisions, exercising choices. Elsewhere the role of will is much less striking. According to social psychology, for instance,

intimate association tends to induce convergence in the social attitudes of the associates; it makes no difference whether the parties
have chosen to become intimate or merely drifted together.

The fascinating aspect of the matter is that man, whose actions can
at least in part be reduced to law, can use those very laws to guide
those actions. The seller, knowing that an excess of demand over
supply will raise the price, may hold his goods off the market for a
while to benefit from the rise. A labor union official, knowing that
intimate association breeds consensus, may avoid close contacts with
businessmen for fear he will betray his fellows. Thus it is that we can
speak of exerting effort to apply social science laws. We are interested
here in applying such laws to lessen moral disorganization.

Unfortunately we sociologists, whose business it is to discover uniformities in the data of moral organization and disorganization, have
not developed a satisfactory body of theory in this field. We have had
many penetrating insights, but these have not been fitted together
to form a system. Sociologists have not paid as much attention to
moral data as they deserve, and this for a curious reason. For a generation social scientists have proudly kept judgments of fact separate
from judgments of value. They have eschewed anything that smacks
of moral criticism for fear that such a stance might harm their scientific objectivity. Although this "value-free" position does not imply
that moral standards and moral conduct should not be studied, there
has often been a disinclination to study them. Despite the fact that
one can be as cold-bloodedly analytic about moral data as about anything else, they have seemed somehow scientifically tainted. Re-
searchers have not thought them as basic, as reliable, as "hard," as
data on matters like social classes or political preferences. From this
standpoint, the present study will be thoroughly out of fashion. It
takes a diametrically opposed position. It assumes that moral phenomena lie at the very heart of society, and that it is above all moral
facts that we need to understand today. I intend to marshal what
we sociologists know—and it is pitifully little—about these focal
matters, so that causes of deficiencies may be understood, and remedial programs soundly based.

The most precious elements in theory are concepts. The fruitful
ones—and they alone survive—point to the crucial aspects of the
reality under examination. They ignore the irrelevant and select what

is essential. Where would physics be today without the concept of the atom? Or economics without the concept of national income, or of purchasing power? No one has ever seen or touched any of these concepts and yet they are elements in theories that are used daily to predict events in the real world.

What we propose here is to set forth a set of concepts, and a theory formulated in terms of them. Both are the fruit of wide reading in the social science literature, and of our attempt to bring order out of the mass of materials dealing with the moral aspects of human societies. There have been many investigations of particular problems in particular cultures, and there have been many "armchair" thinkers who have tried to make generalizations that are valid across cultures. We are indebted to all of them. If our attempt is in some degree successful it should lead to the development of hypotheses that can be tested.

An enterprise such as this risks utter failure. The conceptual scheme may not be capable of generating a theory that will yield suitable hypotheses. But there is no way to know this in advance. The only course is to go through the labor of erecting the scientific edifice, and then use it. The history of science is strewn with the wrecks of systems that have foundered. Ptolemaic astronomy is perhaps the best known of these. The theory of phlogiston in chemistry—that there is a common substance in all inflammable bodies which is lost in the burning—had its day in the early eighteenth century. But each of the wrecked systems has contributed to the process of trial and error by which knowledge advances.

When a scientist of any sort wrestles long and earnestly with a problem, he learns by experience that some aspects of it are more important than others, and that some can be ignored altogether. If he studies falling bodies or what we call the laws of gravity, he learns that the color of falling objects has proved to be irrelevant. He does not even bother to record their color. In such a case we say that the concepts of time and velocity are parts of the theoretical system, but the concept of color is not.

The same holds true in sociology. Concepts mark out the data which need to be analyzed, and guide the analysis. Unfortunately there is no agreement on the concepts that are most fruitful for analyzing problems of moral disorganization. Some writers have assembled one set of conceptual tools, some another. We will put together a set that to us seems capable of ordering the findings of existing research.

A concept which has been little used but which is basic to any consideration of moral problems is the moral order. This points to a general aspect of life, very much as do the terms political order and social order. The aspect here is that of the societally "good" and the societally "bad." Every society develops standards of what is morally right and wrong, and it is the facts in relation to these standards that comprise the moral order. Anything which is relevant to the question, "Are human relations in this situation what the society itself feels they ought to be?" is an element in it. As we shall see in the next chapter, the data that have to be marshaled to answer this question in a modern industrialized society are many and complex. We shall have to consider such matters as common values, moral norms, institutions, laws and their administration, and adherence to or deviation from norms. The moral order is the general scheme of relationships among such data, the manner in which "oughtness" is organized. It embodies a very general theory of what the key elements for the analysis of the problem are. It carves out of the confusion of everyday reality those data that merit careful study. Facts can then be accurately described, relations among them scrutinized, and hypotheses developed and tested.

A second useful concept, and a more analytical one than moral order, is moral integration. This is a concept like temperature: it refers to a continuum rather than to any particular degree on that continuum. We shall speak of high degrees of moral integration and low degrees of it. The continuum itself has to do with the ordering of human relations through common orientation toward shared ends and values. Moral integration is high when institutions and moral norms are adequate and compatible and behavior is guided by them. Moral integration is low when there is either inadequacy or incompatibility of moral norms and institutions, or widespread deviation from norms and disloyalty to institutions. In a society having perfect moral integration all members would understand what social relations are "right" and all would fulfill them. The concept does not assume the absence of all conflict in a society. It merely assumes that whatever conflict there is goes forward in terms of well-defined rules that the parties to the conflicts accept.

Moral integration so defined is a double-barreled concept. It points both to the degree to which the elements of moral structure in the society—standards, institutions and the like—are integrated with one another, and to the degree to which persons incorporate these elements in their action. The concept thus reflects the basic nature of man's social life: on the one hand, he must have the benefit of a vital social system; on the other hand, he must exercise his choice responsibly.

To forestall misunderstanding, we should distinguish moral integration from what may be called interpersonal integration. The latter refers to the degree to which members of any group feel at home with one another and enjoy mutual contacts. Interpersonal integration is high when there is a minimum of strain and conflict in the personal relations of the group members. The importance of this dimension has been stressed by students of "group dynamics." They have been interested in discovering patterns of participation that will result in harmonious adjustment among group members. Such adjustment may accompany moral integration, but it is not the same. Personal animosities are sometimes strong among zealots for the same way of life, and many a clique of hail-fellows-well-met has no distinctive moral orientation. It is the contention here that however important interpersonal integration may be for personal happiness, it cannot take the place of moral integration for the cementing of the society.

The concepts of moral order and moral integration reveal the central orientation of our inquiry. We are going to be concerned with discovering what factors make for integration within the moral order. If we can learn what they are, or at least if we can see exactly what kind of research is necessary to discover them, we will be on the road to intelligent social action against moral degeneration.

Every group that is to any degree self-governing has something in the nature of a moral order. People cannot work together without overt or tacit standards of conduct corresponding to their common values. Even so intimate a group as a family, which one might suppose was unified solely by interdependence and mutual affection, has to have some moral integration. There must be concern for the family unit as an ongoing system, a willingness to take responsibility for the welfare of the whole, an understanding of what is proper conduct for family members and what is not. Without these, the unit soon ceases to be a group at all.

It would no doubt be ideal if we could investigate the moral orders of all important groups, from the family to the society. This would yield a panorama of the whole problem in all its complexity. Unfortunately, the complexity is overwhelming. Something less ambitious must be undertaken. In deciding where to begin, one is torn between the alternatives of studying the society and of studying the small intimate group. A strong case could be made for beginning with what we call primary groups, like the family and the play group of children. Their structure is simple. One would be beginning with the purest case, a procedure usually recommended in scientific work. Furthermore, primary groups have some degree of independence from the rest of society so that they give as well as receive moral influence. Indeed, the sociologist Cooley thought that these primary groups served as well-springs of the morality of the wider society and acted as constant sources of criticism of large-scale organization based on power.

On the other hand, there can be little doubt that the shift to larger units of social organization is what has brought on most of the current problems of the moral order. Investigations at the societal level are therefore most likely to get at the heart of the most crucial questions of our day. Since, moreover, the culture of the society has a profound influence on the life of all groups it includes, any gains in societal moral integration will tend to diffuse throughout the whole web of life, improving the moral integration at lower levels of social structure.

Nor is there an advantage in trying to effect a compromise by choosing to study the local community. The local community has most of the complexities of the society itself, with less autonomy and power; and it is perhaps no more independent than the primary group, yet without the latter's simplicity. When all is said, the society seems the strategic place to begin.

This study is limited not only to the moral order of societies, but to that of a certain type: the civilized and democratic society. This is because civilized societies are gradually inheriting the earth and it is their moral problems that are most in need of solution. Nonliterate societies, because of their small size, their isolation, and their homogeneity have a quite different character. Although some of the very best analyses of moral order are the work of anthropologists studying such societies, they can have only suggestive and analogical value for our undertaking.

The limitation to the democratic society excludes two great sets: the autocratic or totalitarian, and the colonial society. These are excluded not because they are unimportant today—the totalitarian has never been more important—but because their analysis is a separate and herculean task. Totalitarian societies function in accordance with what has been called the audience mode of interaction instead of the public mode; that is, their members are passive receivers of guidance issuing from a central source which uses power and propaganda. Because members are passive, influences do not well up from primary groups to set the standards of societal life and keep the centralized power in check. Though there are rich materials on the experience of Germany under Hitler, we in the West know little about the operation of the U.S.S.R. and Communist China, at present the principal totalitarian societies. It would be fascinating to compare the moral processes in the democratic and the totalitarian types, but that will have to wait until scholars have had a full opportunity to analyze totalitarian moral systems.

Very indirectly the present study does have some bearing, however, on the world-wide struggle between democracy and totalitarianism. The democratic societies are not likely to win the uncommitted areas of the world to their banner so long as they are plagued by many unsolved problems of their own. Social science could perform a great service if it could do anything to help the democracies put their houses in order.

The civilized and democratic societies include a large proportion of mankind: all of Western Europe, North America, Australia and New Zealand, Japan, India, Pakistan, parts of South America and Africa, and some small countries in Asia. These are the societies to which the analysis that follows is intended to apply.

It is a fair question whether societies that have such different cultures as, say, Japan and France can be dealt with as if they are of one type. Their moral orders certainly have many distinctive features.

On the other hand, the development of a democratic, urban type of life has brought great similarities to different culture areas. It may not be too great a feat of abstraction—and this study assumes that it is not—to disengage from the totality of societal experiences in these areas the likenesses of organization and of process which characterize them.

Since civilized, democratic societies are exposed to many external influences through their contacts, they are constantly changing. Their dynamic character must be reflected in the concept of moral integration itself. A static definition might be adequate for isolated, non-literate societies, but simply will not do for the modern, Western type. Built-in mechanisms of smooth moral change have become part of the very conception of integration. Thus, our earlier phrasing should be supplemented to read: "Moral integration is high when institutions and moral norms are adequate and compatible, behavior is guided by them, and *the moral web changes in an orderly fashion.*"

When we come to discuss social change in this work, we shall always be interested in the mechanisms of short-term change, not in historical trends. This is because, once a high level of integration has been lost, it is in the ability to move quickly through a period of low integration or maladjustment to a new stage of high integration that a society shows its moral caliber. We have no scientific criterion by which to set up a model of the perfect society, and therefore no way to measure the "goodness" of one form of moral integration as against another. Each has to be judged—scientifically at least—in terms of its own common values. This being the case, the shift of a society from one set of common values to another through time, the long historical trend, does not concern us. It is certainly a problem of great importance, one to which philosophical thinkers rightly devote their attention; but critiques of history go beyond the sphere of science. Even so fascinating and currently significant a question as how the underdeveloped countries should refashion their processes of moral control as they move into the orbit of civilization falls outside our purview; for no one knows what common values they will come to accept as the basis of their new integration.

No matter how hard an author may try to avoid it, his treatment of a subject like ours is bound to be influenced by his greater acquaintance with his own society than with any other. Our intent is to discuss the moral orders of civilized, democratic societies in general. Yet readers from other countries will no doubt often think that it is only the society of the United States which is being analyzed. Certainly many of my examples will be drawn from the area of my greatest familiarity. Though I deplore ethnocentrism, I cannot fully escape it.

Civilized, democratic societies are highly complex structures. By their very nature they are difficult to integrate morally. It is no wonder that they have so many moral shortcomings. In an earlier work I tried to give a concise statement of just how intricate such a society is. Perhaps it will be helpful to repeat it here:

This American Society is a tremendously complex thing. It not only exists over a great area and includes more than 6 per cent of the world's population, but it has many principles of structure running through it. There is, first, the matter of spatial proximity. Everything else equal, we tend to associate and interact with those who are nearest to us. But so unequal have other things become that this principle is largely overlaid by other ones, except in small towns and the open country. Next is the principle of the division of labor. We come in contact with those who are involved in the same industrial or commercial processes as ourselves. These contacts may be superficial and in some cases hostile, but they help to fashion the structure of our society. A third principle is that of caste or class membership. The Negroes and the Orientals are forced to associate largely with their own kind because of avoidance by the whites. Recent immigrants find themselves in much the same position. Within the Americanized white majority there are class divisions, based chiefly upon income differences, which channel association too. Since so many of the leisure pursuits that attract Americans cost money, those who can afford the same types of recreation tend to mingle with one another. Finally, there is the principle of common values. Cutting across all the other lines of cleavage are religious and political loyalties that determine in some measure the persons with whom one comes in contact.

Underneath all these elements of differentiation in our society runs a current of generalized communication through our mass agencies of diffusion—the newspaper, the moving picture, and the radio. Reinforcing the mutual understanding and the approachability that come from our pioneer background, our national traditions, and our common public school education, this current gives us common topics of interest and thought which cannot but aid understanding, even though it does not stimulate general association.

It is in the cities that these various aspects of societal structure become most entangled and confused. One would need not four but many dimensions to plot them satisfactorily. And as time passes the urban type of life becomes more and more predominant. This fact alone introduces an element of increasing complexity into American society. Nor is this complexity a stable one. Because of the mobility of the people in terms of residence and because of the rapidity of technological advance, social forms are constantly undergoing evolution and changing their relations to one another. It would probably not be worth while to investigate in detail the social structure of one of our great cities, because before one had finished the task the results would be outdated.

It is obvious that the moral order—how "oughtness" is organized —of any such society must itself be most complex. Raising a low level of moral integration is bound to call for patience, but even more for intelligence. This is where social science can make its contribution.

Although moral integration is ordinarily highly regarded, and may therefore seem to be a value concept, it is here used in a strictly scientific sense. It refers to the degree to which the members of a society obey self-imposed standards of conduct. By this definition, a society can be perfectly integrated in terms of its own moral standards, and yet be a thoroughly bad society in the eyes of outside observers. The North Africa population dominated by the Barbary Pirates in the eighteenth century formed a society which was regarded as a blot upon civilization's escutcheon—but it seems to have had considerable solidarity under its own peculiar norms. A more recent example is Hitler Germany. To say that a society is morally well integrated, therefore, is not necessarily to approve it.

Our use of the word moral in connection with societies rather than persons will no doubt trouble some readers. They are used to thinking of moral action as peculiarly private, not public. Now it is certainly true that a man may draw on religious sources for a principle of conduct which he regards as morally superior to that which is practiced in his society. We point out, however, that until he persuades his fellows to adopt his principle it is not an instrument of societal integration. It may even be a source of societal disruption.

Since one aspect of the good life is order, and since order requires moral consensus, it seems legitimate to emphasize the need for shared moral orientations. Individually held moral principles may be necessary for progress, but in times like ours wide acceptance of moral norms is indispensable for the maintenance of order.

What is more, one might argue that creativity and order—seemingly antithetical—are in some degree interdependent. The philosopher, the artist, or the inventor needs social roots if he is to develop. His genius rarely bears fruit unless he has opportunities for orderly growth. Conversely, order itself is hard won and must be constantly renewed. Even those nonliterate societies that seem so stagnant to modern man must occasionally have faced new problems imaginatively.

Sociologists are sometimes accused of fostering a "groupish" way of life. They are thought by definition opposed to a laissez-faire sort of society, or to privacy. Nothing could be further from the truth. Sociologists wish to study how groups work. They are trying to find out what consequences follow from what antecedents. They do make the assumption that enough people are interested in the well-working of groups to make such study profitable. I make the further assumption, and this is not true of all sociologists, that moral integration is an important aspect of the well-working of societies. However, no assumptions are here made about the content of the values and norms and institutions by which the integration is achieved. If there are circumstances in which a system of anarchism results in moral integration, the sociologist will be only too glad to report them.

The upshot of the matter is that the knowledge tentatively formulated here is instrumental only. It may be useful in the hands of men of good will. Even they must be wary, in their attempts to strengthen moral integration, not to lessen the realization of other ends and values. Men legitimately strive for progress, pleasure, and a full stomach as well as for social peace. The improvement of a society is a bewildering undertaking, one that requires not one but many strategies. In each campaign, however, the fund of societal devotion and good intention needs to be joined with an understanding of social processes, and with the application of that knowledge. Only thus can modern democratic societies hope to measure up to their potentialities.

CHAPTER 2

The Anatomy of the Moral Order

The moral order does not stand out in the normal routines of a society. It is so enmeshed with other aspects of life that its pattern is not easily distinguishable. We must look at it through special glasses to bring it into relief. The peculiar power of our moral lenses is to pick out and see clearly all the elements in society that reveal "how oughtness is organized." In this chapter we shall consider the nature of each of these elements, so that later we can understand how they work together to perform society's tasks.

The main constituents of the moral order as here conceived, and their relations to one another, are indicated in the upper half of Figure 1. The lower half indicates other relationships, also of interest to sociologists but not part of the moral order. The whole is meant to show that societal structure and process are resultants of two sorts of forces, one coming from the habitat conditions in which the society has its being, the other from the common moral values of the society, worked out in the past and now guiding its destinies. The first is mediated by demographic and technological factors such as birth and death rates and the state of the practical arts, the second by what we shall call the moral web—moral norms, institutions, and law. The reaction of the people to the moral web through adherence to norms, obedience to law, and loyalty to institutions—or through the opposites, deviation, disobedience, and disloyalty—is also part of the moral order. The political order has roots in the moral order, but spreads beyond it.

The most basic—though not the most tangible—aspect of the moral order is the set of common values that motivates the members of a society. Since this is a key idea for what will follow it calls for careful discussion.

It has been said that man is the only creature who contemplates his own death. Certain it is that members of both primitive and civilized societies use foresight to anticipate the consequences of their acts, and so strive to realize their preferences. These strivings are of many kinds. Some have very ordinary objectives such as enough to eat tomorrow. Others have very complex and sophisticated goals, such as a greater appreciation of painting or music, or a reduction in the rate of juvenile delinquency. Some of the preferences may be

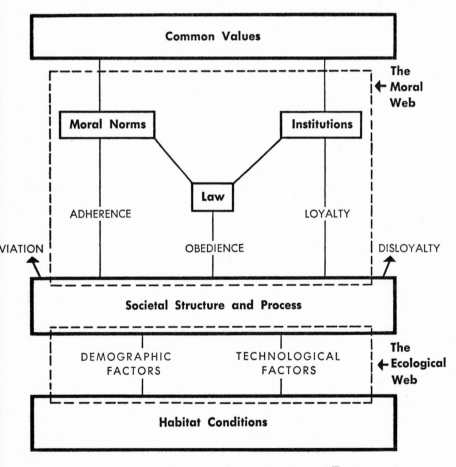

Fig. 1

called ends because we can visualize a definite future state that would represent consummation. Others are better called values because they represent continuing qualities of life which we desire to see realized. Both ends and values run the whole gamut, from the very private and individually unique ones to those widely shared by others. The common values of a society are likely to be intangibles such as democracy and humanitarianism. It is in terms of them that responsible courses of action are justified. Societal members do not so much envision specific future events to work toward, as attributes of the good life as they see it. Batten has well stated it:

> Fundamentally, community depends only secondarily on the perception of common interests and the formulation of common goals. These indeed are the necessary outcome of community, but interests and goals may change with changing circumstances and thus provide only a temporary and superficial basis for social solidarity. The essence of community lies in the general acceptance of the rightness of human relations of a particular kind in the pursuit of any goal.

Since the adjective "common" in the term "common values" is crucial to the theoretical system here developed, we must explore its meaning in some detail.

The word is doing double duty. To make this clear we must identify two dimensions as shown in Figure 2. If values are qualities that are thought desirable, the first question is: "Desired for whom or for what?" We may be oriented either toward the person as a center of life, may have his welfare in mind—or toward the society as a center of life, and its welfare. (Not relevant here and therefore not shown in our figure is orientation toward intermediate groups.) It was the first dimension MacIver stressed when in *Community* (p. 100), he made his famous distinction between common interests and like interests. Thus the interests of college students severally in academic marks are like—that is, each is oriented toward his own personal welfare—but their interest in the success of the football team is common. Applied to values, the same distinction would put the possession of great wealth on the personal side, the desire that everyone be honest on the societal side. Any value that relates to the working of the social system as a system is potentially a common value.

The other dimension involved is the degree of consensus among the people of the society. A common value in this respect is one about which there is a high degree of consensus. If there is not, designs for the society in this aspect of life are either conflicting or nonexistent. It should be noted that when applied to individual orientations, the appropriate distinction is between like values and idosyncratic values. The very general striving in the United States for personal economic success illustrates the former, the seeking of a Thoreau for intimacy with beauties of nature the latter.

SOME DIMENSIONS OF VALUE

Degree of Consensus	Orientation toward Society	Orientation toward Individual
High	Common	Like
Low	Conflicting or Nonexistent	Idiosyncratic

Fig. 2

Thus the term "common values" really means: values relating to the societal system about which there is consensus. But this phrase is awkward, and we shall therefore continue to use the short term "common values." It should never be forgotten, however, that both the desire and the object are common.

A possible difficulty here is that a common value may be a quality that seems to be a personal characteristic like kindliness or truth. However, such qualities are as a rule cherished because they further the kind of relations among persons that make for a desired type of society. Any attitude that links one person to others may be an object of concern to the society.

The culture characteristic of a society may carry like as well as common values. Part of the way of life that is passed on to the next generation almost always concerns traits that represent an individualistic or small group orientation rather than a societal one. Though all societies have to function as systems, there is no need that all human activities gear in. In American society, for instance, traits like playing bridge, camping, listening to the radio and drinking whisky are learned by many people from their elders but are not attributes of the society that are commonly desired. Some have argued that the American emphasis on financial success is a common value—something that is thought good for the system—but it seems much more plausible to regard it as a like cultural attitude acquired by many persons. Only if we did regard such striving by everyone as necessary to the good life would it be a truly common value.

The set of common values of a society has been variously labeled. The most celebrated term perhaps is Emile Durkheim's "collective conscience." Although the meaning of the expression changes somewhat throughout his work, the sense it has in his most mature thought is the organization of beliefs and sentiments which the members of a society hold in common. The term has never been taken up by English-speaking scholars, probably because it suggests a moral unanimity in the group equivalent to the moral unity of the person, a suggestion uncongenial to those in the nominalist tradition of Hume, Mill, and Spencer. Hobhouse, for instance, who was in that tradition, suggests that the unity of the group is one of devotion, while the unity of the person is neural.

The problem of less-than-perfect unanimity on moral values is one we will have to wrestle with when we come to the discussion of moral norms. Common values are so hard to come to grips with that it seems wisest not to broach the question of consensus at this level of abstraction.

A famous psychologist, William McDougall, used the term "collective will" for much the same phenomenon. He rightly pointed out that collective will requires that the volition in each member spring from a sentiment *for* the whole. He holds with Cooley that what occurs is an expansion of the individual selves to include the group. The natural expression for such an expanded self is "we." Perhaps the clearest indication of common values is such expressions as "We do not want our country to be militaristic."

A frequent error is to assume that the possession of a common value by a society means that all of its members act alike over a wide area of life. This may be so, as when the value of truth is generally cherished. Persons then act similarly in similar situations. But suppose that the common value is one of aesthetic tolerance. Then people might wear different kinds of costumes, build different kinds of houses, paint different kinds of pictures, and yet would all the while be expressing the common value. Clearly, it is not the personal behavior which is the crucial point but the orientation toward the social system. Holders of a common value are oriented toward the same kind of system. In *Life and the Student* (p. 143) Cooley dreamed of such a common orientation when he wrote: "Our democracy might be a work of art, a joyous whole, rich in form and color, free but chastened, tumultuously harmonious, unfolding strange beauty year by year. Each of us would be spontaneously functional, like the detail in great architecture."

The difference between what has recently been called loosely and tightly structured societies could be interpreted as the result of the presence or absence of a common value of tolerance. The looseness of both Thai and American societies would then be attributed in part to their tolerance, and the contrast of both to Japanese society would be attributed to the lack of a value of tolerance there. Such an interpretation allows us to assert that a loosely structured society may have as high a level of moral integration as a tightly structured one.

Common values are among the most deep-seated elements of a society and therefore change very slowly through history. What is frequently referred to as national character is evidence of this fact. We shall not attempt to discover the causes of the common values. If that can be done at all, it is only possible for scholars of such tremendous historical learning as Max Weber or Arnold Toynbee. At any rate, the belief of some sociologists, that the current value system of a society can be explained by the contemporary relations of that society to its natural environment and to other societies, does not seem tenable. That view neglects the tremendous momentum of culture, a momentum which renders every society actively selective as it enters new situations. Common values do seem to be more than a mere superstructure which adapts itself passively to physical and technical conditions.

An illustration may give substance to the concept of common values. A number of writers have written about the value system of American society. Drawing upon their work, but keeping in mind the distinction between common and like values, we can formulate the set of American common values as follows:

Dignity of the person including equality before the law
Civil and religious liberties
Responsible democracy—control by the people of their common life
Opportunity for all
Humanitarianism and friendliness
A high level of effort
Competition within fair rules
Technological progress
Peaceful orientation toward other nations
Patriotism

These are characteristics which Americans believe their society should exhibit if it is to function as a satisfactory system. They are valued because they constitute a preferred way of life. Even when they appear to be individualistic by nature, as do civil and religious liberties and opportunity for all, they are thought to be good for the whole quite as much as for the parts. It is apparent that these common values interpenetrate one another at many points, that they hang together. For instance, opportunity and competition work together to elicit and reward effort; civil liberties, democracy, and opportunity produce an active public opinion.

Cooley's theory that the wider values of a society are an outgrowth of the values developed in primary group association was outlined in Chapter 1. He believed that men learn lessons of loyalty, lawfulness, fair play, and the like in small, intimate groups, and then try to make the same principles work in larger wholes of which they are members. We pointed out that the audience form of interaction typical of totalitarian societies interferes with this process. In democratic societies one might suppose that this process would lead to similar sets of common values everywhere. That this is not the case is not necessarily a refutation of the theory. The specific ways in which primary group values are carried into larger group relations may vary a great deal from one democratic culture to another. Fair play in a young, rapidly expanding society and fair play in a mature, stable one may look quite different. Primary group values do, however, perform a selective function by screening out elements of organization that would be flatly incompatible with them. Thus no democratic society generates lasting moral norms which require members of families to spy upon one another. There are too many persons who have experienced the joys of family solidarity, and they have too much power in a democratic society, for such a norm to become permanently embedded in the culture.

The variety in sets of societal common values around the world is very striking. Anthropologists have amply documented this fact. Using such terms as patterns or themes or configurations of culture, they have shown how values as well as other elements vary from one society to another. Ruth Benedict puts it neatly as follows: "The three cultures of Zuni, Dobu and Kwakiutl are not primarily heterogeneous assortments of acts and beliefs. They have each certain goals toward which their behavior is directed and which their institutions further. . . . They are traveling along different roads in pursuit of different ends, and these ends and these means in one society cannot be judged in terms of those of another society, because essentially they are incommensurable."

Perhaps the only generalization that can be made with certainty about all sets of societal common values is that they cannot be inconsistent with loyalty to the society itself. This is true almost by definition: a society is something that must have coherence.

Following Spengler in his use of such terms as Apollonian, Faustian, and Dionysian to describe the spirit or the "soul" of a culture, several anthropologists have of late tried to compare and explain the basic orientations of different peoples. Abram Kardiner, in *The Individual and His Society* (pp. 471–83), has advanced the theory that differences are chiefly due to varying methods of child training. This explanation would have seemed quite inadequate to William Graham Sumner. The thesis in his *Folkways* was that all elements of the moral order respond ultimately to the exigencies of the life of the group as a whole. He would have sought to understand what caused the variations in child training.

We are all aware of the mighty tensions generated between societies with different common values. The "cold war" between Soviet Communism and the West is only the latest example. Less obvious is that there may be a degree of inconsistency even within the set of common values of a single culture. Karl Mannheim has pointed this out perhaps better than anyone else. In his *Diagnosis of Our Time* (Chap. 3) he spoke of the crisis in valuation brought about by the mixture of tendencies in Western nations deriving from such disparate sources as Christianity, the Enlightenment, and the French Revolution. The United States, for instance, has been struggling for a hundred years to make the value of personal freedom and that of a reasonable security compatible.

Modern urban societies are so differentiated that one may wonder whether it is accurate to impute to them any common values at all. Perhaps all that holds them together is interdependence for sustenance and the interlinking of groups that results from overlapping memberships. Certainly in a country like the United States the members of different social classes or the people in different regions tend to put their own interpretations on common values. Whether this leaves anything more than lip service paid to purely verbal symbols is a legitimate question. In times of economic crisis, like the Great Depression, and times of social change, like that ushered in by the U. S. Supreme Court's decision on the desegregation of schools, the clash of opposing viewpoints is far more striking than any underlying consensus. But to most students of American society it seems that there is an underlying consensus nevertheless. No matter how dissimilar the preferences of certain parts of the society are on particular issues, there seems to be a general preference for working out solutions in a democratic and humanitarian manner. True, divisions run deep. But if only ecological and sociable interdependence were opposing them, they would run much deeper. The underlying stratum of common values is what keeps the society from splitting wide open.

There is no need here to discuss whether the common values of a society must have a religious origin if they are to inspire the highest level of responsible behavior. Moderate levels of integration have been achieved without it. "We can conceive of the moral order," Redfield writes, "as equally present in those societies in which the rules for right conduct among men are supported by supernatural sanctions and in those in which the morality of human conduct is largely independent of the religion (in the sense of belief and cult about the supernatural)." Gillin points out that Japanese culture and society have been integrated around the secular concept of honor. Hoebel suggests that among primitive tribes, supernaturalism is marked in strongly integrated societies, whereas in atomistic societies "religion rarely enters as a progenitor of tort." To Sapir there is no such thing as a "genuine culture" unless high levels of integration in morality, spirituality, and aesthetics are woven together; a genuine culture is "the expression of a richly varied and yet somehow unified and consistent attitude toward life, an attitude which sees the significance of any one element in civilization in relation to all the others. It is, ideally speaking, a culture in which nothing is meaningless."

Whether religion is in fact indispensable to a set of moral values that can integrate a society successfully can only be determined by empirical study. There is advantage, however, in facing quite clearly what is implied in each of the two possible answers to the question. When common values relate solely to what happens in the here and now, in the empirical world, there is some possibility of determining whether or not the values are actually being realized. If we believe in honesty, for instance, we can find out how much dishonesty is currently practiced. On the other hand, when common values relate to the hereafter or, more broadly, the unknown in general, there is no possibility of empirical check. The former situation gives rise to what Max Weber calls an ethic of responsibility, the latter to an ethic of ultimate ends. In the extreme case of the second ethic the person centers on one value to the exclusion of all others and is not perturbed if his attempts to realize this value—for instance, salvation—cause suffering to his contemporaries.

Put another way, the society that is real to the actor differs. In the ethic of responsibility, it is the mundane society that counts. In the ethic of ultimate ends, it is the transcendental society.

It is interesting here to note in passing that primitive man not only merges the human with the supernatural, but merges the natural with both. He feels obligation not only to the members of his own society and to the deities, but to nature itself. Redfield says that the attitude is one of mutuality. The moral order here includes inanimate nature. And the obverse of this is that nature is thought of as caring for man.

The extreme opposite is illustrated by the thought of the Encyclopedists in France and the Utilitarians in England. Their writings sharply distinguished the human from both the natural and the supernatural, and ethics was a matter of the rational calculation of effects of conduct in the human realm. After the turmoils of the twentieth century, there has been a partial reversal—a tendency not to identify the human with the natural, but to return to the identification of the human with the supernatural. Two writers who believe that common values can be based only on divine law are Ortega y Gasset and T. S. Eliot—see their books *Concord and Liberty* and *The Idea of a Christian Society.*

A different question is the role of religion in bringing about peaceful relations between societies by supplying common values across national boundaries. Many religions have hoped to convert all mankind and thus cement all societies into a single moral order. Though it has not come to pass—and there is no prospect that it ever will—religions have knit together peoples in various regions of the world. Medieval Christendom united Western Europeans, and the Arabic peoples of the Middle East and North Africa have been brought together by their common faith, Islam. T. S. Eliot sees this kind of linkage as revealing the true significance of religion and as constituting the hope of mankind: "I would assert further that a religion cannot be fully apprehended until it becomes the faith of peoples of different original cultures, and, while uniting these peoples in a common brotherhood, can be contemplated in its transcendence of culture as well as lived in the conditions of each particular culture. Any mere political, legalistic or economic union of humanity is a frail and temporary substitute for the union in the diversity of cultures, which only a common religious faith can create." Eliot would certainly not call Marxism a religion in his sense, yet its ability to bring together people as diverse as the Russians and the Chinese would seem to indicate that political and economic ideologies can also be powerful.

Common values, whether sacred or secular, are strengthened by processes of symbolization, through ritual, myth or folklore, and heroic figures. The importance of ritual is so well known that it requires little exposition. Durkheim has developed the theory of this phenomenon further perhaps than anyone else: "There can be no society which does not feel the need of upholding and reaffirming at regular intervals the collective sentiments and the collective ideas which make its unity and its personality . . . Hence come ceremonies which do not differ from regular religious ceremonies, either in their object, the results which they produce, or the processes employed to attain these results. What essential difference is there between an assembly of Christians celebrating the principal dates of the life of Christ, or of Jews remembering the exodus from Egypt or the promulgation of the decalogue, and a reunion of citizens commemorating the promulgation of a new moral or legal system or some great event in national life?" And again, "So the rite serves and can only serve to sustain the vitality of these [traditional] beliefs, to keep them from being effaced from memory and, in sum, to revivify the most essential elements of the collective consciousness."

One might perhaps object with some justice that modern societal rituals tend to emphasize the unity of the nation generally rather than the particular common values that the nation stands for. This is certainly true of the older European countries with long and varied histories, whose traditions embody many value themes. The United States, born in the intellectual climate of the Enlightenment, with its ringing Declaration and its judicious Constitution, is more aware of the common values on which and for which it stands. Though Memorial Day services pay homage to those who have died for their country, and invoke the continued patriotism of citizens, there is a frequent implicit reference to the values of freedom, democracy, and humanitarianism for which the dead are thought to have perished. And, conversely, there is de-emphasis upon values that may divide the citizenry. In his *American Life: Dream and Reality* (p. 3) Warner puts it thus: "Memorial Day is a cult of the dead which organizes and integrates the various faiths and national and class groups into a sacred unity."

Myths and folk tales alike lend prestige to common values, by connecting them with great events in the distant past. They differ only in that myths deal with the religious or supernatural, folk tales with mundane events. Myths have great power over men's minds because they are beyond the reach of scientific criticism. Current beliefs and practices, by being explained as inherited from gods and goddesses, are given unquestioned validity. Modern scientific skepticism, on the other hand, has tended to undermine most folk tales. Ruth Benedict has asserted, however, that items which originally were folklore become incorporated in religious dogma and thus achieve lasting influence. She says: "The fundamental opposition between good and evil is a trait of occidental folklore that is expressed equally in Grimm's fairy tales and in the *Arabian Nights*. Taken up into the cosmologies of the Hebrews, the Mohammedans and the Christians, it determines some of the most deeply seated world views of western religions and western civilizations. The opposition of God and the devil, of Christ and the Antichrist, of heaven and hell, is part of the fundamental intellectual equipment of those who participate in these civilizations." It need only be added that moral orientations are strongly influenced by such intellectual equipment.

In the folklore of primitive peoples and the sagas of peoples taking their first steps toward civilization the symbols of common values are folk heroes; in the literature of highly developed societies, they are historic figures. The United States has a distinguished gallery of these, three of whom are of giant stature: Washington with his dignity and steadfastness, Jefferson with his belief in the common man, and Lincoln with his humane compassion. There is no need to spell out the role such heroes play in keeping common values fresh and in projecting them, by force of subtle suggestion, into action. Who can say how many Americans have not been inspired in their daily lives by the examples of these great men?

It is interesting that it is our present need for symbols of common values, not the past accomplishments of such men, that keeps their fame alive. Cooley pointed out why legend plays so large a role in fame: "What we need is a good symbol to help us think and feel; and so, starting with an actual personality which more or less meets this need, we gradually improve upon it by a process of unconscious adaptation that omits the inessential and adds whatever is necessary to round out the ideal. Thus the human mind working through tradition is an artist, and creates types that go beyond nature. In this way, no doubt, were built up such legendary characters as Orpheus, Hercules, or King Arthur, while the same factor enters into the fame of historical persons like Joan of Arc, Richard I, Napoleon, and even Washington and Lincoln."

Common values need hands and feet, so to speak, and ritual, myth, and heroic figures serve in that capacity. In *Power: a New Social Analysis* (pp. 152–53) Lord Russell said the same thing in different words when he wrote :"Social cohesion demands a creed, or a code of behavior, or a prevailing sentiment, or, best, some combination of all three; without something of this kind a community disintegrates, and becomes subject to a tyrant or a foreign conqueror."

The more concrete fulfillment of common values is carried out through what I call the moral web. The principal parts of the moral web are institutions and moral norms; an auxiliary part is law. All are assumed to be derivative from common values and effective in bringing those values into actual operation in daily life.

The distinction between institutions and norms is subtle but worthwhile. We can perhaps think of social structure as having different degrees of coagulation at different points. Around some permanent problems, like childbirth and child rearing, all societies develop well-defined roles which combine to form institutions. In *The Integration of American Society* (p. 25) I defined institutions as systems of social relationship to which people feel loyal because these systems embody their common values. The various roles in an institution like the family or the school become established in culture. They are usually slow to change.

At other points in social life there is no such degree of coagulation. Individuals are moving about with more freedom of action, but at the same time it is necessary to keep their behavior in tune with the society's common values. Here moral norms apply. The society formulates with more or less precision what choice is expected in specified situations, and enforces such choices with sanctions.

To express the distinction between institution and norm in another way: the moral controls are put in a different place. Through institutions the controls are embedded in the very social structure itself. Moral norms place them in conscience. In the former, common values are *experienced*; in the latter, *accepted*.

The differential contributions of moral norms and institutions to contemporary American society are well brought out by a recent exchange between Kenneth Boulding and Reinhold Niebuhr over the most effective way to render modern life ethically responsible. Boulding thinks we must put our main faith in moral norms, because large scale organizations have a tendency to become bureaucratic and morally obtuse. Niebuhr, on the other hand, holds that we can keep institutions morally fresh, and that if we do, they are the more effective means to societal regeneration because of their solidity and their incorporation of persons.

Laws are the rules laid down by public authority. There is a close tie between them and moral norms, simply because no authority can stay in power long whose laws flout the moral norms of those upon whom the laws are to be enforced. We do not mean of course, that there is a one-to-one correspondence between laws and norms. Some laws treat matters so technical as to fall outside the moral order altogether—for instance the United States law that requires income tax returns to be made on or before April 15. Other laws represent rules desired by a large section of the population and hence pushed through a legislature, but on which there is not the overwhelming consensus that bespeaks a moral norm. The so-called Prohibition Amendment was such a law.

The term "institution" has often been given a wider meaning than it has here. It has been extended to include all culture traits, as when the flying of kites is called an institution in Chinese culture. Or it is limited to large or influential elements of culture. Thus professional baseball might be spoken of as institutional. Often there is a moral connotation which would make the term encompass all of what we call the moral web, but would exclude nonmoral structure. The great sociologist Durkheim used the term thus in *L'education morale* (p. 181) when he said that institutions both lay down the conditions of action to which people have to adjust or suffer sanctions, and express the common values of the society. A very narrow meaning is that of a public establishment, as when we call a mental hospital an institution. These examples show that we must be alert to the implications of the term in any given context, and explicit about its meaning when using it in scientific discourse.

When we say that the system of roles which forms an institution is part of the moral web we mean that this piece of social organization is just as much "right" as an approved mode of conduct. In a democratic society, for instance, the people think it is right to have legislatures at every level of government; and we Americans believe in the public school in the same way that we believe in honest trading.

Institutions, besides their minor function of symbolizing the common values of the society, have two major functions: that of implementing these common values, and that of inculcating them. One of these functions is essentially operative in the present; the other is educational and disciplinary for the future.

This is clearly seen in the institution of the family. On the one hand, the family is a way to carry on the day-to-day life of the population in a way that is morally approved. Men work to support their wives and children. Women care for the home. The desires of husband and wife for sexual response receive expression. Children are brought into the world and cared for during a long period of dependence. In short, some of the major aspects of an orderly, on-going life are accomplished through the role-structure called the family. Each person learns what his role is and, normally, carries it out.

The family also performs an inculcating function, especially with respect to children. It is the place where they get their first and probably richest indoctrination in the common values and the moral norms of the society in which they live. In the jargon of the social psychologist, the family mediates the moral culture of the society to the child. It teaches him how to behave—not only at home, but in many other situations he may encounter in life.

Some institutions are mainly operative, others mainly educational or disciplinary. The capitalist enterprise as a pattern for getting the society's work done is almost exclusively operative, the school is chiefly educational. The family combines both functions in somewhat equal proportions. Government inclines to be largely an implementation of common values, but has its training aspects as well.

The main inculcating processes of a society are two. The broadest one is the moral indoctrination of children. It takes place largely through groups like family, school, and church which, because they express established institutions, are especially suitable for the purpose. The children enter well defined roles in these structures and are morally molded by their regular relationships to adults and other children there. Being fundamental to the society's welfare, this moral indoctrination is not left to the hit-or-miss processes of casual interaction. We do not mean to say, however, that no indoctrination can occur outside of institutional groups. Children learn a great deal from the informal groups of their peers, for example, including much that reflects the moral order of the wider society.

The other principal process of moral inculcation is professionalization. Those men and women who are going to fill roles in the society that are both powerful and difficult to monitor are given ethical training in the course of their education so that they will perform their functions with due regard for the society's welfare. Professionalization is carried out in large part by the educational institutions that specialize in the various fields of training. In recent decades many occupations have been added to the four traditional professions: law, medicine, the ministry, and teaching. Hence a much extended network of professional training.

To the layman the connection of an institution with the moral order is much more apparent if it carries on the inculcating function. Family, school, and church seem unquestionably moral in character. When the main function is an implementing one, that connection is less obvious. The government seems to many a largely technical agency with only a tenuous relation to the society's common values. The linkage of economic enterprises to the moral order is often completely overlooked. We think of them as ways of mining coal, carrying freight, making automobiles or selling groceries, or, from another and more general standpoint, as ways of making money. We rarely stop to consider that they are ways of performing these functions in accordance with the common values of our society. But unless they are in fact suffused with these values they do not deserve to be recognized as institutional.

The institutions of society tend to fit together into a system. One evidence of this is that they cure each other's dysfunctions. If the family fails to do an adequate job, school or church or a charitable organization tends to take up the function and perform it. Thus at any particular time the tasks of any one institution are functionally related to the responsibilities of all the others.

A notable difference between the institutions of nonliterate and those of modern societies is that the former are geared to a static, the latter to a dynamic order. Modern societies are learning more and more how to build problem-solving machinery into their institutional structure. It is not necessarily true, therefore, that a high level of moral integration connotes inflexibility.

Closely related to institutions is the concept of legitimate authority. What differentiates such authority from crude power is exactly that it derives from the common values of the society and is accepted by the people who obey it. The most clear-cut examples of legitimate authority are found in political institutions. A constitutional monarch, a president, a governor, a mayor have the ultimate backing of the state, because they express the people's will. But legitimate authority is found in other institutions as well. Parents have it over their minor children, bishops over priests, the president of the corporation over his subordinates. Wherever there is an accepted hierarchical relationship that reflects the common values of the culture, the superior has legitimate authority over the inferior.

One of the burning questions throughout civilized history is whether the state should have legitimate authority over all other institutions—or whether the church, the university, the guild, and the family should have "liberties" that give them some measure of autonomy. Whitehead has given a fascinating overview of this contest in his *Adventures of Ideas* (Chap. 4). In fact, each society solves the problem in the manner most compatible with its value system.

Moral norms are the other principal part of the moral web. They develop in every society to influence the decisions of conscience to accord with the accepted common values. In primitive and peasant societies these norms are part of a transmitted body of custom. In civilized societies, where change is endemic, they undergo frequent modification. Conditions peculiar to our century, for instance, have produced the norm that forbids a driver to leave the scene of an accident until he has identified himself to the injured, witnesses, or the authorities.

An interesting difference between institutions and moral norms is that the former have both implementing and inculcating functions, the latter only implementing functions. This is because an institution is a role structure in the midst of which persons receive moral training. A moral norm, accepted by the individual in his conscience, tends to implement the common values but does not necessarily have any educative effect on others.

The moral norm needs to be distinguished from other types of norms and from modal behavior, and ideals.

Cognitive, aesthetic and technical norms would seem not properly to belong to the moral order. Rules of scientific thought such as are listed in textbooks of logic are clearly not matters of conscience in the ordinary sense. Nor are canons of beauty. It seems equally legitimate to regard norms of efficient technique, such as assembly-line production, as distinct from moral norms. In all three cases, those in whom the norms operate undoubtedly feel them to be in some sense "right." But they are right for relations among cultural objects—ideas, percepts, physical operations—not for relations among people and groups as actors.

By modal behavior we mean the most frequent response of people to a given situation. Thus, if on a highway where there is no speed limit, half the cars travel between 50 and 60 miles an hour, one-sixth travel more than 60, and one-third travel less than 50, driving between 50 and 60 miles an hour is modal behavior. If there is a speed limit of 60 miles an hour, modal behavior corresponds to the norm; if the limit is 50 miles, it does not. The question of whether moral norms *should* follow modal behavior has been much discussed in all ages, and usually the answer has been negative. A positive answer would seem to imply that moral norms can make no distinctive contribution. The two Kinsey reports on sex behavior in the United States raised this question in acute form since they purported to show a very wide divergence between traditional norms and actual conduct. It is not unreasonable to suggest that, although norms should not be slaves of modal behavior, they cannot be effective if they are greatly discordant. This, however, is not a matter on which science can speak with authority.

The comparison of moral norms with modal behavior brings out two meanings of the term "expected behavior." The word "expect" can refer to what in fact will happen—modal behavior—as when we say "I expect that there will be ten conventions in the city this month"; or it can refer to what ought to happen—the moral norm—as in Lord Nelson's famous injunction at Trafalgar, "England expects every man to do his duty." A good deal of confusion in sociology has arisen from this ambiguity.

The distinction between moral norms and ideals is a distinction of degree of practicability. Ideals are formulated without a comprehensive appraisal of the situation and of the obstacles to their realization. Moral norms, on the other hand, specify what can reasonably be required considering all the conditions. An ideal is a standard to which the members of a society are asked to aspire; a moral norm is one to which they are obligated to conform. Americans would like their people to live up to American ideals, but they count on them to live up to moral norms. Hobhouse, in *Morals in Evolution* (p. 23), speaking of the comparison of a norm with an ideal says: "But there is this immense difference: that one rule has behind it the forces of society, and so in fact becomes the normal conduct of the average man, while the other rests on the teaching of the idealist and is perhaps practiced only by the best men in their best moments." Another way of saying the same thing is that the violation of a moral norm will bring sanctions down on the head of the violator; not so failure to live up to an ideal.

While a moral norm is comparatively easy to define conceptually, it is very difficult to identify in practice. Some analysts do not recognize moral norms at all as an independent set of phenomena between common values and law. They believe that there are very diffuse principles on the one hand—common values; and very concrete implementations of those principles on the other—laws. They see no point in setting up an intervening concept. Although it is true that there are real problems of empirical identification, there are great advantages in giving conceptual status to moral norms. Only thus can problems of legitimate and illegitimate authority be clearly delineated and analyzed. It is inconclusive to lay a law alongside the common values to determine its moral legitimacy; there is too much room for differences of interpretation of the values. When moral norms are the criterion for legitimacy, analysis is more conclusive.

How does one discover a moral norm? How can one be sure that a standard, once discovered, can be properly so classified? These are questions about which there is much room for argument. The theoretical answers are not difficult but the practical application of the theory is problematical.

Since norms are found in the common sense of oughtness among members of a society rather than in behavior, they are hard to observe. Their positive aspect is much more elusive than their negative aspect; for when they are breached, people do tend to go into action: they impose negative sanctions. The normal accompaniment of such sanctions is indignation. On this theory one could define a moral norm as a standard whose violation entails reactions of indignation and negative sanctions on the part of the other members of the society.

This definition is weak chiefly at one point. What proportion of the members of a society has to behave in the indicated ways to say that a norm exists? Certainly no quantitative answer can be given.

Expressions like "the great majority of the people" do not take us very far. What is actually requisite for a norm to continue to exist is that enough people feel so intensely about it that it is recognized as the prevailing standard, as one which, because it fits with other elements like institutions, is part of the continuous moral web. More briefly, a moral norm exists when a standard expresses the dominant moral forces of a society. However difficult this definition may be to apply in practice, it is a clear idea.

Several writers have called attention to the fact that a moral norm not only sets a standard of conduct but implies the necessity of setting such a standard. There is danger that the society will not function satisfactorily. There is an obstacle to be overcome, one that the consciences of persons can deal with. Therefore, a norm develops to guide conscience.

Since the most effective moral norms are accepted in conscience, the typical attitude toward such norms is a mixture of obligation and devotion. A person feels a duty to conform because the society to which he feels attached needs that conformity. His broadest self is being expressed when his behavior follows the norm.

The great majority of moral norms seem to be what might be called conduct norms. They are addressed to the consciences of actors in particular situations. They either prescribe a positive action or forbid a negative one: "Honor thy father and thy mother" or "Thou shalt not kill."

Ford has analyzed clearly the components of conduct norms. He finds five elements: a person, a condition, an emphasis, behavior, and sanctions. His example of a norm, arranged in this order, is: Any married man in the society at any time and in any place, must not (emphasis) speak to his mother-in-law, thus receiving credit for respecting his mother-in-law (positive sanction), and avoiding illness (negative sanction). A sixth element, meaning, can be read into the norm. In our example the meaning is that speaking is a sign of intimacy and to be intimate with one's mother-in-law is shameful.

Rarely are the components of norms specified so completely. "Honor thy father and thy mother," for instance, assumes that the injunction is to all persons at all times, and there is no indication of sanctions. Under such conditions of elision the same norm in different cultural situations may have quite different meanings since the elided elements may vary as well as the sense of a verb like "honor." It has been suggested to me that this particular norm has one meaning if it is part of a traditional Jewish culture, another if it is part of a medieval Christian culture, and still another if it is part of contemporary democratic culture. Perhaps, despite its imperative form, the statement represents a common value rather than a moral norm—a value which can be interpreted differently.

Conduct norms are, of course, generally derived from the society's common values which in turn are usually compatible with primary group values. It can happen, however, that the demands of loyalty to the larger system are in conflict with the demands of loyalty to the family, particularly when one system is degenerate from the standpoint of the other. In Hitler Germany, children were encouraged to report on the loyalty of their parents. From the viewpoint of the Nazi state, this was legitimate because critical parents might be traitors; from the viewpoint of a non-Nazi family, such behavior on the part of children was contrary to the essential norms of family solidarity, norms which the state was wrongfully challenging. Such a situation is, of course, a sign of grave weakness in the society's moral integration.

In addition to conduct norms there are what may be called situation norms. Here the focus of attention is not so much the action of the individual as the adequacy, or goodness, of a set of conditions. It is true that persons are responsible for maintaining the situation, but the persons are not clearly identified and are not the focus of the norm. This type of norm is most clearly exemplified in civil rights such as freedom of speech and freedom of religion. The center of attention here is the person who may want to discuss some public question or worship in a certain manner. No one has an obligation so to do, but the norm states that the situation ought to be such that he will be permitted to. No particular person is charged to do anything specific. One could not name the persons who must refrain from interfering with freedom of speech or religion, or the persons who have a duty to protect its exercise. Our American values simply require that the individual be untrammeled in these respects, and all relevant persons are so advised by the norm.

Of the same generic sort but slightly different are norms like "all communities ought to have health officers." In one sense the right of the community to be free of epidemics and health hazards is being recognized. However, the chief responsibility for securing this right rests not on outsiders, as in the case of personal freedoms, but on the local citizens themselves or their representatives. Once a health department is established, the norm merges imperceptibly into an institution. In other words, coagulation of moral structure has occurred around a basic situational norm.

There is no definite number of moral norms that are necessary to the successful functioning of a society. All that can be said is that the "problem areas" must be properly covered so that conflict and friction are kept within manageable limits. The number probably does not increase in proportion to the complexity of the society, because as differentiation proceeds some areas of interaction become partly autonomous, and much of the control in them becomes a function of subcultural rather than societal norms. The professions, for instance, do a great deal of self-policing, and trade associations often enforce standards to a degree that makes societal concern with some problems unnecessary. It would be wrong, however, to conclude that complex societies evolve into congeries of self-governing segments. There always remains the necessity of weaving the various segments together into a firm moral web through society-wide norms. Moral integration requires the meshing of human lives across the society even if only in a few and rather general ways.

Variation in the content of moral norms from one society to another is of course, tremendous. Despite the fact that cross-cultural study shows considerable similarity among the values which cluster around primary group experience, and among the norms that implement these values, the differences in habitat, economy, social organization, and religion are so great that standards of conduct of necessity vary markedly. Not only the content but the coverage of life activities by norms is different. In general, the greater the margin of subsistence the more free play is possible without risking societal disaster; hence a greater segment of life is left outside of normative control.

Although positive sanctions in the form of rewards of all kinds play a role in the moral order, they tend to be much more conspicuous in smaller groups like families and schools than in societies. In the United States, for instance, we have few specific societal rewards outside wartime military and civilian decorations. There seems to be an increasing tendency to name "doctor of the year" or "mother of the year" or "teacher of the year" but such honors are so rare as to have little effect. Much more important is the vague positive sanction of general prestige. The desire to be known as a leading citizen undoubtedly induces many persons to undertake activities supporting the moral order.

At the societal level negative sanctions are much more prominent than positive ones. Societal norms tend to be minimum standards supported by various degrees of punishment. As a matter of fact, one of the best indications that a moral norm exists is the presence of a negative sanction.

The close relation of the moral quality of an act to sanctions is brought out clearly in *Power and Society* (p. 50) by Lasswell and Kaplan: "When a practice ceases to be treated or symbolized as subject to sanctions, we say that it has become 'technical.' It has become a matter of expediency, not of morality." This quotation makes us also realize that sanctions are not something added to the natural functioning of the social order; they are an essential part of that order. They represent the control of the parts in the interest of the whole.

We said at the start that we were going to center our attention on societies rather than smaller groups. Reference needs to be made, however, to the variety of relationships that may exist between the norms of the society and those of the groups it includes.

The most common situation is that societal norms are carried down into the life of the smaller unit, with additions appropriate to the narrower situation. Thus a Boy Scout troop inculcates the general norms of the society in which it functions, but has a code of honor that goes beyond them. In tightly organized societies, such would be the pattern for almost all included groups. In loosely organized societies, however, another relationship is common: the included group fosters norms of its own that are compatible with the societal norms but makes no effort to reinforce the latter. Most leisure time organizations in the United States are cases in point. Finally, there are groups such as criminal gangs whose norms are flatly incompatible with the societal norms. These groups we shall call deviant.

Since moral norms are problem-solving devices they are always attributes of groups that have some degree of integration. A social class whose members are not in communication and who therefore do not feel problems to be common is not likely to develop moral norms. Its members may have many similar traits as a result of similar experiences, but whatever norms they hold will be due to their participation together in other groups, not in their class.

Just as we raised the question of the relation of societal norms to those of included groups, we can raise the question of the relation of moral norms at all levels to the conscience of the person. Is conscience merely the adherence to the norms of the groups to which the individual belongs? This is a philosophical question. But some factual statements can be made about it.

In general, it appears that conscience is molded by other factors than norms. First, since norms tend to specify minimum standards, persons in whom devotion to common values is strong make an extra effort to embody them in their action and thus exceed the requirements of the norms. They seem to be acting on a "higher" morality, to be expressing ideals rather than moral norms. Second, if moral norms have become rigid they tend, in a time of social change, to drift away from the spirit of the common values which they are ostensibly expressing. Sooner or later persons arise who perceive this disjunction and feel it their moral duty to criticize the norms. Third, influences may become powerful in conscience that represent norms of groups in which the person does not participate in the ordinary sense. Thus, a student of other cultures may draw from them moral ideas which lead him to doubt the validity of his own society's common values and hence its norms. Finally, a peculiarly sensitive person may feel moral strains and moral possibilities developing in his own society long before others do, and may thus espouse a creative morality.

Despite these tendencies for conscience to be more than a mere reflection of moral norms, no society can maintain itself if the consciences of most of its citizens are out of tune with the norms. The everyday operation of the system requires that these be a high degree of moral consensus.

Earlier, we distinguished law from institutions and moral norms.

We must now turn to a fuller consideration of law as an auxiliary feature of the moral web.

Law has been defined in many ways by many scholars. We give it here a meaning that represents a distinctive function in relation to the other concepts which have been set up for understanding the moral order. Many aspects of that order which are often subsumed under law have here been parceled out to other concepts. The whole notion of the moral imperatives necessary to societal functioning, for instance, has been embodied in the concept moral norm. One of the chief objectives of law is, of course, to express such norms in terms that can be enforced, but this is not true of all law even in democratic societies. Some of it is morally neutral and merely provides rules of thumb to render acts like the making of contracts effective. Again, it has been pointed out that there are many roles involved in the making of law, its application, and its enforcement and that actually law-and-government is one great system of social activity. But this aspect of the matter is covered by our concept of institution. It is proper, therefore, to give the concept law a narrower meaning than is customary, and to study the relation of this restricted set of data to moral norms and institutions.

For our purposes law will mean those rules for the conduct of persons and groups, and for the control of situations, which are laid down by public officials and backed by the power of the state. Law in this sense is little in evidence in the most primitive tribes, because there the moral norms and institutions have such power over the relatively simple pattern of social life that the specialized functions of spelling out rules and enforcing them are largely unnecessary. On the other hand, the satisfactory regulation of life in a complex, urbanized society is unthinkable without the proliferation of specifically legal norms and the machinery for their application.

The central theoretical problem is the relation of law to moral norms. Clearly when the two are perfectly compatible there is a high degree of moral integration. The law gives precision and power to the moral norms that express common values. When the two are not compatible, there may be several reasons. First, the moral norm may try to maintain a standard of conduct that is above the minimum which is feasible for the law to enforce. In most societies norms of truth exact a standard of conduct superior to anything required by law. It would simply be too cumbersome to attempt legal enforcement of this standard. Secondly, some moral norms are outside the field in which we think it is necessary for the law to intrude. There may be very general indignation over unsportsmanlike conduct on the athletic field—which indicates a norm—but no legal recourse. Thirdly, the selfish interests of those who make the law or of their constituencies may lead to the neglect or distortion of a moral norm. This is obviously true with despots, and often to a lesser degree with dominant groups in other systems. The landed gentry in England, for instance, used its power in Parliament to maintain the use of spring-guns against poachers long after there was strong revulsion among the general public. Fourth, a law may be passed during a period of public discussion before public opinion on the issue has crystallized into a moral norm. In his *Recollections* (p. 143) Viscount Morley says of this situation: "Great economic and social forces flow with tidal sweep over communities only half conscious of that which is befalling them. Wise statesmen are those who foresee what time is thus bringing and try to shape institutions and mold men's thought and purpose in accordance with the change that is slowly surrounding them." Fifth, a law may be maintained by the inertia of institutional machinery after the moral norm it once expressed has changed. We are not speaking here of laws no longer enforced—they are dead letters that can hardly be called law at all—but of obsolescent laws. South Carolina's recently abandoned prohibition of divorce for any reason was a case in point. Finally, it is obvious that when the society is itself so divided on an issue that in different regions or different classes incompatible norms develop, the law cannot be compatible with all of them; it may actually represent a compromise which is fully compatible with none of them.

The degree to which those in power can successfully, through law, flout the moral norms of the people over whom they rule varies with many factors, including the enlightenment of the population, the development of channels of communication among them, the monopoly of military weapons in the hands of the rulers, and the like. But in every case such abuse places great strain on the moral order. De Jouvenel's *On Power* (p. 308) puts the matter as follows: "The necessary cohesion of society cannot be procured by Power alone.

There must exist, rooted in a common faith, a deep community of feeling, passing into an acknowledged ethic and maintaining an inviolable law." Political figures who ignore the common values of their people do so at their own peril. They invite either revolution or societal disintegration. Here is the reason why democratic systems provide legal means of holding power in check.

Although it is by and large true that law is the handmaid of moral norms, it has distinctive characteristics not possessed by the norms themselves. One of the great services performed by law is to publicize the existence of norms and give them solidity in the public mind. The freedoms protected by the Bill of Rights in the United States Constitution, for example, could hardly be so easily understood and would certainly not be so easily communicated to the rising generation if they were not embodied in law. Again, law can deal with the complexities of a modern society in a way that norms cannot. The latter are formulated in the common-sense terms natural to the man in the street, whereas law can be couched in technical terminology equal to the task of controlling delicately-balanced social machinery.

The institutions and moral norms which are the main components of the moral web reinforce each other. Moral norms are kept alive and vivid in the person's mind by his institutional roles; and institutions are kept fresh and vigorous by the participation of persons who have internalized moral norms.

A high degree of moral integration means not only a well-woven moral web—it means conduct in conformity with that web. Loyalty to institutions and adherence to moral norms are indispensable. Most people must be playing their roles as parents or workingmen or citizens faithfully, and must in their conduct show the expected degree of friendliness or honesty or tolerance. It does not suffice to have appropriate patterns in the culture if they are not put into practice. Actually the moral web itself cannot long remain intact unless it is given overwhelming support by the members of society.

The only additional concepts that need discussing at this point are those that connect persons to moral norms. We shall speak of genuine adherence, expedient adherence, and deviation. A genuine adherent obeys a moral norm because it is part of his conscience. He has accepted the values it expresses and is therefore only true to himself in conforming to it. Genuine adherence is what keeps most of us from committing murder. I doubt whether the homicide rate would rise much if there were no policemen.

From our present viewpoint, it makes no difference whether the adherence is of the devout sort, where the norm is clothed with the sacred character of ultimate value, or of the rational sort, where it is seen as a well designed instrument for attaining that value. What is decisive is the fact of the genuine acceptance of the common value.

The term "expedient" is here used with that slightly derogatory meaning it has acquired in daily life. Expedient adherence implies that one is motivated by a calculation of the consequences for oneself rather than for society, including the possibility of sanctions. To the expedient adherent the police, courts, and prisons act as deterrents, though of course he also responds to the milder sanctions of public disapproval and shame.

Finally, when conduct does not conform to the moral norms we speak of deviation. We would include here any violation of the norm, for whatever reason. In the great majority of cases deviation springs from the desire to obtain personal advantage of some sort—pleasure or wealth or power. Sometimes reformers who are strongly opposed to an existing norm feel that they must go beyond criticism and actually violate it as a symbolic act. But however lofty the motive, we would still call it deviation.

The most delicate distinction in this analysis is that between expedient adherence and deviation. The former represents a very unstable and precarious social situation—any weakening of the sanctioning machinery will change the calculus of consequences and increase the amount of deviation. It is of the greatest importance therefore that a society keep to an absolute minimum the number of expedient adherents, and convert them as rapidly as possible into genuine adherents.

Before closing this preliminary discussion of concepts, it may be worth while to consider briefly the role of one of the prime enemies of moral integration—nonmoral power. It is a form of deviation. It must be clearly distinguished from legitimate authority, which is the exercise of power within the moral web. Unlike legitimate authority, which derives from and is responsible to the public interest, nonmoral power thrives on public apathy and is indifferent to the public weal.

Nonmoral power may show itself at any points in the processes of a society. It is particularly likely to appear in dealings with other societies because of the lack of a world moral order with recognized common values, institutions, and established norms. Imperialism, colonialism, and war offer striking examples. Internally, nonmoral power is most frequently evident in three forms. First, persons who have political or military power may behave, not in accordance with the common values of the people—this would be legitimate authority —but in terms of their selfish interests. The extreme of this is despotism, or tyranny. Second, ordinary citizens who find themselves in powerful economic positions for the control of which adequate moral norms have not yet developed may go against the spirit of common values. We recall the conduct of the so-called "robber barons" in fields like railroads, steel, and oil, at the end of the nineteenth century in the United States. Third, unscrupulous persons may use coercion in direct violation of well established norms and law. Racketeers who threaten physical violence unless they are paid "protection money" illustrate the type.

We have sketched the main components of our conceptual scheme. It is obvious that our approach to society in terms of the moral order is selective. Out of the chaos of reality it picks a few elements believed to be of key significance for this aspect of social life. We shall center on the relations among these in the hope of discovering truths helpful to those who would improve the processes of civilized, democratic societies.

In concluding, I wish to repeat that the concepts of a moral web, and of moral integration based upon it, do not imply that the person is somehow subordinate to a social leviathan. In a democratic society the moral web is the product of the people's own experience— it is their common values clothed in an outward form. In conforming to it they are conforming to their own principles and standards. If they are inclined to toleration of differences as a principle, this can be implemented through the moral web. If any feature of the web becomes obnoxious to them, they have the power to change it. What is really being emphasized is that, however morally integrated a person may be who is a societal nonconformer, a society is not morally integrated unless it has a firm moral web.

CHAPTER 3

The Problems of the Moral Web

Social science, like natural science, finds its main justification in its value as an instrument: it gets things done. What it chiefly does is to help men fashion social life to their desires. One of sociology's major tasks is to minister to the needs of societies as wholes. This in turn requires that a society be understood as a system, not merely as the field of action of co-operating, competing or conflicting parts. As do all systems, a society adjusts itself to its problems as a whole; its parts perform functions for the whole, and in the process become interrelated with each other in complicated ways.

The analogy with the biological organism is suggestive but not definitive. The individual behaves as a unit; there are elaborate mechanisms—neural and circulatory—which keep the parts of the body in touch with one another; each organ, like the heart, the stomach, and the brain, has a special job to do in the service of the organism as a whole. When external pressures are exerted on the system, resources are mobilized to meet the challenge.

The notion of a society as a system implies, then, not a nominal unity that yields to every stress, but a real unity that pursues its established way of life by means of the structure it possesses. Lewis Mumford has made this point forcefully: "Every form of life, as Patrick Geddes has expressed it, is marked not merely by adjustment to the environment, but by insurgence against the environment: it is both creature and creator, both the victim of fate and the master of destiny: it lives no less by domination than by acceptance. . . . As a being with a social heritage, man belongs to a world that includes the past and the future, in which he can by his selective efforts create passages and ends not derived from the immediate situation, and alter the blind direction of the senseless forces that surround him." Mumford is here referring not merely to individual man but to collective man, to societies. They too, are real units in the real world. They too are insurgent and creative.

As Radcliffe-Brown has pointed out, the analogy between the organism and a society breaks down in two respects: (1) one can observe the structure of an organism independently of its active functioning, but this is not true of many aspects of a society; and (2) most organisms do not change their structural type in the course of their lives, while societies do. Both points have led to doubts regarding the propriety of labeling societies structural-functional systems. There seems to be no impropriety, however, provided we remember that both the structures and their functions in the whole may change through time. American society, for instance, has remained a system throughout the last century despite the fact that large-scale industrial organizations have risen where there were none before, and despite the sharp curtailment of the functions of so central an institution as the family.

Actually there are two degrees of dynamism in a system as complex as an industrialized society. The first degree is manifested in the constantly balancing inputs and outputs. This makes such a society what is called an open system. Energy from plant and animal sources goes in and skyscrapers, automobiles, and the fine arts come out. Or, babies go in and corpses come out. All the time the society maintains a recognizable and operative structure which fulfills its tasks. At any particular time this structure is carrying on all kinds of elaborate processes such as feeding babies, teaching children, growing crops, manufacturing furnaces, distributing commodities, running baseball leagues. But beyond this first degree of dynamism, a modern society is always changing. It is putting into practice new ways of growing crops, of organizing higher education, of laying out cities.

It is a basic assumption here that one of the functions which always needs to be performed is moral integration. Without a moral center of gravity, there is no society. There must be some agreed social patterns to which conformity is secured—otherwise orderly life is impossible. We also assume that institutions and moral norms—what is here called the moral web—are always needed to perform this function. They prevent the war of each against all that Hobbes postulated as the state of nature. Generally speaking, however, the moral web is fashioned to cope with the first degree of dynamism much better than with the second. This is what we mean by saying that the moral web can maintain a "steady state" but can hardly guarantee that, when changes become necessary, the transition will successfully be made from one steady state to a new one.

A steady state or stable equilibrium is defined by Homans (*The Human Group*, p. 303) as a state in which a shift in one factor produces results that tend to decrease the shift in that factor. The changes, in other words, are self-limiting. This is possible only for biological or social wholes in which structural parts complement one another. When an outside stimulus exerts pressure at some point, the message is relayed by a communication system and the services of the relevant parts are brought into play to protect the integrity of the whole. The type of reaction in the human body, for instance, varies all the way from manufacturing antibodies to combat some kinds of danger, to running away in the face of others; but the constant objective is the maintenance of the ongoing system.

If the danger is warded off and the system returns to the original steady state, there may remain no clear trace of the experience that the whole has passed through. It may look and act very much as it did before, or as does a similar whole which has not been through the experience. This is the principle of equifinality enunciated by Bertalanffy, that the present state of a biological or social whole does not allow us to discover its previous history. The system may have been subject to no pressures worth mentioning or to severe ones. A city that has overcome a crime wave may appear much like a city that has never had one. In other words, there are alternative causal routes to the same steady state.

The concept of a steady state does not imply, of course, that the social body can always resist successfully. When external pressures pass beyond a threshold, defenses break down and readjustments of the system take place. Theoretically, only two results are possible: either the system, after appropriate reorganization, attains a new steady state, or else it disintegrates.

Nor does a steady state mean that nothing new can be incorporated without breakdown and reorganization. In social wholes at least, traits can be added to an existing steady state so long as they are smoothly compatible with whatever is already there. There may even be a smooth replacement of one way of doing things by another. So long as no problems occur that raise moral issues, the old steady state continues.

It may help us to see the very complicated processes involved in the control of a society if we compare the moral web to the thermostatic circuit familiar in modern systems of heating. The essential elements of such a circuit are the thermostat itself, which is sensitive to changes in temperature, the electric wires that carry impulses to a furnace control, and the furnace which produces the heat that is conveyed to the room where the thermostat is located. The thermostat is so set as to turn the furnace on when the temperature of the room falls below the set minimum level and to turn it off again when the temperature rises a certain amount above that minimum level.

Just as the thermostatic circuit maintains house temperature within tolerable limits, so the purpose of the moral web is to maintain human behavior within tolerable limits. It may not be stretching the analogy too far to say that just as the circuit keeps producing warm air for the house, the institutions and moral norms keep producing well-behaved and conscientious people for the society.

There is also the problem of reinforcement. If someone opens a window in the wintertime the furnace has to exert extra effort to meet the added burden. Similarly, if the social system becomes disorganized at some point, the moral web has an added burden to cope with. The moral web would actually try to cure the disorganization, to close the window so to speak. Household thermostatic circuits do not now do this, but from an engineering standpoint there is no reason why they shouldn't.

What are the events or conditions that call for processes of reinforcement? In general, they tend to be quantitative increases in obstacles which the system is used to deal with though in smaller numbers. Elsewhere I have shown that in American communities one such obstacle is the national and racial heterogeneity of the population. The more heterogeneous the population of an American city, the more likely that the city will score low on moral integration. This seems to indicate that the more minority members there are in a city, the greater the strain on the existing steady state. Part of this is undoubtedly due to the cultural pressures between the various groups.

How much of it is due to the prejudices of the native-born white majority is not known, but certainly it is a good deal.

Another factor which my earlier study indicated as an obstacle to moral integration is the spatial mobility of the population. The larger the proportion in a city of people that had moved in or out in a given time period, the lower the city tends to score in moral integration. The reason is probably that the development of solidarity in any group takes time. Transients are not likely to take deep interest in the welfare of the city through which they pass.

A whole society, too, can be strained by increased heterogeneity of population. In the same way, mobility in or out of the society as a whole should be a handicap to integration. Internal migration, however, may not be a handicap. From one point of view, it would seem to be disintegrating in its effects—people need roots. On the other hand, to the degree that it acts to bring the various parts of the society to understand one another, it might be found to make for integration.

Just as back of the thermostatic circuit there is the desire to keep the house at a constant temperature, so back of the moral web are the common values of the society. These are what the machinery is designed to implement. An interesting feature of the situation is that the very operation of the system tends to pass those values on to newcomers. We shall see in the next two chapters that this applies not only to children growing up in the society but equally to immigrants from outside.

Thus far we have recognized two aspects of the operation of the moral web. One is its efficiency in doing its central task. Do the institutions and norms operate so as to keep conduct within the tolerance limits of the system? Or in the terms of our analogy: Does the thermostatic circuit function sensitively, accurately, and quickly so that temperature is maintained within narrow limits?

The other aspect is the question of recuperation: When the "normal" processes under extra stress fail to accomplish the necessary control over social behavior, does the moral web include processes of reinforcement which can recapture the steady state? Are supplemental processes on call which will cope successfully with the new exigencies? Are window-closing mechanisms, so to speak, built into the thermostatic circuit? These questions will be discussed below in Chapters 6 and 7.

Up to this point we have assumed that the moral web is fitted to the situation, that if the machinery connected with its operation is in order, all will be well with the society. The questions of efficiency and reinforcement have to do with a steady-state analysis, for they do not raise the problem of changing the moral web itself.

A human society, however, is subject to far more unpredictable vicissitudes than is a house and heating system. We know pretty well what outside temperatures our furnaces will have to counteract. A society, on the other hand, may be subject to altogether unforeseen cultural influences from other societies. These may seriously disrupt the way of life if there is not some means to ward them off—to maintain the society in the face of external pressure. This problem is neither wholly static nor wholly dynamic. Insofar as the moral web enables the society to resist the outside influence and maintain its pre-existent steady state, one might say there is no change. But the very act of coping with new types of pressure usually means that new kinds of defenses are built, and this does imply change. In short, reinforcement processes are set up, but this time they are directed not against foreseeable emergencies but against unanticipated threats. There is no analogy here to the thermostatic circuit, for to meet new challenges requires intelligent adaptation which a merely physical system lacks. One could hardly imagine, for instance, a thermostatic circuit that could take effective action if mice started to gnaw the wiring. Perhaps because of its partly static, partly dynamic character this situation of resistance to outside pressure is one of the least studied problems of moral integration. We shall consider it briefly in Chapter 8.

A civilized society does not always view outside stimuli as threatening. It may welcome the change as bringing something it desires. Even so, the new features that are brought in are likely to upset the existing steady state. They may call for readjustments throughout the societal structure. This phenomenon of the second degree of dynamism in human societies was mentioned earlier. How does a society remain a system under these circumstances? How does it reach a new equilibrium?

Asking these questions is like asking how the owners of the house obtain a remodeled thermostatic circuit when the old one is rendered obsolete by additions to the structure which overtax the furnace. For the householder the answer is easy. He employs a heating engineer who can take account of the new conditions and design a new layout that will function satisfactorily. In the same way a society may need to refashion its moral web. We shall call this the problem of readjustment. So far in man's history it has been met largely on an *ad hoc* basis. Whatever social machinery was available has been used to solve the problems as they have arisen. More and more, however, man is institutionalizing social change, is learning to build into the moral web itself the institutions of moral decision and social planning which render the transitions to new steady states less jarring. Some day, perhaps, we shall have learned to preside over a moving equilibrium.

The readjustment process gets under way only if there is a problem that is seen as such by the members of the society. Nothing will take place so long as only outsiders perceive some area as problematic. This is well illustrated at the community level in a recent evaluation by Solon T. Kimball of a Health Inventory project in an Alabama town. Here there was a diffuse feeling in the traditionally dominant segment of the community that a health survey would be a "good thing," but no widespread belief that matters were in any way critical. No machinery existed for close co-operation between the dominant group and organized labor on the one hand and the Negro caste on the other—hence no chance for the development of a really broad view of health problems. Only those changes were recommended which fitted the subcultural values of the dominant segment of the town. Kimball concludes: "The Health Inventory worked successfully to the extent that it conformed to prevailing values and worked according to existing patterns. The Community Council and its program had strength where it gave expression to the prevailing order. It failed in exactly those spots where there were no traditional procedures or where values kept social groups apart. The Health Inventory moved the town off 'dead center,' but not so far off as to upset the balance of power and the system of intergroup relations." Which is to say that not enough of a problem was felt to move the community out of its existing steady state.

Readjustment implies adjustment to something. It implies that an appropriate relationship to something external to the moral web itself is possible. What is this something? We answer that it is not one thing but two. On the one hand, the moral web is connected with the dominant common values of the society; if there is a failure of the web to express those values, there will be a strain to achieve a better meshing. On the other hand, the moral web adjusts itself to the basic conditions under which the society operates. These conditions consist of its natural habitat, and of other societies with which this one is in contact. This conception of the place of the moral web makes it a mediating element. It sets up the controls that make possible the realization of the common values under the existent conditions. By adjusting itself to each, it adjusts the one to the other.

This view of the moral web as an intermediate element is consistent with a growing appreciation on the part of social scientists of the bipolar character of social life. Clyde Kluckhohn has said: "We require a way of thinking which takes account of the pull of expectancies as well as the push of tensions . . . which emphasizes culturally created values as well as the immediately observable external environment." In our terms, both the expectancies and the tensions strongly affect the moral web, one from the side of values, the other from the side of conditions.

Although Sorokin does not put the matter in quite the same way, it seems that his position in his great work, *Social and Cultural Dynamics* (Vol. 4, Chap. 6), is also compatible with that taken here. He believes that all social systems have their meaningful or value-laden aspects and their causal or ecological-empirical aspects. Change may come in either aspect, and is likely to cause concomitant change in the other.

It is worth noting that our conception of the moral web does not require us to adopt any dogmatic position as to whether causation in history flows from the material to the ideal or vice versa. It simply assumes that there is a mediating process at work. No issue of causes arises unless the common values and the habitat-bound factors cannot be reconciled. Such irreconcilability is indeed rare. A particular set of common values can be realized under widely varying conditions, and a particular set of conditions becomes part of life under widely varying value schemes. Usually, therefore, neither has to give way. It is altogether exceptional that the moral web is so strained by its relation to each of the poles that one of the poles forces change in the other. History seems to show that influence has in fact been exerted in both directions. In the famous case of the Tanala of Madagascar (discussed in Chapter 10), the discovery of the wet method of cultivating rice changed the property norms from a communal type to a small-family type and ultimately affected the system of common values. On the other hand, when the Pilgrims could not find a way to realize their common values either in England or in Holland, they migrated under great hardship to a different habitat in the New World. We shall be concerned, then, not with the adjustment of the dominant set of values to the material conditions of life, nor with the adjustment of the material conditions to the common values, but with the adjustment of the moral web to both.

The position taken here is, of course, in violent disagreement with Marx, who saw the relations of production as the instigating force of social change. Common values, to him, are merely resultant "superstructure." The viewpoint of this study is closer to that of Max Weber, whose *The Protestant Ethic and the Spirit of Capitalism* and other writings on religious sociology hold that the value orientations of a culture constitute a variable which is partly independent of the material conditions of life. It is also compatible with Toynbee's emphasis on the role of religious values in the rise and maintenance of a civilization.

Although we give great weight to common values as they have been crystallized in the past and come into the present as a part of culture, we shall make little attempt to account for their content. We shall assume that different peoples have worked out different sets of values from their collective experience in the past, a process which appears so complex as to be almost inscrutable. Furthermore, we shall assume that there is no scientifically valid criterion by which to judge the common values of a society. Various writers, claiming a knowledge of the nature of man sufficient to serve as a criterion, have pronounced judgment. Most recently Erich Fromm in his book, *The Sane Society*, has offered a profound critique of American society and its values. His touchstone is his concept of mental health. He says (p. 69), it "is characterized by the ability to love and to create, by the emergence from incestuous ties to clan and soil, by a sense of identity based on one's experience of self as the subject and agent of one's powers, by the grasp of reality inside and outside ourselves, that is, by the development of objectivity and reason." In terms of this concept, he finds so many shortcomings in American society that he describes it as sick.

It is obvious that the view here taken is opposed not only to Marxian materialism but also to any interpretation which derives common values exclusively from contemporary societal experience. Our main point is that societal culture acts as a strong selective agent, permitting to each new generation certain types of experience and withholding from it other types. For this reason, common values have a strong tendency to be self-perpetuating, since all subordinate groups are molded by them. One school of investigators who have not always guarded sufficiently against the implication that all group standards are the product of the immediate social situation are the followers of Kurt Lewin. These students of group dynamics have perhaps been carried away by their enthusiasm over their success in producing changes of standards in small groups.

The tremendous momentum that a set of common values can acquire is illustrated in John W. M. Whiting's book *Becoming a Kwoma*. He shows very clearly that the members of the tribe achieve status by upholding the traditional values, and that these values therefore have great appeal to the coming generation. Desire to inculcate is matched by eagerness to absorb.

We shall, then, be concerned not with what causes change at the poles—conditions and common values—but only with what occurs between them. However, the situation is more complex than has so far been stated. Although the moral web does adjust itself to the common values on the one hand and to the conditions on the other, there is a further aspect of the social system that needs to be taken into account. This we may call the ecological web. As we saw in Figure 1 it lies between the moral web and the conditions. It consists of all that great complex of relationships which have been built up to provide sustenance and satisfy the recreational needs of people. The effects of current technology are strongly reflected in it. When we think, for instance, of the character of contemporary American society, technology is what chiefly comes to mind—the elaborate division of labor, the great cities, the factories, the chain stores, the systems of transportation, the baseball and football leagues.

One can think of the moral web and the ecological web as cushions between societal common values on the one hand and societal conditions on the other. They both mediate the relations of the two poles. Because of the freedom thus implicit in the system, different theorists incline to see one or the other of the intermediate elements as dominant. Human ecologists are prone to believe that the ecological web develops out of the conditions and strongly influences the moral web. Normative theorists, on the other hand, are likely to believe that the moral web derives from the common values, and selectively patterns the ecological web. That both are right is easily demonstrated. The ecologists need only point to the many changes in the moral web that have followed upon the widespread use of the automobile. New norms have developed concerning drunken driving, for example, and new institutional machinery for policing traffic and licensing drivers. The normative theorists, on the other hand, can point to situations like that reported by Vogt and O'Dea. They concluded from a study of two adjacent villages in the southwestern United States that the differences in their ecological webs must be largely attributed to the religious differences of their populations. "It is clear," they conclude, "that the situational facts did not determine in any simple sense the contrasting community structures which emerged. Rather, the situation set certain limits, but within these limits contrasting value-orientations influenced the development of two quite different community types."

As conceived here, problems of readjustment of the moral web are generated from either of the elements that impinge upon it—the ecological web, or the common values. If a change occurs in the habitat or in the pressures from surrounding societies, it is immediately reflected in the ecological web. If any of these changes are judged to be dangerous to the welfare of the society, they may be checked by controls from moral norms and institutions; if they gain ground, they may exert pressure for change in the moral web itself. Problems of this sort will be discussed below in Chapter 10.

Readjustment in the moral web may be generated from the value pole chiefly in two ways. First, the values themselves may change. Few would deny that history shows examples of attempts to incorporate into one society common values borrowed from another. Witness Masaryk's attempt in 1919 to embody American concepts of democracy in the newly created Republic of Czechoslovakia. More frequent is the influence on values exerted by a large influx of immigrants. In addition it is at least arguable that there is spontaneous growth in sets of common values, resulting perhaps from the ability of the human mind to extrapolate. If the members of a society have found that an emphasis on justice has had gratifying effect on their common life, they may come to embrace equality of opportunity as a common value—a considerable step ahead. If social science studies had been as frequent in eighteenth century France as they are in the United States today, more evidence would perhaps have been collected concerning changes in common values as a source of influence on the moral web.

Even if the values themselves do not change, there may be changes in the moral web because it is found not to be in perfect accord with them. New evidence may crop up showing that institutions do not accomplish what they are aiming to accomplish. Or, different sections of the population, usually social classes, come to interpret the values differently. Then incompatible norms develop, posing a problem that has to be solved by a society-wide reinterpretation of the common values. These and similar matters will be discussed in Chapter 11.

If it is true that there is a measure of free play in the relations among common values, the moral web, the ecological web, and the conditions, it is of great practical importance to find the point at which leverage for change can be applied most effectively. On the basis of general sociological knowledge, there seems to be no doubt that this point is somewhere in the middle of the range, where the ecological web and the moral web meet and interpenetrate. It is clearly extremely difficult to bring about change at the poles directly. Conditions are by definition the relatively basic and permanent aspects of the situation. Common values are deeply rooted and almost impossible to attack successfully head on. People are seldom permanently converted to a different set of values. In the middle of the range, however, we can manipulate social structure. New types of organizations can be started, old ones can be given new emphases. Institutions and norms can be modified. New functional positions can be set up and new channels of communication created. These are the kinds of changes that can be brought about by rational effort.

Since they have effects upon moral integration, he who would improve the moral integration of civilized societies should gather information about them. If we can find the patterns that produce high and low levels of integration within the dual framework of common values and conditions, we will have the basic information needed to try out new courses of action.

Many students of modern societies have noticed that such a process of trial and error is to some extent already provided for by the differentiation of classes, groups, and associations. This differentiation has produced within these complex societies subcultures that have distinctive norms. Although the norms cannot be out of key with the essential societal common values, they may stress different implications of those values for specific situations. Conduct with respect to these subcultural norms provides an opportunity for the social scientist to study their probable effectiveness if applied to the wider society. He cannot assume that what works well for the farmers or the city wage earners will work well as a broad societal norm, but he can get some sense of the strong and weak points of these subcultural trials and evaluate their probable worth for broader application.

What we have been saying thus far is quite abstract. We have considered broadly how the moral web functions to keep a society in a steady state and how it must be readjusted when the society is carried by change beyond the threshold where the old moral web can function successfully. This is all very well, but before proceeding further we need to see matters more concretely. We need to get some sense of the underlying characteristics of industrialized democratic societies that make both for the steady-state difficulties of deviation from moral norms and malfunctioning of institutions, and the dynamic problems of readjustment of the moral web.

It is perhaps not an oversimplification to say that the distinctive underlying attribute of twentieth century societies is the geographical scope of functional co-ordination. Things are organized on a new scale. Production is for far-flung markets. Distribution is accomplished through great transportation networks. There has been a sharp rise in the accessibility of both goods and people.

There have been many effects of this new scope of co-ordination.

Two of them appear to be particularly important for moral integration.

On the one hand, there has been a tendency for social structure to nucleate. Where formerly there were thousands of small towns with small firms related to the local market, there are now in addition hundreds of large cities with great corporations producing for and distributing to regional, national, and international markets. Although many small units are still operating, they are parts of great networks of production and consumption dominated by units of gigantic size. The proportion of the total structure which is included in these industrial and commercial giants has steadily risen. Thus, nucleation seems an appropriate term to describe what has been happening.

A correlative effect of the increased scope of co-ordination is the growth of differentiated areas of residence, so that whole communities or city districts are now inhabited by families of a single social class. Formerly classes tended to live together in the same local population like slightly separated layers in a cake. In the large cities produced by modern co-ordination, the layers have been so displaced that one can hardly speak of a cake at all.

Each of these two developments has posed a problem of great difficulty for the moral web. These problems are utterly unlike in their immediate nature but both are linked to the same basic change in society. The nucleation of social structures spells concentrated power. Those who make the decisions for large economic units hold in their hands the welfare of hundreds or thousands. The temptation to use such power selfishly is hard to resist. Moreover, one form of concentrated power calls forth other forms as counterweights. Big business has been offset by big labor unions and big farmers' organizations. The interests of the several parties being diverse, titanic struggles ensue which are sometimes hard to keep within the bounds of law and order.

Institutions and moral norms fashioned for a society whose structure was less nucleated have long since been outmoded. This has been very generally appreciated and many changes have in fact been made. So-called "big government" is only one indication that the people of modern democratic societies have tried to cope with the challenge by fashioning political controls to keep concentrated power in check. But nowhere has the problem been successfully met, for the nucleation constantly runs ahead of the attempts to subordinate it to the moral web. It remains a challenge to those concerned over the moral integration of industrialized, democratic societies.

The development of homogeneous and socially independent areas of residence constitutes a problem at the other end of the scale. Whereas nucleation requires that powerful men, the decision-makers in big bureaucracies, be brought under moral control, the second problem concerns little men, those of low socio-economic status. Essentially what has happened is that the sliding apart of social classes in large cities has left the lower classes exposed in a manner they have rarely experienced before. When they were integral parts of villages and towns they benefited from the leadership and cohesion of the whole community. The better educated and more prosperous elements of the population enfolded them in a common way of life. Now they are stripped of these guiding elements, left in large measure to work out their own destiny. The so-called "blighted areas" of great cities constitute the most notorious example of this denuding process, but a similar phenomenon can be observed in areas where depletion of the soil has been followed by migration of the more prosperous farmers, leaving those without capital on the impoverished land.

The two areas of difficulty that have been singled out do not, of course, include all the problems of the moral web in industrialized, democratic societies. In the course of our analysis we will run across others that have little relation to nucleation or the exposure of lower class elements. But these two will provide a sort of contrapuntal thread running through our study. And even the elements that seem but slightly related to either are tied in one way or another to the most fundamental trend of our times, the increasing scope of co-ordination.

CHAPTER 4

The Transmission of Values and Norms

The tasks that make up the daily round of any society have to be performed regularly, or the whole structure falls apart. This requires the
acquisition not only of the skills called for by the tasks but also of the
rules or standards for conduct in the various roles. The society's skills
need to be brought into play in an orderly, interlocking manner. It
is neither productive nor pleasant to have men working at cross
purposes.

The usual word for this process is socialization. For our purposes,
moralization is more acceptable because more specific. There are
many aspects of socialization, like the learning of language, which
do not determine one's role in the moral order.

The two principal elements that need to be transmitted are the
common values of the society and its moral norms. They exist, of
course, before the new member comes on the scene and simply have
to be effectively transferred to him. This is not a matter of objective,
rational learning like memorizing the multiplication table. The
values and norms have to become a part of conscience, which is to
say they have to be incorporated in the self. If the new member
merely knows what the standard of conduct is but does not feel any
devotion to it, he will obey it only so long as he sees some immediate
advantage in doing so. He will become what we call an expedient
rather than a genuine adherent.

Since moral norms are derived from the underlying common values
and are merely applications of them to particular situations, one
might suppose that the internalization of either the one or the other
would be sufficient. This is not true, however. Life is so complex,

situations are so multifarious, that it is impossible to have well-recognized and universally known norms for all contingencies a person may encounter. There must be a set of more general principles to which he may refer when confronted with a set of circumstances for which there is no norm, or for which the norm is unknown to him.

On the other hand, common values are vague at best. Hence it is societally desirable to have members act in accordance with specific norms in all the frequently encountered situations of life. Only then can we anticipate the behavior of others with sufficient accuracy to allow close co-ordination.

There are two principal categories of newcomers to a society. One is its native children. The other is made up of immigrants. As we shall point out in Chapter 11, if immigrants arrive in large numbers and settle together, they are likely to give rise to morally readjustive changes in the host society. Some of their common values and norms may influence the moral web of that society. But if they are few and scattered, their assimilation to the new society will be somewhat comparable to that of the native children. Where the latter must merely be moralized, immigrants must be partly demoralized and remoralized. But in both instances the common values and the moral norms of the surrounding society tend to be accepted.

The moralization both of children and immigrants is hampered in modern democratic societies by the tendency, noted at the close of the preceding chapter, for the less educated and less prosperous elements of the population to be "morally uncovered." To the degree that both lower class children and newly arrived immigrants are particularly in need of the fostering care of a community with strong moral leadership, the settlement pattern of modern cities is often inadequate and even maladjustive. We shall discuss this point later in the context of juvenile delinquency.

It is too easy, perhaps even dangerous, to speak of the common values and moral norms of a society as if they were all perfectly adjusted to one another—a seamless web. To the civilized onlooker this seems frequently true of primitive societies—but probably he is mistaken. Though Sumner's strain for consistency has had much opportunity to work itself out in such societies because of their slow rate of social change, there is probably always some degree of incompatibility between norm and norm, norm and value, and value and value. In all complex, urban societies, at any rate, this incompatibility exists. They are so dynamic that new elements are constantly developing that are out of harmony with moral elements already present. We must realize, then, that when we speak of the internalization of common values and moral norms we may be referring to a process by which, occasionally at least, incompatible elements are brought into conscience.

There is nothing mysterious or surprising about the child's acceptance of common values and moral norms. He is surrounded by a society and its contained groups, with the members of which he must live. He is a growing, plastic, receptive organism. It would be odd indeed if he did not come to cherish these cultural elements which, typically, his parents, older siblings, and friends are only too willing to teach him. His social acceptance and approval, which every child desires, depend upon it. It would be a mistake to conclude, however, that effort on the part of adults is unimportant in the internalization process. Though it is too strong to say that they must systematically indoctrinate the child, they certainly must make the important moral elements salient in his life.

Cahn has explained how children come to share the moral world around them as follows: "They learn group standards from the tone their parents use to say 'liar' or 'thief' and the excited whispers their playmates reserve for gutter-talk about obscene occupations and supposedly shameful natural functions. They are taught impressively when wrong conduct is followed by some group gesture of rejection, for rejection is a rod that even the most favored child will feel at one time or another.

"All these kinds of external policing are designed to make themselves eventually unnecessary by creating and training an internal monitor alert and strong enough to take over. The objective to be gained is a disciplined conscious self or conscience, who will speak within on behalf of the outer community and enforce standards. The external police cannot always be on the scene, to arrest every offender and punish every infraction. Fear of being caught, powerful as it is in the operations of morality, is not enough to maintain the process. . . . The enforcement process must do more than announce certain mandates and illustrate the danger of disobeying them. It must build up the varieties of moral habit it identifies with 'good character.' The habit and character so developed are expected to be there on guard whenever an occasion arises for making a moral decision."

The acquisition of moral culture is slow but continuous. Norms are probably learned first, and common values become meaningful only later. This is because the notion of a requisite for the general good is difficult to grasp, and is understood first for particular types of situations. Thus a child will learn that he must not take his play-mates' toys or the neighbors' milk bottles, before he has any notion of private property in general. It takes considerable social sophistication to realize the connection between situations which are on the surface very different.

Piaget, whose *Moral Judgment of the Child* is the outstanding research monograph in this field, shows that a child first thinks of moral norms as completely objective, like things in the environment. He accepts them as commands from those for whom he has respect, but he has no real appreciation of their significance. External con-formity is the only obligation he feels. Since, to him, a lie is a state-ment that departs from the truth, even an error made in good faith is no less a lie. A "white" lie told to save someone else anguish is as bad as a lie told for selfish gain. No matter what the motivation, that falsehood is bigger which is further from the facts.

All this begins to change at the age of about eight. Now norms are appreciated more and more as expressions of fundamental values that make the smooth operation of society possible. Piaget says the child is beginning to appreciate the principle of reciprocity. He realizes that rules are not given in the nature of things and imposed by adults but represent solutions to mutual problems. They are internalized in this stage as in the former one, but now they are being built into a self which is conscious of its social participation and even aware that rules may be changed if circumstances make it desirable. Thus, ulti-mately, moral norms are seen to be embodiments, for special types of situations, of underlying common values which are more general in character.

A society's oncoming generation is, then, competent to acquire the necessary moral norms and common values. Whether the members of that generation do so in sufficiently large proportion to give the society a high level of moral integration depends entirely upon the

success with which the moral web is organized. If it enfolds the growing child with a consistent pattern of moral elements, all will be
well. If it subjects him to inconsistencies or does not offer him
guidance at all in crucial areas of his life, the society's moral integration will be weak.

This is tantamount to saying that moral integration tends to perpetuate itself. If a society is well integrated to start with, the acceptance of common values and moral norms is easily accomplished. The
societal institutions act as powerful instruments. They provide roles
into which the young can fit while the necessary process of internalization is taking place. Especially in a complex society these roles can
rarely be features of the social structure in general but must be features of definite societal organs—institutions. The family, the church,
and the school are places where acceptance of common values and
moral norms goes forward. In fact, the society delegates to these
institutions the moral tuition of the younger generation.

In his studies of Australian aborigines set forth in *The Elementary
Forms of Religious Life*, Durkheim was struck with the importance
of another instrument for reawakening the sense of moral obligation
in the adults and of kindling it in the young: the large societal gathering. He says (p. 427), "Now this moral remaking cannot be achieved
except by the means of reunions, assemblies and meetings where the
individuals, being closely united to one another, reaffirm in common
their common sentiments. . . ." In the tribes he was studying, these
assemblages solidified sentiment for both political and religious custom. Although modern societies still attempt to gather their members in large assemblies on national holidays, the immensity of these
societies and their highly differentiated character militate against it
as a successful means of internalizing common values and moral
norms. Any particular gathering is too small a segment of the national
society and too heterogeneous in itself to give the strongest sense of
national fellowship. In *The Loyal and the Disloyal* Morton Grodzins
has recently argued that one common value at least, patriotism, is
fostered by all the rewarding experiences that the individual has had
within the confines of his society. According to the author (p. 29),
the Englishman's "patriotism results less from the direct internalization of national ideals than from linking to the nation the love and
joy he derives from all the diverse activities of life. . . . Populations

are loyal to a nation as a by-product of satisfactions achieved within nonnational groups, because the nation is believed to sustain and symbolize those groups." This argument would seem plausible only for patriotism—other common values do not involve the nation directly.

For the "moralization" of any particular young person it is not enough, however, that the society in general be well integrated. The milieu in which he himself lives must be free of strong contra-moral influences. The web of life must offer support while he is internalizing the common values and the norms of his society. This truth has been well documented in two recent studies: Bernard Lander's *Toward an Understanding of Juvenile Delinquency* and Albert K. Cohen's *Delinquent Boys*. The former is a statistical monograph based on 8,000 Baltimore cases; the latter develops a theory of what the author calls the delinquent subculture.

Lander analyzes the delinquency rates for 155 census tracts in Baltimore in relation to certain socio-economic variables. Although he finds that there is a close correspondence between delinquency and the two factors of residential crowding and substandard housing, the correspondence is evidently produced by the relations of these factors to others, since it disappears when the others are held constant in the comparisons. On the other hand, home ownership correlates in a strongly inverse manner with delinquency even when all other variables are held constant. Lander concludes that home ownership can be interpreted as an index of social stability, and that it is the degree of instability which is a prime cause of delinquency. Another finding that tends to confirm this interpretation is that delinquency rates are highest not in the areas of highest Negro residence (as most people suppose) but in the areas where whites and Negroes are most evenly mixed. Given existing white attitudes, these areas of maximum racial heterogeneity would have the greatest social instability. Pointing up his finding that the delinquency rate is not related specifically to the socio-economic level of an area, Lander (p. 89) states: "The delinquency rate in a *stable* community will be low in spite of being characterized by bad housing, poverty and propinquity to the city center. On the other hand, one would expect a high delinquency rate in an area characterized by normlessness and social instability. In such sections there is a deficiency in the traditional controls which maintain conventional behavior in stable communities." Most sociologists conclude from such studies that deviation can best be countered by re-rooting young persons in stable communities. But David Riesman believes this solution impossible in a modern, mobile society. In his *The Lonely Crowd* (Chap. 15) he looks to the development of autonomous persons who can cope with life without being thus rooted.

Sociologists have generally assumed that the stability which is important in this connection is of the social if not sociable variety. Riemer, contrasting village and metropolis, suggests that it is not only neighborly solidarity which is effective but economic solidarity too. He believes that one thing which keeps people in the village morally in line is that the deviant suffers in his pocketbook. In the metropolis, unfavorable neighborhood opinion does not so ineluctably result in immediate economic sanctions.

Instability is almost certainly the reason why areas of high population turnover prove to have the highest rates of deviation. In my study of U. S. cities of more than 100,000, I found that an index of crime correlates + .45 with the rate of in-and-out-migration. Within cities it is usually the areas surrounding the business districts that have both the highest population turnover and the most crime. Transients are attracted by low rents here. In-migrants who successfully establish themselves in the local economy tend to move out of such areas as soon as they can.

There is another kind of instability that comes from fluctuations in prosperity. In his *Suicide* (Chap. 5), Durkheim pointed out that it was not only economic disasters which raised suicide rates, but sudden affluence. One of his examples is that the highest suicide rate between 1874 and 1886 in France was precisely in the most prosperous year, 1878, when a great World Exposition was held in Paris. It is axiomatic, of course, that a decline in prosperity can also be very unsettling. The chapter on Hilltown in Homans' *The Human Group* gives a vivid description of such a situation. As the mills that were the backbone of this New England town failed, the whole spirit of the community declined. Organizations lost vitality; entertaining and visiting dwindled; deviation from norms became more common. Social disintegration set in.

It is interesting that the role of social instability in creating moral problems was not adequately appreciated in the first half of the nineteenth century when the industrial revolution was changing the character of English life. Bentham and his disciples argued for a science of morals through legislation, in the belief that men of good will, acting rationally, would solve all problems. No stress was placed upon the importance of the continuity of social relationships, probably because up until the opening of the nineteenth century there had been little social instability. Men did not then appreciate the great contribution settledness makes to the moral order.

It is rewarding to fit together Lander's findings on instability and Cohen's theory of the delinquent subculture, mentioned above. According to Cohen, subcultures tend to arise when a large number of persons feel maladjusted to the dominant pattern of life and seek new solutions to their problems. They explore the situation and gradually develop a new pattern. He emphasizes that the process is not one of each person reaching a new adjustment and then communicating it to others, but rather a joint exploration throughout.

To Cohen, the principal maladjustment to which the delinquent subculture is the solution is the inability of many lower-class American boys to find social acceptance among middle-class children or to participate easily in public activities conducted in accordance with the competitive values of the middle class. But delinquency is six or seven times as frequent among boys as among girls, raising the question why the girls too do not develop a delinquent subculture. One would think that they would find good clothes and good manners just as hard to come by as the boys find a start toward a good occupation or wealth. The answer Cohen gives, which seems somehow insufficient, is that it is the man and not the woman who, by his breadwinning activities, is responsible for the class position of his future family. A lower-class girl need not feel so frustrated in her adolescence since she can always hope to "marry up" in the future. Lack of success in terms of middle-class standards in her teens does not so clearly foreshadow dissatisfaction as it does for boys.

The connection between Lander's results and Cohen's theory is presumably that a stable neighborhood is likely to be one where even lower-class children find enough warmth and support not to feel severely frustrated by their inability to acquire middle-class badges of achievement. In an unstable neighborhood there is a double disadvantage: first, the web of life is not well woven; and second, there is more likelihood that middle-class points of view will be inter-mingled with the dominant lower-class orientations. These are the reasons why an accepted caste situation, such as exists in most peasant societies, rarely gives rise to a delinquent subculture.

A delinquent subculture, once developed, is a source from which the growing children in the area draw emotional sustenance. As they become part of it, they find the acceptance of societal values and norms more and more difficult, and those that they had already accepted slip away for lack of reinforcement. Similarly, the hold of institutions weakens because they represent a way of life that has become meaningless to the youthful delinquents. Interesting con-firmation of these points comes from a study that contrasts the moral ideas of middle-class and lower-class children in an American city. Adolescents were asked why it is wrong to steal. Only 16 per cent of the middle-class children answered "because one might get caught," whereas 54 per cent of the lower-class children gave the same answer. This would seem to indicate that more than half of the latter are either societal deviants or expedient adherents.

Writers on the subject of character development have emphasized the important role of the family. It is certainly true that the transfer of attitudes from the older to the younger generation takes place largely during the early years of life in the home. This being the case, the reader may wonder why so much emphasis has been put upon the stability of the community or neighborhood in which the family lives. The truth of the matter is that stability or instability affects the rate of successful internalization of values and norms in a whole geo-graphic area. There are in any area some families that perform well, and some that do not. But the area will determine the proportion of families that are successful—though not, of course, their identity.

The family has both a creative and a transmissive function in the moral development of the child. Parents and children form a small, intimate group, usually with strong bonds of affection—a prime source of moral experience. Here the child learns to take into account the needs and aspirations of other members of the group, and to identify his aims with theirs and with those of the group as a whole. He learns through experience the rightness for all group activity of such simple virtues as loyalty, kindliness, and responsibility. To the growth of these human values in young people the family makes an indispensable contribution all over the world.

Besides generating common values and the simpler moral norms, the family plays a great role in transmitting the moral attributes of the enveloping society. During the first years of life most of what the child learns about the wider world comes to him through his family; and for at least another decade the family shares with school, church and other agencies the task of interpreting the wider world to the child. What is more natural than that parents who embody the society's standards in their own conduct should inculcate those standards in their children? If the society is democratic, the child will learn the rudiments of democratic citizenship; if it is aristocratic, he will learn the peculiar duties and responsibilities of his station in life.

In both its creative and its transmissive roles, the character of the relations within the family makes a great difference. The situation is most favorable for internalization when the child feels that he is a member of a warm, co-operative whole. Emotional security gives him pleasure and self-confidence. From co-operative activity he learns the worth of effort. He reciprocates with love and respect for those who enfold him in a satisfying round of life. The acceptance of common values and moral norms in these circumstances is but incidental to a larger process, is but to play his part in the common enterprise.

In the modern world, and perhaps particularly in the United States, there has been a widespread failure to come close to this ideal situation. Growing ranks of juvenile delinquents attest to the inadequacy of the internalization process. Many families are obviously failing to provide an emotionally satisfying home life.

Another significant factor is the transition of millions of families from farm to city. As long as the family is a relatively isolated unit performing most of the functions necessary to its life, the child has a lively sense of an ongoing social group, and is able to participate in joint endeavors, often in exciting ways. In addition, the round of life together produces many family rituals which have an integrating influence. But in the metropolis the family is stripped of many of its functions. Its only product is children—otherwise it is merely a consuming and recreational unit. The work of the father is unseen by the child, and completely disconnected from that of the wife. The children are only rarely drawn into the domestic economy. In terms of subsistence at least the urban family is not a well-knit group. This very looseness offers fewer occasions for ritual.

That the family can become a strong co-operative unit even in the metropolis is proved, however, in numerous cases. When parents bring their interests into the family circle and encourage their children to do the same, each becomes concerned with the problems of the others and all participate in working out solutions. Instead of co-operation in meeting subsistence needs, the focus of the family is the sharing of the experiences and aspirations of its members. This is a more sophisticated task which calls for a more intelligent level of family life. Unfortunately many families have so far been unable to reach it.

Another reason for failure to provide the sort of home in which the acceptance of common values and moral norms occurs naturally is that the family is severely strained by the crosscurrents of a complex life. Husband and wife develop incompatible interests, often with desertion or divorce as the consequence. Or, the parents may squabble in the home until the child loses his emotional security.

As the children grow up, another source of strain is the gap between the generations. In epochs of relative stability, this gap is small—the world into which the children are going is much the same world as that into which their parents went. In periods of rapid social change like the present this is not so. Parents, for instance, who did not have television when they were children now find their own children acquiring habits and attitudes they never had. Frequently, they are at a loss to cope with those that seem to them objectionable. This makes for confusion and strain.

Again, parents may become so beset by anxiety or so enamored of new-found pleasures that they fall prey to the vices and excitements of the metropolis, neglect their children, and set them a bad example. "In many homes," a municipal judge has recently written, "parents have viewed their responsibilities in a detached and indifferent manner, and their children could really be said to have been left to bring themselves up. . . . A substantial portion of the young offenders brought to court come either from broken homes where the parents are living apart, from homes rendered destitute by the chronic alcoholism of one or both parents, or from homes presided over by parents with long criminal records. The stories disclosed by the police about conditions in these homes are unfit to print. Some are beyond belief. If the conditions which exist in some were ever brought to light, the public would wonder why the delinquency problem is not worse. It can be said with truth that some of the children never had a chance."

Finally, the internalization of common values and norms sometimes does not go forward because the parents refuse to let their children experience the discipline that comes from bearing the normal responsibility of participation in a joint enterprise. They are extremely "permissive" for fear that the creative energies of their children will be frustrated. This notion, popularized by one school of child psychology, has had immense influence on our schools and homes. The judge just quoted is among its many critics:

"A generous application of liberal principles, so called, has resulted in parents' overindulging children and allowing them to do as they please. That they should gratify every whim, express themselves freely, do just as their 'little hearts' desire, and have everything they want has been not only tolerated but encouraged. Instead of inhibiting violent tendencies and molding character by strict supervision and guidance, parents have deliberately refrained from stifling the impulses of youth lest some latent talent be frustrated. . . . Children can hardly be expected to respect the property of strangers when their destructive tendencies have known no curb in the home." Perhaps the judge does not give enough weight to the danger that stern and authoritarian treatment would rob the children of confidence in their parents' affection, but one can certainly agree that children need to learn that the common good is furthered by conformity to reasonable rules.

Although the various reasons given for the failure of the family as an agency of moralization are fairly independent, they often relate to the point previously discussed: the instability of the surrounding community. Because modern urban life is not congenial to the large kinship unit so common in primitive and peasant societies, the conjugal family has become the prevailing form. Because conjugal families start anew in each generation, and because they are small social units, they tend to take the impression of the environing conditions more easily than would a large family composed of several generations. Disorganization in the neighborhood then introduces discord into the family. This is certainly one reason that unstable census tracts were found in Lander's study to produce the highest delinquency.

Besides offering worthy models of behavior, the family must be capable of leading the child out into the wider reaches of life which he will face as an adult. This family function is wholly neglected by those who concern themselves only with the emotional side of family relationships. It is equally important that the family do what it can to adjust the child to society's life. Obviously this function can be performed successfully only by parents who themselves have a solid grasp of the meaning of the societal values and moral norms, which they must have acquired by participation as well as by communication. For all practical purposes, the parents must themselves have internalized the values and the norms before they can provide the family atmosphere within which the child can do the same. But this is not the whole truth. Nor does a warm relationship between parent and child guarantee results. A third factor, a certain pedagogic skill, is needed in addition.

The interpretation and explanation of the normative elements of a complex society's culture are tasks which, though later performed by other institutions, must be begun at home. They are tasks best performed by parents who are deeply rooted and well educated. A book like *The Education of Henry Adams,* despite the author's disclaimers, testifies to the superlative achievement here of families of what might be called the intellectual aristocracy. Perhaps one of the reasons why there is so much delinquency among the children of immigrant parents in the United States is that these parents have not been able to lead their children out into the American moral order. However affectionate and close the family, the home has not been a moral springboard into adult waters.

Let us take a common value on which Americans pride themselves—the dignity of the person. What in fact does it mean? That one should never make fun of another? Or that persons should never be excluded from organizations they wish to join? Or does it simply refer to the rights accorded by the Constitution? Children are likely to be confronted quite early in life with situations where an interpretation of this value is sorely needed. If their families do not give them guidance they are not likely to receive it until habits and attitudes have already been formed.

Next to the family itself, children's play groups and associations probably have the greatest influence for good or ill. This has been demonstrated by psychologists and sociologists in the past half century, but must have been known to observant adults in all times and places. Piaget reports that the child first learns moral autonomy in the fellowship of his own age group—first realizes, in other words, that moral norms are not just handed down from on high but are produced by the members of groups and can be altered by group consensus. This is the reason why the play group has sometimes been called the school of the citizen.

Unfortunately many play groups, particularly of older boys, do not live up to their moral potentialities. Frequently the code fostered among their members is not consistent with the common values and moral norms of the society. Juvenile gangs are particularly vicious in large urban centers where they often carry on in open violation of the law. Many, perhaps most, adult criminals have been started on their lawless careers by participation in such youthful fellowships.

Probably the chief cause of morally deviant play groups (as of morally deviant families), is general instability in the neighborhood. Children are not likely to rise above the moral level of the life that surrounds them. If there is anomie or normlessness among the adults with whom they come in contact, they will lack guidance; or if, still worse, crime and vice are highly organized in the area, they are likely to receive positive misguidance. We have spoken of the tendency in modern urban life for the lower socio-economic groups especially in the so-called blighted areas to be deprived of the moral tuition of higher groups in the society. Societal institutions do not reach effectively into these areas with the result that institutional groups there distort if not betray the patterns they are supposed to express.

Carr's diagnosis in his *Delinquency Control* (pp. 79–81) squares with ours. He sees two main causes of delinquency, both stemming from a disorganized environment. In the first place, such an environment makes possible the growth of deviant subcultures which in better organized areas would be curbed. Children growing up conform to these subcultures as the only way to enjoy self-respect among their peers. Secondly, disorganization in the environment creates a confused and maladjusted personality which then falls into deviant behavior to escape frustrations.

Still, all the blame for delinquent gangs cannot be laid on the areas where these children live. Children from well-educated families, living in relatively prosperous neighborhoods, also become involved in car thefts and holdups. When this occurs, it would seem to stem from a combination of inept handling in the family, wide acquaintance through mass communication with the ways of the underworld, and perhaps rejection by popular or admired contemporaries. The family may have erred either on the side of sternness, alienating the child, or on the side of a permissiveness that spoiled him. Criminal suggestions may have come from comic books, movies, television, or detective fiction. Boys in whose lives these ingredients have been mixed are particularly likely to fall in together if they have been excluded by other groups. They then may develop a group pattern that is in strong contrast to the law-abiding culture of their immediate neighborhood.

A thoughtful report on a project of delinquency prevention in Chicago has this to say:

A pattern of delinquent conduct first gets established in a community because its adults have compromised their own moral standards. . . .

Where the struggle for material advance is most intense, and where means for achieving position and recognition are lacking, even adults will frequently stifle their scruples. The cumulative effect of such acts is to breed an attitude of indifference with respect to the opinions of conventional society. With this attitude comes a falling away of interest in the character and reputation of the community. There develops a kind of personal isolationism in which people enter into an unspoken agreement not to meddle in the affairs of their neighbors in return for a free hand in carrying on their own affairs.

In such a situation it is easy for the greatest variety of moral views to spring up and exist side-by-side in the same neighborhood. Honesty and frugality exist side-by-side with cheating and waste. . . .

What we see in children as delinquent conduct is often no more than the inevitable effect of such a community atmosphere. When children are confronted with conflicting systems of moral values they themselves fall into conflict and confusion. Parental admonitions to tell the truth and respect the property of others lose their effect when the child is able to see others making their way through life, often more successfully, by lying and stealing. . . . Under these conditions children inevitably develop habits of delinquent behavior which, as they are passed along to the younger children, become neighborhood traditions.

The church and the school, as established institutions that come in close contact with children, have a dual responsibility in the moralization process.

First, they are in a position to influence the play groups of children in constructive ways. If they are to succeed, however, they must have informed and imaginative leadership. It is all too easy to alienate young people by seeming to break in upon activities which they cherish as their own. Youth likes to feel its independence, and may take unrequested advice as an encroachment on its private preserve. Great understanding and great tact on the part of school and church staff members are essential. To offer help quietly and then wait patiently for a response is more effective in the end than to take initiative that will almost certainly be resented.

The second responsibility of school and church is, of course, to perform their own principal functions in such a way as to facilitate the acceptance of the society's values and norms. If the findings of social psychology can be trusted, church and school are more likely to succeed here in proportion as they rely less upon verbal exhortation and indoctrination, and instead shape the social life of the child so that he is actually participating in morally operating groups. Experience is still the best teacher. The more the life of the church and of the school can reproduce in microcosm what the moral order is trying to produce in macrocosm, the more successful the internalization. And, incidentally, the more adequate the child will feel as a person.

It is clear that the moralization of the younger generation in modern society is no easy task. No simple set of conditions can be relied upon to do the job. No single agency can be assigned all the blame when there is failure. Many permutations and combinations of factors occur, with results all the way from outstanding success to utter failure. If what has been set forth is a correct reading of current social science thought on the subject, the optimal set of conditions can be stated somewhat as follows: A child is most likely to internalize the common values and moral norms of his society when (1) that society is itself well integrated; (2) he lives in a stable neighborhood or community; (3) his family is a warm, co-operative fellowship in which he is trained to accept responsibility; (4) his family is well enough integrated into the society to guide him in his adjustment to the wider world; (5) he is accepted into peer groups that conform to societal norms; and (6) school and church give him opportunity to experience a group life that is morally well organized.

The problem of transmitting the values and norms of their host society to immigrants is different from the one we have been discussing. Immigrants have already been moralized in another society. They are now confronted with a different culture carried by people to whom they are strangers. They labor under the difficulty of having to unlearn as well as to learn. Nor do they find their teachers within the bosom of an intimate group like the family. On the other hand, adult immigrants are normally aware of the problem that confronts them and can try, if motivated to do so, to move rapidly forward with their own acculturation.

The host society is usually somewhat ambivalent toward nonassimilated members. On the one hand, as strangers who have queer ways the immigrants are held at arms' length and often driven back upon their own group; on the other, the host society, fearful of nonconformity to its moral standards, wishes to bring powerful influences to bear upon the newcomers. The compromise actually adopted in most cases is that the native citizens try to have the immigrants assimilated through such instrumentalities as settlement houses and adult education classes in language and citizenship, while avoiding personal contact with them.

The processes by which immigrants come to accept the common values and moral norms of the host society vary according to circumstances. S. N. Eisenstadt, drawing on his researches in Israel and on his wide knowledge of the literature, has discussed many angles of the problem of the absorption of immigrants, including the normative aspect that interests us here.

One of the crucial factors is the attitude toward the immigrants of the communities in which they settle. If the local residents are actively hostile, they may provoke a belligerent response from the newcomers. When the latter constitute a cohesive group, they may isolate themselves and thus retard markedly their acculturation. If they have little solidarity, their belligerence may result in futile negativism leading at times to personal instability and embitterment toward the new society. On the other hand, my colleague Werner Landecker, himself an immigrant to the United States, believes that a mild distrust of immigrants on the part of natives may further the acculturation process by stimulating the newcomer to added efforts to fit himself into the host society.

The rate at which the immigrants are plunged into the strange society is an important variable. There are dangers at both the slow and the fast extremes of acculturation. Migrants to rural areas, for instance, frequently try to preserve their old culture by isolating themselves from the host society. Germans have done this in many parts of the world, particularly in the Balkans and in Latin America. They hardly acculturate at all. At the other extreme are immigrants who come to live in large cities without savings and without an established group of compatriots to help them. They have to swim or sink. Without the language and customs of the natives, they must find some kind of adjustment to survive. This is so painful a process that it may leave permanent scars of criminality, disillusionment, or disloyalty.

Usually, however, these extreme paths are not followed. Eisenstadt points out that many peasants, migrating to rural areas in other countries, do in fact at first work out a way of life that is much like their old one; but that they do participate enough in the life of the local communities for a slow but steady process of acculturation. Speaking of nineteenth-century migrations to France and Belgium, Eisenstadt (p. 283) says: "The pattern of peasant culture was well fitted to the rural framework of the absorbing countries, with relative isolation from the modern industrial economy. Within this framework the very slow process of change of customs, acquisition of language, and so on, did not deter the immigrants from achieving a more or less accepted place in the new setting." Whether or not these immigrants accommodate themselves to those values and norms which regulate the national—as distinct from local—life, depends on how strong is their orientation toward the country of origin. If it remains strong, it will interfere with the development of patriotism, the acceptance of military service, and the like. If it is weak, the immigrants can become thoroughly acceptable members of the society while yet remaining a distinct group in the population.

The readjustment of immigrants to urban areas is usually facilitated, in the United States at least, by formal ethnic associations oriented toward the adaptation of the migrants to the surrounding culture. A classic exposition of the role of such associations is given by Thomas and Znaniecki in *The Polish Peasant in Europe and America*. Other analyses are those of Warner and Srole and Mary Bosworth Truedley. The latter suggests that autonomous ethnic organizations have six main functions. It is interesting that three of these are related to moving forward into the life of the host society, while the other three relate to the maintenance of enough solidarity within the migrant group to prevent demoralization during the transition.

The first acculturation function—at least for the Greeks in Boston, the group Miss Truedley studied—"is the solving of the specific problems of a group in transition from a European peasant society to an American one." Financial help for the needy compatriot is one example. A second function of such organizations is "that they permit the practice of American behavior at various levels of sophistication. Americanization is both hastened and made easy by allowing the ethnic individual to practice behaving in terms of his new personality among his own kind, where he is not overwhelmed by a sense of inferiority. . . ." Third, the individual is helped to choose between Greek and American cultural traits and patterns. "While conflict in allegiance is not an issue, every ethnic individual is forced to consider over and over again his relation to Greek and to American culture. 'Shall we dance Greek or American?' is one way in which adolescents phrase the basic question of the culture conflict."

On the other side, autonomous organizations perform what might be called morale-maintaining functions, so that the new migrant does not feel socially isolated in the new situation. These functions are listed as cushioning the shock of transition, maintaining interaction among Greek Americans, and making ethnic social structure overt. The first two are obvious. By the third the author means the "people need the sense of belonging to a society and of knowledge of their relative position in that society." She says further that "these formal organizations make more explicit the climbing systems within the Greek community" and "serve to reward the successful climbers."

Comparing the acculturation of one immigrant group with that of another, it is clear that the group which has value orientations more similar to those of the host country will accept the norms of that society more quickly. As Florence Kluckhohn says, "The slow rate of assimilation of Spanish-Americans (and more recent Mexican immigrants also) and the low level of understanding as well are in large part attributable to a wide disparity in all major orientations of Anglo-Americans and Spanish-Americans."

Children of immigrants are in a particularly confusing situation. Since their parents usually still have much of the normative orientation of their original society, while the children get out more into the surrounding American culture, they are faced with numerous incompatibilities just at the age their character is being formed. This is no doubt the cause of the well-known fact that the second generation tends to run afoul of the law more often than the first. A striking example is furnished by the Molokans who settled in Los Angeles a generation ago. Such cases are peculiarly difficult because any attempt by an outside agency to help the children internalize the society's values and norms will only serve to increase the tension between generations in the family. The public school has often been criticized by immigrant parents for having done just that.

The optimum process for the acceptance of common values and norms by immigrants might be summarized as follows: Acceptance will proceed most satisfactorily when (1) the community into which the immigrants come is friendly, (2) the new social situation has enough features in common with that they left behind to give them some sense of familiarity, and (3) they can benefit from organizations and programs designed to bridge the transition from the old culture to the new.

Thus far, we have been concerned only with the internalization process. It is obvious that common values and moral norms not only need to be implanted—they need to be made to stick in the consciences of men. All we have said about the importance of institutions in setting the stage for internalization could be repeated here with respect to maintenance. There is need for reinforcement from as many sides as possible all through a person's life. Backsliding is all too easy and too frequent, especially in modern societies where the normative system is constantly bombarded by selfish interests.

In a justly famous essay, Robert K. Merton has suggested that in American society it is the cultural goal of achievement which, acting very strongly on the individual, often leads him to deviate from institutional norms in the area of means. In order to rise in the world, he cuts moral corners. According to Merton, this is because much greater stress is put upon the achievement goal than upon the standards of honesty and fairness in the competitive struggle. Though there is no doubt about the fact of widespread deviation, care should be taken not to equate Merton's term "cultural goal" with our "common value." Individual achievement is certainly stressed in American culture but it is extremely doubtful whether it is a property of the social system which, by general consensus, is essential to it. It would rather appear that the strain here is between the common values of honesty and fairness and their implementing norms on the one hand, and the like value of personal achievement with its implementing manipulations on the other.

Another obvious peril to the retention of societal values and norms is the possible entrance of the individual into groups whose norms are not fully compatible with those of the society. Our earlier analysis of the effect of deviant groups here becomes relevant. Most persons, however, in whom values and norms have been well internalized originally are not tempted to join such groups. They find more satisfaction in the companionship of those who are morally integrated into the society.

This leads us to the general point that the less social solidarity or cohesion there is among those who genuinely adhere to common values and moral norms the more deviation there will be. Closely related is the unfavorable influence of an ineffective sanctioning machinery. There are always those in whom the values and norms have obtained only a precarious hold. Since they are on the verge of becoming expedient rather than genuine adherents, the prospect of sanctions for violation is decisive for them. In general, the anonymity of the modern metropolis greatly decreases the opportunity of seeing sanctions imposed on others. Offenders often flee their areas of residence after committing a crime, and certainly many of the youth there never learn whether criminals are caught and, if so, how severely they are punished. Under these circumstances deterrence is very weak.

A general point, implicit in our discussion, should perhaps be recognized explicitly. It is that different people may without harm to society accept values and norms of subcultures that are inconsistent with one another, so long as they are not inconsistent with the overall societal moral order. A simple example will clarify the thought. Certain religious sects believe that to play cards is sinful. Adherents to other religious faiths join clubs and associations whose sole aim is to play cards. These two sets of persons may exist peaceably side by side in the same society so long as that society neither prescribes nor proscribes card playing.

Although childhood learning of common values and norms is the most general process of moralization, a process of special importance for the elite is professional training. Through it, modern societies powerfully reinforce the moral order. A profession is an occupation that performs a function requiring abstract learning. By this very fact, the service of professionals has a fiduciary character; the client must trust the professional to do the job competently because he himself is incapable of evaluating the performance. For much the same reason, the professional must so conduct himself as to uphold the moral standards of his society. His relation to his client, or patient, or parishioner is so intimate that it can rarely be obvious to the general public whether or not the public interest is being adequately protected. The doctor who is asked to perform an illegal operation must be trained to refuse; likewise, the attorney whose client wants advice on how to evade the law. Professional codes of ethics have thus developed in response to the needs for safeguarding both the recipient of the services and the general public. Usually these needs go hand in hand, as when a doctor treats a sick patient, but at times they are potentially in conflict. In that case the public interest takes precedence. A recipient has no right to a service, however competent, which his society regards as wrong.

A code of ethics is a set of professional norms which, like any other norms, must be internalized to be effective. Indoctrination is usually begun during the professional training, and, one would hope, reinforced during a lifetime of practice. Yet the expectation that the norms will be built into conscience is often disappointed, and that for two reasons. First, the individual is already an adult when he begins his professional training. His moral standards are set and, though he is as a rule strongly motivated to become a competent professional, that motivation does not always accomplish the rectification of conscience. Second, the moral tuition does not take place under primary group conditions. There are few mechanisms that can mediate professional norms to the novitiate, as the family mediates societal norms to the child. Classroom lectures are a poor substitute for intimate association. It is probable that the code of ethics is transmitted mainly in situations of a master-apprentice kind involving older and younger practitioners. Hospital internships offer such opportunities for fledgling doctors. A young lawyer may be taken in hand by the head of his firm. A graduate from a theological school may serve as an assistant to a revered pastor. But the difficulties the ancient professions of law and medicine are experiencing in keeping their members in line testify to the frequent failure of the internalization process. Since the professionals are looked up to as the elite of modern industrialized societies, their moral lapses have serious implications for the moral health of the social system, all the more so because the only alternative to self-control by the professionals seems to be control by political means. Most analysts of the modern scene fear such control because of what it might mean in terms of arbitrary actions and red tape. Indeed, the great philosopher Whitehead so dreaded the extension of political controls that he urged increasing professionalization as the most promising way to tighten the sagging moral web of contemporary societies. He felt that if more and more occupations became professions, the leadership of all societal institutions would fall to men of high moral principle.

If professionals are to fulfill the destiny which Whitehead pictured for them, their moral training must become more effective than it is. The only answers the sociologist can give are the old familiar ones—intimacy of contact and stability of relations. If aspiring professionals were early thrown into close contact with practitioners of high ethical standards, and if they maintained their relations with these moral models for a period of years, they would themselves develop sound professional consciences. The difficulty of such an arrangement in a shifting and impersonal world are all too obvious.

Nothing less than careful and imaginative planning for the attainment of a higher level of professional conscience—a planning which might require the whole restructuring of professional training—will suffice.

In discussing the transmission of values and norms to children, immigrants, and fledgling professionals we have spoken in what might seem unduly static terms: internalization and acceptance. Little has been said of the creative influence of fresh personalities upon the existing moral code. The reason is that this is part of the dynamic process analyzed later on.

CHAPTER 5

The Maintenance of Institutions

An institution is a structure of related roles which embodies the common values of a society. It differs from a moral norm in that it is more complicated and at the same time more manifest. These two qualities spring from its nature as a structure. Whereas a norm can lie latent in the conscience of each person in the population until the moment for its application comes, interrelated roles have to be practiced to be maintained. Even a voluntary fire department needs an occasional drill.

The term institution, like so many concepts in sociology, refers to the phenomena near one end of a continuum. There is no sharp break but only a rather arbitrary cut-off point between what is institutional and what is not. Who can say which role-structures implement the common values of a society and which do not? In American society there would be no doubt about the institutional character of the family and the public school. But what about the generalized religious form called the church, or what about the labor union? There is room for considerable difference of opinion here. Some would interpret the common values of the society so as to make the church or the labor union essential to their realization, others would not. This kind of uncertainty is inevitable in a dynamic society where perspectives are constantly shifting.

In most societies, however, there would not be as much dispute over the roster of institutions as there is in the United States. The more homogeneous and settled a society, the more clearly its institutions stand out. The people of such a society have a high degree of consensus on what the pillars of its social structure are.

Since an institution is a role-structure, it may have many exemplars or only one. There are some forty million American families but only one Federal Government—yet both are institutions. Both are ways of getting the functions of the society performed in the manner its members believe to be right. The institution is always a cultural fact —a pattern of roles, not a social fact—a pattern of particular people.

The number of exemplifications of an institution does, however, affect its operation as part of the society's normative system. The fewer the number of groups that embody an institution, the more likely it is that the institutional pattern will be accurately reproduced in these exemplifications. Public sentiment is the most influential guardian of institutional patterns, and the more public sentiment can be focussed on a few instances, the more likely that the pattern will be followed. Extreme cases of deviation from the institutional pattern occur wherever the embodying groups are embedded in a local web of deviant behavior into which the normative standards of the wider society reach but weakly. Examples are families in the blighted areas of large American cities, and local governments in vice-supported communities such as occasionally grow up around large military camps.

Because of these same subcultural influences, efforts to reinstate the institutional pattern are less likely to be successful when there are many supposed exemplars than when there are few. Reform energies are frittered away by having to be scattered. It takes a well-co-ordinated, long-term plan to affect the standard of family life in a deteriorated neighborhood, whereas the public schools might be brought up to snuff in a comparatively short time and with less effort.

The function of institutions in a society might be likened to that of the poles supporting a circus tent. They produce high points in the web of life from which the rest of the social fabric hangs. They organize the areas of human experience most essential to the ongoing of the system in such a way that less significant areas tend to fall into place. Or, to change the figure, they are like the nuclei in cells, controlling the process in the surrounding cytoplasm. We hasten to add, however, that the ordering of life in the area between institutional groups also requires the presence there of persons carrying in their consciences moral norms that are relevant to the problems in those areas.

It follows that when institutional groups are for some reason unusually weak and ineffective, the surrounding life is prone to disorganization. But this is difficult to prove. Usually the whole texture
of a society decays at the same time, and we cannot assign causal
priority to any one factor. We may argue that failure in the internalization of norms brings degeneracy in non-institutional areas which
in turn undermines the institutions, but we may argue with equal
justice that the precipitating cause of a general decline is degeneration of institutional groups.

There have been some notorious instances, however, which seem
to prove that institutional groups *may* be primarily at fault. One is
that of the Catholic Church during the early eleventh century—
long before the Reformation, at a time when the Church was still
the most cohesive influence in Europe. France under Hugh Capet had
practically withdrawn from the Holy Roman Empire, so that the
ecclesiastical organization was more unified than the secular one.
One might expect the Church to play the leading role in maintaining
standards. Yet just at this time the Church fell to its lowest moral
level. "Immorality was rife in the monasteries; the clergy were often
amazingly ignorant; . . . The Church was riddled with pluralism,
simony and nepotism; clerical celibacy was an almost forgotten ideal;
many of the higher clergy were merely rough warriors or ambitious
schemers, the creatures of their lay backers. In such circumstances
civilization, culture and peaceful industry were almost impossible.
The crowning evil was that the very class that should have raised
the moral standards by their teaching and example were so entirely
under lay control, that little could be expected of it."

Another small piece of evidence on the same score is given in
my *The Moral Integration of American Cities*. It was there (p. 112)
found that churches and schools were both probable factors in producing the level of moral integration of their communities.

Another way to express the contribution institutions make is to
say that they are the guardians of the steady state of a society. Un-
wonted strains and pressures may momentarily throw a society off
balance, but if the institutions are in a healthy state their embodying groups will draw upon their reserves of wisdom and energy to
re-establish order.

Since institutions derive from common values, and since societies differ in these values, each society is likely to have a unique set of institutions. Sociologists have pointed out, however, that some functions are so necessary to any society that certain types of institution tend to be universal. The family, for instance, occurs in some form in every known society. Some kind of control machinery also seems essential. But in fields like education and religion the structures that develop differ so greatly that it is stretching matters to claim them to be universal institutions. The truth clearly is that man's life everywhere is somewhat alike—but only somewhat. Though common threads run through different cultures, they are woven into such different patterns that it is largely a matter of terminology whether the patterns should be called by the same name. Are primitive sorcery and the Christian churches different types of institution, or two examples of the same type?

Institutions have three possible roles in the achievement of moral integration. They may serve to perpetuate an existing steady state of the moral order in the presence of random fluctuations in societal processes; they may reinforce and defend the existing steady state when it is under the pressure of forces from outside the society; and they may pioneer change in the process of transition to a new steady state. The first of these roles will be discussed in this chapter. The second is considered in Chapter 8, and the third in Chapters 9, 10 and 11.

All sociological writers from Comte to the present have stressed that society is a very elaborate web of interadjusted parts. Each part both serves the others, and is served by them. The tentative manner of societal evolution makes it inevitable that in times of comparative stability Sumner's strain for consistency will have worked itself out pretty well, so that in fact institutions will then be helping to maintain a steady state: this indeed is their "natural" function. There is no need to explain why or how it is maintained. We are concerned here only with processes that get in the way, only with the obstacles to its successful maintenance. These are of two main types: those that act from within—that constitute weaknesses in the institution; and those that represent interferences from other parts of the social structure.

Since institutions are culturally developed role-structures which are exemplified in particular groups, their weaknesses will not appear in the model, so to speak, but only in the copies. This we can assume because by definition a steady state is one in which the moral web is already properly fashioned.

If we liken an institution to an iron worker's mold and the groups that exemplify it to castings, then the task of the present chapter is to consider why the mold produces imperfect castings. The mold is a good mold; it needs to be realized or incarnated.

Before considering the forces that impede its realization or incarnation it will be well to suggest what resources the society has at its command to offset weaknesses in institutional groups and keep them up to par. Two such resources stand out: professional leadership, and monitoring.

Alfred North Whitehead, we noted in the last chapter, strongly holds the view that professional leadership in institutional groups would not only keep them functioning satisfactorily but give moral stability to the whole society. The same line of thought is elaborated in the important recent work *The Quest for Community*. Its author, Robert A. Nisbet, attributes many of the woes of the Western World to the fact that modern political thought has cherished the individual on the one hand and the state on the other, but has shown little concern for the groups in between. It is precisely the more important of these groups that are ordered by institutional patterns; and, according to Nisbet, it is in the decentralization of state power to these groups that salvation lies. Neither Whitehead nor Nisbet denies that institutional groups already wield a great deal of influence; they merely advocate a policy of purposely giving them more influence provided they are guided by professionals with a sense of responsibility to the enveloping society.

So far as keeping an existing steady state is concerned, institutional groups need to be continually supplied with professionals adequately trained for the roles they customarily fill. Under normal circumstances, churches, schools, colleges and universities, government departments, social agencies and great corporations recruit such professionals in a systematic manner. The assumption is that when any unusual strain occurs in the functioning of these enterprises the professional leaders, because of their training, imagination, and societal responsibility, will rise to the occasion and keep the group functioning in accordance with the institutional pattern.

The family institution exists in so many thousands of examples that it can hardly have the sort of professional leadership which schools, churches, and government departments enjoy. Perhaps at some future time most mothers and fathers will have something like professional preparation for child care and homemaking. In the absence of such societally oriented training, we will have to depend mainly on parental affection.

By the monitoring of institutional groups we mean watchfulness over their policies and activities. Monitoring may be done by persons outside the group who realize the importance of maintaining the institutional pattern—or, in large institutional groups, by insiders not immediately involved in important events. An example of the former is the watchfulness of families upon one another in the old-fashioned neighborhood. However unpleasant and sometimes vicious such monitoring may be, it does serve to keep institutional groups from deviating too far from the accepted societal pattern. Inside monitoring is illustrated by the interest with which lay parishioners often follow the proceedings of the national assemblies or sessions of religious denominations. They want to be sure that the decision-makers are not carrying the collective body in an unacceptable direction. Because the relation of the citizen to public institutions like schools is often distant, monitoring here falls between "outside" and "inside." The residents of a school district do have some responsibility for the conduct of the schools, but rarely feel that they are members of the school group.

Inside monitoring represents the workings of what communication engineers call "feedback." The members of the institutional group are being "fed back" information about what is going on at levels different from their own. Such arrangements have come to be regarded as standard for the effective functioning of large democratic groups of any kind.

Participation by the common people in the direction of institutional groups has been viewed by some with a certain mistrust. Selznick, for instance, feels that only a trained and cultivated elite has a real feeling for the ethos of a society and should therefore alone have a dominant voice in the control of institutional groups. To him the participation of "mass man" in this control is dangerous. Because "mass man" is only dimly aware of the ethos of his society, he can be misled by clever demagogues like Hitler into betraying the democratic institutions his society has established. A similar view is expressed by Ortega y Gasset in *The Revolt of the Masses*. Whether these strictures would apply to monitoring also is not clear. Perhaps those who distrust the moral orientation of the masses would admit the value of their criticisms so long as they were not active in decision-making.

One of the weaknesses to which all groups are prone is formalism. This means essentially the dull routine that ensues when the vital spirit of an enterprise fades away. People "are going through the motions," but their "heart is not in it." As Cooley has put it in *Social Organization* (p. 343): "Underlying all formalism, indeed, is the fact that it is psychically cheap; it substitutes the outer for the inner as more tangible, more capable of being held before the mind without fresh expense of thought and feeling, more easily extended, therefore, and impressed upon the multitude. Thus in our own architecture and literature we have innumerable cheap, unfelt repetitions of forms that were significant and beautiful in their time and place." A good example is the condition into which American schools had drifted at the close of the nineteenth century. Subject requirements were rigid, rote learning was emphasized, discipline was mechanical. The public school, in attempting to carry out its societal responsibilities, had met the problems of rapid growth and insufficient funds by over-systematization. In consequence, certain common values of American life for which the school ostensibly stood—personal dignity, freedom of thought, creative citizenship—were not well implemented.

Bureaucracy has become a word of opprobrium because large organizations are frequently beset by formalism. The public, whether correctly or not, suspects the members of the organization of being apathetic time-servers. It believes that complex organizations have a tendency to spin out red tape which serves only to fetter the participants. To the degree that large-scale organizations require detailed and explicit co-ordination there is an element of truth here. The elaboration of rules may acquire a momentum of its own that is hard to stop. Besides, those who are seeking to rise in the hierarchy, as many are, quite naturally think it best to be on the safe side and conform to the rules even when these seem inappropriate to the situation.

Generally speaking, one would not expect the contemporary urban civilizations to foster much formalism in their institutions. The last two or three centuries have been a period of such rapid social change that there has been little time for formalism. Steady states themselves were of short duration. Institutional groups, like other groups, did not have much chance to get into a rut, and were soon jarred loose. However, just because institutions are the pillars of society, the groups that express them have perhaps had greater stability than others, and thus did come somewhat under the influence of formalism.

In a famous chapter on formalism and disorganization in *Social Organization* Cooley pointed out that the two are closely related. Disorganization is the decay of a body already dead. He cites the later period of the Roman Empire as a time when the system became so rigid that the people grew unpatriotic, disorderly, and sensual.

In the interest of maintaining a steady state of society, it is desirable that formalism in institutional groups be detected quickly. If allowed to persist it may lead to disorganization, with consequences that may upset the equilibrium of the society. But if it is checked early, the affected group may recover its institutional health without jeopardizing the societal equilibrium. We see this when an alert electorate senses complacency in its government and cleans house at the first opportunity. The trouble has been only temporary, and no basic changes in the society are called forth.

Much has been written about human relations in industry and government to the effect that the cure for formalism lies in an adequate recognition of the sociable needs of the group's members. T. N. Whitehead, in *Leadership in a Free Society*, maintains that the "natural" informal organization of workers in shop groups must become part of the formal structure of large economic enterprises.

From the standpoint of the theory of moral order this view is questionable. The chief mark of the healthy state of any institutional group is that its members feel a common devotion to the objectives and values of the institution, that they play their roles willingly because they appreciate the institution's contribution to a cherished

way of life. Such loyalty usually goes with friendship and helpfulness—persons who are engaged in a common enterprise tend to find
fellowship in the process. But moral integration and interpersonal
integration are two different things. Members of a group may experience "togetherness" in a common opposition to the demands of
the institutional pattern, or in complete indifference to it. Conversely,
getting a common job done does at times involve a good deal of friction. The healthy state from which formalism is a departure is a
common enthusiasm for the joint task.

Robert F. Bales, working with small groups in the laboratory, has
shown that, when such groups are given a task to perform, there are
two types of leadership that tend to emerge—one that initiates ideas
and action, and another that keeps the group integrated as a social
unit. These two leadership functions may be performed by the same
person, though usually they are not. The second type requires a person skillful in social relations who can negotiate, compromise, maintain morale, and generally oil the wheels of interaction. At first blush
one might draw the conclusion that the prevention of formalism is
the sole responsibility of the second type of leader. However, a group
might come to enjoy its sociability to the detriment of its mission.
If so, it is the leadership of the first type that is inadequate. It appears, thus, that the avoidance of formalism requires both forms of
leadership.

Since professionals are presumably trained to understand the value
of their own and other types of service, and to exercise rational criticism, their leadership in institutional groups should help to avert
formalism. They should exact high levels of performance of themselves and symbolize excellence for others, be sensitive to the growth
of indifference and dead routine and alert to check them quickly.
Whether they always live up to this ideal is another matter. Professionals enjoy considerable prestige. This renders them less subject
to surveillance and criticism—monitoring in short—than other men.
Basking in the sun of public admiration, they may become enervated,
forget their professional standards of devoted service, and perform
listlessly. Luckily, that is not the rule. Usually the professionals are
alert to the first signs of formalism, and try to deal with it intelligently.

Feedback mechanisms can contribute in two ways to the defense against formalism. First, they can keep the leadership in constant touch with all phases of the group's operations. Leaders can check on the success in achieving collective goals and on the morale of the members. They may learn of tendencies toward time-serving or red tape in time to take action which can trigger recuperative processes.

Secondly, feedback can also serve to facilitate the monitoring of the leadership by lower level group members. If the leadership cadre becomes complacent and lackadaisical, the lower members need to know it. They need regular channels by which information about the workings of the whole body is conveyed back to them. Otherwise affairs may be hopelessly mismanaged. Thus feedback mechanisms are valuable whether formalism occurs at high levels or low. It is important for teachers to learn of the activities of principals and superintendents as well as vice versa.

Institutional groups are different from all other groups in that they express a societally approved pattern. This renders them subject to, and needful of, what we call outside monitoring. Common values are the soil in which institutions must grow. Once a steady state has been reached by the development of an appropriate set of institutions, the guardians of those common values, the people, have a responsibility to see to it that the institutional patterns are followed in practice. Three things are essential here: interest, information, and criticism.

Interest is generated by all the forces that play upon people in society. A well-knit moral order would be one in which people are interested in the welfare of institutional groups. Modern life, however, makes peculiar demands on societal members in this connection.

In tradition-bound societies where the moral order is static, institutions are the subject of myth and caught up in ritual. Interest in the sense of public opinion is unnecessary because involvement is so complete. In industrialized, democratic societies, however, the forces of impersonality, of mobility, and of differentiation are so strong that emotional attachment to the elements of the moral web is attenuated. It would be a gross exaggeration to say that the family is regarded as just another clique, but today for many people the distinction between morally central and morally peripheral groups is blurred. To counter this the moral web has to become the object of conscious development and rational criticism. Interest among the lay public is the first requirement. It may have to be stimulated through education and the mass media. At any rate, if there is no interest among the public the whole system will bog down.

Once interested, the public needs information. In the complexities of modern society, it is hard to keep in touch with developments inside institutional groups. Much has been written on the difficulty of keeping informed of what the goverment is doing, but the problem applies equally to other institutions. The family may serve as an instance. In modern Western societies, well-functioning families have little conception of how inadequately the societally approved pattern is expressed in other family groups. This ignorance is due partly to the separation of social classes, partly to norms of privacy. Our example shows that better and better means of communication are not a complete answer. The undoubted advantage of having the public know about the functioning of institutional groups has to be balanced against the desirability of their self-reliance. Only to the degree that a society's values and norms permit or demand public inspection of institutions, only to that degree should the flow of information be arranged. Under modern conditions the trouble is not so much that we lack such channels, but that we do not use them effectively.

Max Weber pointed to another influence at work in larger institutional groups: professional secrecy. In a conscious or unconscious effort to protect their status, professionals tend to elaborate their technique and develop a private jargon by which the general public is effectively shut out, and which incidentally lessens public information about the institutional group within which they operate.

There has been much criticism of the mass communication media and particularly the newspapers for paying so much attention to events that the public learns little about conditions. It is conditions that first of all have to be understood if there is to be adequate evaluation of institutional groups. The monitors need to know not just the latest scandal within government departments, or their latest spectacular achievements, but the general results of their day to day operations—the balance sheet of routine success and routine failure. The public must somehow get more solid grasp than comes from the reading of spot news.

Another weakness in the contemporary situation, at least in the United States, is that the decline of the neighborhood as a vital social unit has reduced the reliability of information that comes through informal channels. The instability and anonymity of the great city make for uncritical acceptance of rumors and distortions. Though neighborhood gossip may have been a cruel game of idle busybodies, neighbors could evaluate and winnow it. There may be less gossip today, but those who listen to it are less well placed to discount what is false. Information concerning institutional groups may be distorted in the very process of communication.

Public interest and information will produce the kind of criticism that can secure adequate performance of their duties by small institutional groups like families. Such diffuse public criticism is not enough, however, to deal with large and complicated bureaucracies. The critics must somehow penetrate the shell of the organizations. One institution, government, can be so penetrated by the periodic election of new officials. The newly elected officials can implement public discontent by cleaning house. There are obvious disadvantages in too frequent and too sweeping changes of officials, but a moderate use of the method does at least make public criticism effective. The same procedure, with modifications, can be applied to many types of institutional groups. Most churches and private welfare agencies, for instance, rotate the membership on their governing boards.

If the first of the hazards to the successful functioning of institutional groups is formalism, the second is the exercise of nonmoral power.

That power corrupts was known long before Lord Action coined his famous phrase. Yet no society of any degree of complexity can operate without differential allocations of power. The solution that has been worked out in democratic societies is to grant legitimate authority to certain key roles, and to limit strictly what might be termed illegitimate or crude power—coercion, intimidation, manipulation. What power is exercised is then in large part an expression of societal common values. Whenever a power-holder begins to act in some illegitimate way, disciplinary forces of greater power than his are supposed to come into play.

Max Weber's famous analysis of legitimate authority was concerned with essentially political and economic problems, and did not consider authority in the family, the school, and other tuitional institutions. Still it is profitable to consider his three types of legitimate authority in relation to institutions generally.

The tendency of our age is to emphasize what Weber called rational or legal authority, authority respected because the holder of power has been elevated to his position under rules that are themselves regarded as valid. Systems of selection and promotion are integral parts of the usual operation of this kind of authority. Governmental, religious, industrial, and commercial bureaucracies typically possess them.

In the family at least, there is still a trace of Weber's second type —the traditional authority which has always been so prominent in stable societies. Children probably see their parents as wielders of legitimate authority partly because it is customary. Traditional authority has little place in other institutions because they have changed so radically in the past two hundred years that tradition itself has lost its validity.

Charismatic authority—the power of a leader because of his seeming superhuman qualities—plays a minor role in modern institutions because they tend to be highly secularized. Even among religious institutions only the leader of the small sect is likely to be regarded as having charisma. Leaders of denominations reach the top by such a long series of steps of rational selection that they are regarded as office holders rather than superhuman persons. In political institutions charisma again seems rare. Hitler tried to wield charismatic authority, but, as Wolpert says, he possessed only a pseudocharisma —calculated and ideological rather than the spontaneous fruit of a powerful myth. More genuine examples may be found in Britain and the United States in time of crisis—Franklin D. Roosevelt who called the people to banish fear and take new hope at the depth of the Great Depression, Winston Churchill who rallied the British after the evacuation from Dunkirk.

Legitimate authority may operate at all levels of a complex organization. The army corporal's sphere is small, but his authority is just as valid as that of the general, and both can fail to perform in accordance with their institutional role and exercise crude or nonmoral power.

Since legitimate authority represents at once the moral orientation of the society and the principle of co-ordination, it is a fit means for maintaining a steady state. When it is operating smoothly in all institutional groups, they will not only be administered efficiently but will mesh smoothly. Rome just before the first Punic War seems to have enjoyed a period approaching this happy condition.

Modern large-scale economic organizations raise a difficult problem of analysis for a theory of institutions. It is not clear whether or not there is an accepted pattern for them, one that is thought to implement the common values of the societies in which they operate. If there is such an institutional pattern, the discontent shown by the laboring people at the bottom of these organizations would mean that those in higher positions are exercising, at least in the minds of their subordinates, a great deal of illegitimate power. If there is no institutional pattern in this area, then no particular role-structure is "right," and the concepts of legitimate authority and crude power are inapplicable.

Crude power is usually thought of as an aggressive force. It often is, breaking through the close-knit social fabric, but it can also act by omission. To refuse to perform a duty may be just as much an act of crude power as to coerce a subordinate illegitimately. And because it does not involve positive, overt measures, omission is less easily detected and therefore potentially more dangerous. It is hard to prove that law officers deliberately turned their backs on a lynching mob.

Nonmoral power may be exercised unwittingly by a person who carries over into an institutional role the orientations natural to another role he has held. The big business executive who takes a government position, perhaps at a great financial sacrifice, may unconsciously favor the interests of the business class with which he has been identified most of his life.

Crude or nonmoral power cannot successfully be asserted by those in institutional roles unless there is apathy either within or without the institutional group. Either the participants on superior or subordinate levels are not asserting their rights as guaranteed by the institutional pattern, or else the public is not carrying out its monitoring function. There may be a power vacuum into which energetic persons move, enhancing their legitimate authority by crude power. Simultaneous apathy both inside and outside the group is not necessary for this to occur. Institutional groups are delicately adjusted to the rest of the social structure. Either of the two main checks on nonmoral power may prove inadequate when the other fails. If the public becomes apathetic, and if the offenders are high up in the power structure, the other participants in the institutional group may be unable to control them; conversely, when the participants lose interest in maintaining the approved allocation of power within the group, the public may find its efforts to redress the balance ineffective.

The consequences of the use of crude power by one who is expected to exercise legitimate authority are manifold. If he is near the top of the institutional hierarchy, they may be disastrous. The whole organization may become, not a way of doing something which society needs to have done promptly and well, but a way of bringing personal profit or social status, or the sheer joy of dominance to the individual and his henchmen. The political regime of the late Huey Long in Louisiana between 1928 and 1931 is a telling illustration. Crude power at a lower level in the hierarchy may not be quite so catastrophic, but is still bound to disrupt the efficiency and lower the morale of the institutional group.

The best safeguard against the degeneration of legitimate authority into crude power is the decentralization or diffusion of power. The controllers must be controlled. In political matters this is the principle of democracy. Not only must the controls be there in theory, they must be exercised.

The weak, decentralized power of the individual citizen is not usually called legitimate authority—it is rather a legitimate check on those who have authority. When leaders are corrupt, the assertion of power by those below in order to restore the institutional pattern is certainly necessary and proper. If the authorized channels of influence are blocked by the leaders, perhaps even an uprising is legitimate. Jefferson asserted the right of revolution, though the term he used suggests change rather than restoration.

In most institutional situations, the check of crude power in high places is extremely difficult. The whole history of labor's struggle against exploitation indicates that success without the outside help of favorable legislation is almost impossible. Public interest in the preservation of an institutional pattern is crucial. Those who have legitimate authority cannot be trusted to resist the lure of power, and those who suffer from it cannot always effectively organize.

On occasion, however, those who are individually powerless succeed in organizing and thus gaining power. They, too, may then become guilty of its selfish use. Unreasonable limitation of output and "featherbedding" practices by labor are two instances of such abuse.

Power that violates institutional patterns may come from outside as well as inside the society. In Chapter 8 we will consider an extreme instance of this—attempted subversion by those loyal to an alien society. Here we will be concerned with forces acting from within the society but outside the institutional group affected.

An illustration is the pressures that build up around the adoption of school textbooks in parts of the United States where state-wide adoption is the policy. Book publishers and other interest groups have in the past exerted illegitimate, as well as legitimate efforts to influence the choice, ranging from threats to bribery. Crude power has been exerted on anyone who might affect the issue—teachers on advisory panels, school superintendents, state school officials.

Illegitimate power is not always asserted for such crass reasons. Someone who feels that his group has been dealt with unfairly may seek redress by threat or violence. Thus a single member of a racial group whose members have been excluded from political participation may take revenge on the leaders of the dominant group.

Most power exerted from outside is probably not so malevolent. Injury is often done with the elbows rather than the fists. The family life of many a young executive has suffered because of the demands made upon him by a boss wholeheartedly devoted to the success of an enterprise. Farm families may demand so much of their children that school work suffers. Here the assertion of power in one area makes impossible satisfactory participation in another. Any complex society is bound to show imbalances of this kind.

The antidote for power from without is, first of all, vigilance. The group must be alert. But halting the intrusion is usually beyond its capacity. The general public, as protector of society's institutions and the arbiter of power conflicts, must come to the rescue.

Since law is a buttress to moral norms, illegitimate power used to distort the functioning of legal institutions is particularly dangerous. The responsibilities of the legislature that lays down the law, the judges who interpret it, and the executive departments that carry it out are crucial. They must be personally incorruptible and must receive adequate protection against blackmail and coercion. Because it is the machinery that the society has constituted to order its life that is under attack, the sanctions against the use of illegitimate power here need to be severe. In the statute book they usually are, but history shows that they are often mollified in practice. The reason is that the sanctioning apparatus may at some time come under the influence of the guilty parties or their associates. This has been one of the greatest stumbling blocks to the reform of "machine" administrations in American cities.

In addition to the preventive value of vigilance, the public often has the power to "throw the rascals out." The constant threat of doing so if legitimate authority is breached is perhaps the most effective control. The fact that the rascals do not always stay out but find their way back in as soon as the public becomes apathetic again merely illustrates the difficulty of safeguarding the moral order in complex societies.

Crude power exercised in the political sphere has repercussions throughout the society. It undermines the confidence of the citizenry in the whole institutional structure. It is said that Hitler systematically used his knowledge of this fact to break the traditional loyalties of his people, so that they should ultimately turn to him as the charismatic leader who would save them from chaos. Whether or not this analysis is sound, there can be no doubt that widespread illegitimate power pulverizes the moral order.

Formalism and crude or nonmoral power are not the only threats to proper performance of institutional groups. A third type arises from an increase in any of the normal ecological obstacles. In an earlier chapter we indicated that, in the United States at least, heterogeneity and mobility of population make moral integration difficult. Presumably these conditions operate to balk in some degree the operation of institutions. A sharp accentuation of either heterogeneity or mobility would certainly require the reinforcement of institutional patterns. These conditions are illustrated by the situation in large cities, and it is indeed just there that the most ubiquitous of all institutions, the family, finds it most difficult to function.

It would be impossible to treat at length all the difficulties in the way of institutions caused by the tremendous growth of cities. We can, for illustrative purposes, consider briefly the public schools. The task of any school is relatively easy when its children have considerable solidarity because of their adherence to the same set of norms outside of school. They then are already a group; the school has only to guide them. This was essentially the situation in the small villages of pioneer America. Under modern urban conditions the school has to weld the pupils into some semblance of a cohesive group before it can teach them. The obstacles are tremendous. The children may come from the most diverse backgrounds. Some are the children of immigrants; some are from rural areas; some are racially different from the majority; some differ markedly in class status. Many of them have changed status in their lifetime so that they are not at home at their present social level and are consequently unsure of themselves. To bring such a motley set of children to a common devotion to the institutional purposes of the school is well-nigh impossible.

The maintenance of a steady state is threatened also from a totally different source: the occurrence of a disaster. Fire or flood or explosion or tornado may throw the whole social structure into disorder. The normal channels of communication and means of co-ordination may be seriously impaired. The control which flows from the moral norms internalized in conscience may fail because no well-defined norms exist for this situation. Institutions, as the role-structures intended to safeguard the public interest, bear the principal responsibility for reinforcing the moral order during the period of strain.

One of the best studies of the process of community control during disaster was made by Prince on the occasion of the great explosion in Halifax harbor during World War I. It is entitled *Catastrophe and Social Change*. Others have been made in connection with civil defense problems. It is clear from these accounts that in the face of disaster the welfare of the community often tends to be subordinated to the welfare of primary groups. In such a crisis, a person's first sense of duty is to his family and his friends. He will often fail to perform some much needed public service because of his anxiety for his loved ones. Even policemen and firemen sometimes go to the aid of their families before resuming their community responsibilities. In the Halifax disaster, many of the first leaders in co-operative rescue work were visitors to the city. The problem of the community-as-a-whole struck them more forcefully because they had no close personal ties in Halifax.

A recent study of Arkansas disasters comes to the tentative conclusion that middle-class people are better able to see the problem from the broader perspective of the community than lower-class people, probably because of their greater experience with diverse social frames of reference. If this is true, the task of reinforcing institutional controls in time of disaster is not unlike the transition to a new steady state in time of change: in both cases, the more rational and socially mobile middle class are best able to see what needs to be done.

Reports from all sources underline the importance of well-disciplined organization. Among the first groups to react in an organized way in Halifax were army units. A state patrolman in an Oklahoma town hit by a tornado was the first to drive to a near-by town and recruit an organized rescue team. In summarizing some of its work in this field the National Opinion Research Center has said: "It is not the irrationality or maladaptiveness of individual behavior that raises the major control and logistic problems in disasters; rather it is the lack of co-ordination among the large number of actors who are acting on the basis of relatively private definitions. The restoration of organized, concerted behavior requires the re-establishment of the channels of communication and the substitution of a common or collective definition for the multitude of private definitions. . . ."

Those trained to act in concert are likely to perform effectively in a disaster; they will perform even more effectively if they have had some preliminary orientation toward this type of problem. "The possession of specific, well-defined role responsibilities, pre-rehearsed plans of action, the possession of disaster-related skills . . . are factors positively related to the maintenance of self-control and organized response to disaster."

The service of institutions to the maintenance of a steady societal state is more readily safeguarded in the case of disaster than in the cases of formalism, the exercise of illegitimate power, or ecological change. It is easy to urge vigilance with respect to these three, but it is very hard to keep the defenses against them strong and vital. The preparation of institutional groups to meet the problems that follow disaster is at least something concrete. Specific plans can be made, specific training be given; the goal is clear and the means are understandable. Communication and transportation networks make quick and effective action possible; and a growing rationalization of life makes disaster just one more item which can be foreseen and the effects of which can be mastered by organization.

There are no easy roads to the maintenance of vital societal institutions. The complexities of modern life put great pressure on them, be it formalism, nonmoral power, ecological change, or disaster. Social scientists have no sure prescriptions for the relief of these pressures. The patient application of what little we do know, and a gradual accumulation of more expert knowledge, are the best we can do.

CHAPTER 6

Reorienting Deviant Groups

The usual ways to perpetuate a steady moral state are the transmission of values and norms and the maintenance of institutions. If they worked perfectly nothing more would be needed. But in all known societies failure does occur. Not all people behave in terms of the common values of their culture. This is especially true in a modern complex society with its many cross-pulls on persons and groups. Such failures call for a second line of defense. Those who have strayed must be brought back into the fold. Remedial efforts must be organized.

The great majority of rehabilitation efforts have been aimed at deviant individuals. Almost all writers on penology assume that the restoration of the moral status quo is accomplished by individual regeneration. This certainly is of great, perhaps the greatest, importance; it will be discussed in the next chapter. Here, however, we shall consider a process that is in some ways sociologically prior—the reorienting of deviant groups.

It is prior because, as modern research indicates, a very large percentage of those who become delinquent and criminal learn their behavior in such deviant groups. Edwin H. Sutherland has developed a theory of "differential association" to explain the research findings. In an earlier chapter we noted that societal norms are often not well internalized to begin with because of the deviant subcultures into which children are inducted early in life.

These subcultures are carried by groups of varying degrees of organization and structure. Deviant groups are numerous in modern urban life largely because of its widespread tendency toward anomie, or normlessness. The whole bent of economic rationality toward contract rather than status, impersonal rather than personal relations, mobility rather than rootedness, social change rather than stability, specialization by task rather than by skill has diminished the sense of belonging and weakened the hold of common values and moral norms. As we said earlier, these effects are especially pronounced in lower class areas "denuded" of any moral leadership from better educated strata. Thus many people are not held firmly by groups that are carriers of societal mores. That is to say, societal institutions are unable to exert their influence over large areas of life, leaving many holes in the moral and social web. In such holes, deviant groups arise and flourish.

Not every bare patch of land produces weeds, and the mere existence of anomie does not fully explain the development of deviant groups. One must assume the presence of tendencies which, like airborne seeds, take advantage of the opportunities they find. Such tendencies are the culturally stimulated desires for pecuniary gain, the exercise of power, or the thrill of adventure. When unchecked by the restraints of the conventional moral order, they grow luxuriantly.

The term deviant as applied to groups covers the whole gamut from the occasional mildly reprehensible to the viciously criminal. Groups that are still close to conventional standards in their conduct usually orient themselves by the common values of the society but interpret them so as to distort moral norms from their customary meaning. The effect is to make the norms more permissive, so that the deviant group condones acts that the larger society condemns. Such seems to be the nature of the groups described in Whyte's perceptive *Street Corner Society*. The corner boys are well organized; whatever recurring tendencies toward anomie there are in the area are masked by athletic clubs, the policy racket, and political machines. Most of the youthful groups that develop in this soil hover just outside the pale of the societally acceptable. Their members find it difficult to get a start toward conventional achievement as have the "college boys," but they do not turn completely away from the respectable way of life. As Cohen has put it, they withdraw into a sheltering community of like-minded working-class children—and, we might add, of working-class adults. Societal norms are twisted but not ruptured.

At the other extreme are the deviant groups of adults engaged in crime for gain, the so-called underworld. Well on the way to membership in this underworld are the gangs of youths who engage in bloody fights—the worst fruits of the delinquent subculture. The young men who make up these gangs are, according to Cohen, severely frustrated. They live in a society that stresses equality of opportunity; but the wealth and power dangled before their eyes by the dominant middle-class culture are beyond their reach. "We surmise," Cohen writes, "that a certain amount of hostility is generated among working-class children against middle-class persons, with their airs of superiority, disdain or condescension and against middle-class norms, which are, in a sense, the cause of their status-frustration. . . . We would be blind if we failed to recognize that bitterness, hostility and jealousy and all sorts of retributive fantasies are among the most common and typically human responses to public humiliation . . . For the child who breaks clean with middle-class morality . . . there are no moral inhibitions on the free expression against the sources of frustration. . . ." He goes on to suggest that the phenomenon of "reaction-formation," the unconscious buttressing of one's moral position against feelings of guilt, helps to explain the savagery with which gang members destroy property. "The cavalier misappropriation or destruction of property, therefore, is not only a diversion or diminution of wealth; it is an attack on the middle-class where their egos are most vulnerable. . . . It expresses contempt for a way of life by making its opposite a criterion of status. . . . In the delinquent subculture, the stolen dollar has an odor of sanctity that does not attach to the dollar saved or the dollar earned."

Moral evaluation of a deviant group depends on the group's position in the continuum that stretches from the edge of the normal to the depths of viciousness. Mildly deviant groups are probably preferable to the anomie which they supplant. They give meaning and structure to the life of young men that otherwise would have little of either. On the other hand, groups that engage in frankly criminal pursuits like robbery, and burglary, and in war-to-the-death with other gangs, have so destructive an effect on the character of their members as to make any degree of anomie preferable. If their members are rootless, there might be some chance of guiding them into constructive ways. At a minimum their deviation might be changed to expedient adherence. As it is, such gangs have a solid structure which offers strong resistance to the bringing of the members into the moral web of the society.

Obviously, reorienting of deviant groups would be tremendously significant—if it could be done. Untold waste of property and, more important, of human potentialities could be stopped. But so far all attempts to reorient seriously deviant groups have been unsuccessful. The first and simplest reason is that many such groups are dominated by and at times completely composed of adults. The pattern of such group activity is an expression of a kind of social maturity of which deviant behavior is an integral part. Vice and crime have become normal phases of the way of life of these adults. Whatever success they have won has been achieved in large part through their membership in underworld organizations. The reorientation of such a group in line with societal standards would rob it of its essential function. It is not likely that a criminal gang can be made over into a legitimate business concern, or a house of prostitution into a garment-making establishment. The required skills would be lacking —even if we could imagine the necessary transformation of motivation. Adult deviant groups are likely to disappear through disorganization, atomization, and individual reform rather than by reorientation.

Prospects for success are brighter in respect to youthful groups— but even here the difficulties are great. One of these is the difficulty of early detection. Reverting for a moment to the analogy of the thermostatic heating system, deviant groups are like pockets of cold air in rooms far away from the central thermostat. To bring moral forces to bear early would require thermostats in the most remote parts of the house. In fact, however, modern societies find it difficult to set up moral thermostats in blighted areas just because firm outposts of the wider moral web are lacking there. Adolescents get deeply involved in deviant groups before those who might be interested in reorienting them know about the deviancy. What is obviously needed here is something like the air raid warning systems. To date, the school has served better than any other institution in spotting problem children. Where visiting teachers have been employed to counsel with the parents and get at the causes, the existence of delinquent gangs has often been detected early in their career.

Churches and social agencies have rarely been of help in spotting deviant groups. They tend to come in contact only with the "good" people, and to be shunned by those mixed up in shady activities. And this is true in spite of their devoted and concentrated efforts (at least in the United States) to have it otherwise. From the earliest efforts of the Y.M.C.A. and the Y.W.C.A. in the nineteenth century, through the attempts of social settlements and of Boy Scouts and Girl Scouts, to the founding and growth of the Boys Club movement, the constant aim has been to reach all classes of young people. This has rarely been achieved, however, probably because the activities of these groups do not seem sufficiently exciting to the morally deviant. Only an organization like the Boys Club movement, which is specifically aimed at finding and working with the delinquent boys, is likely to dig deep enough into the youth activities of a disorganized area to discover the groups that need reorientation.

Once the youthful delinquent groups have been spotted, however, the battle has only begun. As a rule it is a losing battle. The final reason for general failure to reorient such groups is that they put up very strong resistance. True, young people do not have the same investment in the group activities as adults; nor would the group lose all functional significance if it were reoriented to law-abiding pursuits. But the tendency of the delinquent subculture is to make a hero of the "tough guy," and to consider the usual pastimes of ordinary children "sissy." For such a group to acquiesce in efforts at reorientation is to risk losing status among its rivals. Even the Boys Club movement is usually unable to reorient the deviant groups it has discovered. It generally sets up a competing organizational structure, which may become focal for the more law-abiding boys and whose recreational activities may even interest the less law-abiding; but it rarely succeeds in shifting the prime aims and interests of the groups led by the latter. Several studies show that delinquent gangs will use club facilities for recreation, but will otherwise go right on with their anti-societal activities.

The studies of Festinger and Kelley, though in a different field, support our view. They found that systematic efforts to increase friendliness in a new housing project by increasing the number of contacts among residents did not work unless the residents had favorable predispositions toward new social activities. If they did not, contacts produced no favorable change. Hostility rather tended to increase. Similarly, we must expect delinquent boys to be little affected by contacts with church groups, social agencies, or Boys Clubs—unless they already feel a want of such contacts.

The reorientation of deviant groups, then, is likely to be successful only if they have not yet hardened into an anti-societal mold. But while they are freshly formed and not too set in their ways, or if they have adopted the "corner-boy" accommodation to life, there is real hope that they can be brought into line with common values and moral norms.

One principle that has emerged from the experience of all sorts of charitable organizations is that reorientation is more successful in proportion as it comes from within the neighborhood. It was this principle that motivated the formation of social settlements like that of Henry Street in New York, or Hull House in Chicago. Great as have been their services, however, they too have found it difficult to give the local inhabitants the feeling of control over settlement activities. Neighborhood residents have often come to regard the work of the organization as meddling by "do-gooders" from outside. This frame of mind does not give rise to real moral reorientation among deviant groups.

Yet there is another side to the picture. Sometimes it seems that the more closely a reform agency is identified with an area, the more it has to compromise its ideals. The local leaders often have strong personal interests in other enterprises in the area—businesses, political organizations, and the like. Since these organizations may have to deal with the underworld in order to survive, the local leaders try to keep the reform agency from "rocking the boat."

Whether the leaders are outside professionals or interested adults from the neighborhood, their relation to the deviant group is a delicate one. They cannot bring about improvement unless they are on terms of intimacy with the members of the group, and trusted by them. On the other hand, they are citizens with public responsibilities. What are they to do if they learn that gang members have committed a felony? To inform the police means to lose the group's confidence; not to do so, even though not illegal, means to follow an ethically doubtful course. It is reported that the New York City police department has had to instruct its officers working with youth groups to grasp the second horn of the dilemma, and to inform on the culprits.

The most hopeful account in the literature of reorientation of deviant groups is that which describes what was done in St. Louis in the fifteen years following World War I. Forty clubs were formed there from as many existing boys' gangs, each club sponsored by a substantial citizen interested in helping youths with inadequate opportunities. The author sums up the work as follows: "We go to the gang, capture it, sponsor it, encourage its growth, require no financial allegiance." From the account it is evident that the successes achieved resulted from strong neighborhood support which the sponsors managed to enlist.

Undoubtedly the most intelligent and thorough attempt at reorientation on a broad scale in the United States is the Chicago Area Project. It was inaugurated in 1934 after eight years of study of delinquency in low-income areas of Chicago by the state-supported Institute of Juvenile Research. Its purpose is to test out new methods of treatment and prevention of delinquency in neighborhoods where social agencies had had little success despite concentrated efforts. The Chicago Area Project is a private corporation organized to provide funds supplemental to those made available by the State. "The method of the Area Project has been to encourage and aid the residents of neighborhoods to organize themselves into co-operative self-help units and through these groupings to initiate, finance, and operate programs of social and educational activities; to assist local institutions and public officials to enlarge and make more effective the services which they render to the community; to take action in an effort to eliminate from the community conditions or practices contributing to delinquency; and to attempt to establish such relationships with individual offenders and delinquent groups as might facilitate their assimilation into the conventional life of the community. The procedure followed by the Area Project was designed to arouse in residents of delinquency areas a greater sense of their responsibility for the welfare of children, and a realization that their united efforts may contribute significantly to the welfare of the children and young people of the community."

The aim has been to help neighborhood and community groups to organize and then to help them help themselves in devising and operating programs that will capture the imagination of those prone to delinquency. If the "branches" of some community committees are counted, some twenty-five areas in the most blighted sections of Chicago are now covered. Each local committee is self-governing, and the state personnel act either as consultants or as community workers. The aim, however, is that each neighborhood should develop its own workers. This self-sufficiency has already been achieved in some areas. Central to the whole project is the idea that only those intimately a part of the situation can improve it.

No one who reads the accounts of what the Chicago Area Project has been doing can doubt that the neighborhoods within which the committees operate must be better for their presence. A large number of important services are performed, among them recreation centers for children, summer camps, film programs, and committees that work with young people placed on probation or parole, or find foster homes for orphans, or try to destroy a ring selling narcotics to children. One committee states: "An important phase of the Committee's work included close work with eight neighborhood youth clubs or so-called 'natural gangs.' These clubs are composed of teen-age boys who have taken part in some sort of delinquent activity or boys who are very likely to do so. Some of these activities are gang fights, petty larceny, unusually noisy horse-play, neighborhood disturbances, truancy from school, sex offenses, etc. This phase of our attack on delinquency was initiated about seven years ago and we have since systematically and continually worked with these groups by using community leadership, both adult and boy leadership, in an effort to create effective personal relationships with these boys so as to influence their behavior and become a positive influence in their life."

Despite these diligent and intelligent efforts the success of the Chicago Area Project in reducing delinquency has been modest only. In some areas and at some periods real improvement has been noted, but there has been little overall decrease. No one knows how much delinquency rates might have risen had the Area Project not been in operation, but the failure of the program to achieve striking success is discouraging. Rarely will cities be fortunate enough to be served by so imaginative and seemingly sound a program.

The experience of the Chicago Area Project should give rise to critical thought about approaches to delinquency. Indeed it is doing so. Why does a program so well conceived not have dramatic effects on the rates of juvenile deviation? What has been left out of the reckoning?

As one immerses oneself in the literature on juvenile delinquency in the United States—and an extensive literature it is—one gets the feeling that juvenile delinquency is the price Americans pay for other things that they want. They believe in progress, with all it means in the way of social change. They believe in a free labor market, with all it means in the way of population mobility. They want children of all classes to aspire to a higher level of living with all the envy which this entails. They want the economies that come from mass production and distribution, with the great cities thus created, the hierarchy of occupations, and of rewards. They want their children to enjoy life, which often means that the children are not given enough responsibility. The parents themselves want a "good time" which sometimes spells parental neglect. Some parents foster prejudiced attitudes toward minorities, which make for conflict among children. Once one begins to enumerate the qualities of life Americans seek—some of which are merely like values, some of which are common—it is easy to understand why certain areas of American cities are shot through with juvenile misconduct. To use a colloquialism, the American people are asking for it.

The last paragraph was written before I made the acquaintance of the following discussion of a crimeless society in Donald R. Taft's *Criminology.* His analysis is so similar to mine that I cannot refrain from quoting him:

No pretense is made, of course that the exact nature of a crimeless society can be foreseen. Nor is it urged here that a reversal of *all* processes tending toward crime is either necessary for marked reduction of crime, or in itself desirable. Still we may summarize, in terms of our previous argument what, in part, such a reversal would seem to entail.

Since social change implies maladjustment, a crimeless society had best be static. To avoid culture conflict it should be internally homogeneous.

On the economic side a crimeless society must avoid excessive competition and greed for material gain and must be planned rather than chaotic. This would be essential to avoid such sources of maladjustment as relative failure, city slums, struggle for speculative gains, monopolistic advantages and various types of exploitation.

A crimeless society might have to reverse the trend toward impersonal relationships and restore the personalized culture of the past. It might need to restrict human freedom. It might resort to a return to religious superstitions as agencies of social control. Though different in some respects, such a crimeless society would seem more nearly to approximate primitive or peasant society than does modern society. The reader may well query, however, whether such a society would attract a population which had tasted of the thrills and satisfactions of our modern dynamic, complex and crime-ridden existence.

Such deep-running influences obviously call for fundamental remedies. The American people cannot hope to reduce juvenile delinquency by a little tinkering with the social structure here and there. There must be some basic rebuilding. It is a fair question whether they are ready to change their way of life sufficiently to accomplish the task.

It would be unrealistic to expect renunciation of some of the most deeply entrenched ends and values. The analyst can do no more than estimate how far it is feasible to go in certain directions, and devise a strategy which will cope with delinquency even while as many of America's cherished goals as possible are left intact.

The most promising strategy now used is urban redevelopment. This is the program of changing the pattern of great cities sufficiently to remove family dwelling areas from close proximity to demoralizing influences such as vice and the cruder forms of commercial recreation, and to plan dwelling areas with adequate play space and a complement of institutions serving children. One of the few careful research studies of the beneficial effects of this strategy was made by F. Stuart Chapin. Minneapolis slum dwellers, he reports, who moved to a new public housing project were leading a more satisfactory and useful life after a year than were a matched group of families who remained in the slums.

Although redevelopment will often take the form of a decentralization of the metropolis, with many of the present residents of the inner rings moving out to new neighborhoods on the periphery, there may also be planned rehousing in the central area provided that effective barriers against the influence of the underworld are erected. One of the forces encouraging redevelopment is the growth of industry around the periphery of many large cities. Lewis Mumford foresaw this twenty years ago. In his *Culture of Cities* he painted an attractive picture of small communities built around light industries, where work, education, and play could be fused into a way of life in the best democratic tradition.

Such redevelopment would not interfere with the progress of the society. The free labor market would not be disturbed, though probably some people would be loath to move once they found themselves integrated into a pleasant community. Children would still aspire to a higher level of living, but perhaps this phrase might come to include intellectual and aesthetic values as well as material ones. There would be little effect on the efficiency of production and distribution, or on the hierarchy of occupations, though opportunities for children might become less unequal. More yard space and pleasanter surroundings would encourage families to keep up their property and afford occasions for delegating responsibility to children. Because of the separation from demoralizing influences, there would be less anxiety about teen-age boys doing part-time jobs. Parents would spend more time in and around their homes, thus growing closer to their children. Whether or not conflicts between youths of different races and nationalities would be lessened would depend in part upon the housing policies laid down for the new developments. Evidence points to the lessening of tension when people move from segregated to mixed housing projects.

In this chapter I have strayed from the course I charted at its beginning. I asserted that one of the most important ways of maintaining a steady moral state was the reorientation of deviant groups to conform to the moral web of the society. It has been shown that though many attempts have been made to do this—some of the most carefully conceived and enthusiastically executed—all have failed to reduce juvenile delinquency sharply. The reason for this was that the underlying conditions leading to deviation were too strong, that the drag of the negative forces overcame the positive ones. If, however, some fundamental change could be made to lessen these negative forces, and urban redevelopment was suggested as such a change, then positive forces—as represented in the Chicago Area Project—might win the day.

The theory that we propound is an application to moral deviation of the concept of the threshold. Below a certain threshold of neighborhood life, the reorientation of deviant groups is so difficult as to represent an unsound approach to the reduction of delinquency; above it, such reorientation becomes feasible. It is probable that all areas in most small cities, and the better residential areas in larger cities, are above this threshold. Only the most deteriorated areas in the metropolis seem beyond redemption by this method.

Reorientation of deviant groups was considered as one of the ways for the maintenance of a steady state. We assumed that the moral web—the norms and the institutions—was adequate; the deviants needed merely to be brought into line. Our analysis seems to indicate that this is an optimistic view. Some at least of the youth groups of large cities cannot be reoriented without more basic changes. If and when these changes come, they will not be the continuance of the present steady state but the development of a new one. This takes us into the sort of problems discussed in the later chapters on dynamic processes.

CHAPTER 7

Punishment and Retraining of Individual Deviants

We have discussed why modern societies produce so much deviation. Some of it can be handled within institutional groups, without removing the deviant from his normal social context. Some of it may be dealt with by the reorientation of deviant groups. Much of it, however, seems to require more drastic measures. A severe breach of the moral order calls for dramatic and specific action.

The people of civilized countries tend to think of such action in terms of punishment of the wrongdoer. They are concerned that misconduct shall be inhibited. They want the offending individual controlled as long as he is likely to repeat the offense; they want him so treated as to discourage others from following his example; and they want him reformed before he is returned to society. We moderns think of these as the "natural" reasons for the society taking action. But Paul Fauconnet in his book La responsabilité has made a strong case for another reason for societal action, one which is so covered up in contemporary life that we can appreciate its continuing influence only by looking at the actions of more primitive peoples.

Fauconnet points out that in preliterate societies the attachment of the sanction to the crime itself is close, the attachment to the criminal often vague. He cites cases where a murdered man's relatives may murder, not only a relative of the culprit in retaliation, but the first stranger they meet or, in the extreme instance, the first person they meet. He believes that the only possible explanation for this is that society has a deep need to react to a crime, to impose a sanction, even though it finds difficulty in seizing upon a proper subject. The reason, he thinks, is that the moral order must be re-established at all costs so that the members of the society can continue to believe in it. "It is the social confidence in the authority of moral rules, the moral faith, which needs to be fortified." It is really the crime at which the punishment is aimed, only incidentally the criminal. Men try to destroy the crime, or at least heal the breach, by quickly doing something about it.

Although "an eye for an eye, a tooth for a tooth"—the *lex talionis* —does not at first glance seem to fit Fauconnet's theory, it does in fact do so. It appears to have been the rule in what are called segmental societies, societies made up of loosely related bands. Each of these bands constituted the principal unit of social organization for its members, and its moral order was jealously guarded. Revenge for assaults from members of other bands was regarded as re-establishing the moral equilibrium. Reciprocal retaliations often resulted in a feud. But as the devastating effects of such practices became apparent, the larger society of which both bands were parts developed a strong enough moral order of its own to control the retaliatory processes by seeing to it that wrongs were fairly compensated rather than returned. This way of refereeing a dispute between bands gradually grew into a criminal law, based upon the interest of the society as a whole in the peace and security of all its members.

The development of a common criminal law was aided by the close connection made between crime and sin. The criminal had jeopardized not merely his own relation with the unseen powers but the standing of the whole group. Hence punishment meant expiation. It is only one step from the fear of the gods' displeasure to a desire for reassurance concerning the integrity of the moral order.

Though citizens of civilized countries may think that they have long since outgrown the need for the immediate re-establishment of moral equilibrium at the risk of punishing an innocent bystander, the behavior of lynching mobs in parts of the United States has in the past been quite consistent with Fauconnet's theory. White men, acting in terms of the regional mores of the "untouchability" of white women by Negroes, have often taken law into their own hands and put to death any Negro upon whom the least suspicion has fallen.

According to the theory we have been discussing the moral web of a society is something highly prized. It is what enables the society to operate at all, what preserves its way of life. Preliterate men, living close to the margin of subsistence and beset by fears, need continual reassurance about the moral web that supports them; hence their eagerness to reassert the moral order. If civilized men show less of this tendency, it is perhaps because they have a greater sense of security. In that case one would expect the primitive reaction to reappear in times of crisis, and there is in fact considerable evidence that it does. Most observers believe that the rise of "McCarthyism" in the United States during the Korean War can in part be interpreted as a demand for complete political conformity voiced by less informed elements of the population rendered fearful by the mounting cold war with the Soviet Union.

Sociologists are inclined to believe that in Western societies at least the sense of the importance of a firm moral order is most marked among persons of the lower middle class. Members of this group, the theory runs, have ambitions to climb up the social ladder, but are in fact in constant danger of falling into the lower class. Generalized anxiety is thus thought to give them a greater need to feel surrounded by a strong moral web. They contribute to such a web themselves by being very circumspect and disciplined in their own conduct, and require a similarly strict adherence to moral norms from others.

The general growth of rationality and the scientific attitude has strongly affected men's thinking about punishment. Jeremy Bentham tried to make an exact science of it in the late eighteenth century. His *Principles of Morals and Legislation* enunciated the famous principle of "the greatest happiness of the greatest number," from which he derived a sort of calculus for determining the severity of punishment. Although modern penologists do not hold with his system, his general notion—that the effects of punishment on the man himself, on others who are potential offenders, and on the law-abiding citizenry should be carefully weighed—would be accepted. In trying to assess these various effects, more and more weight has been given to the intent of the deviant, because if he did not mean to commit the act, a much lighter punishment will keep him from doing it again than if he intended it. Whereas in earlier times even young children, the feeble-minded, and inanimate objects were held responsible for anti-social acts, they are now excused for lack of intent to injure.

Ignorance of the consequences of one's acts and carelessness are by no means fully exculpating in civilized systems of law, but they do constitute extenuating circumstances.

Some light on the problem of punishment can be gained if we think of the control of deviant behavior as an aspect of a society's steady state. Every modern community expects a certain rate of deviation, and is equipped to take care of that much. The existing conditions are creating a certain number of deviants, some of whom are not apprehended and remain in their communities as a menace, while others pass to societal agencies for control, stay varying lengths of time under the guidance of these agencies, and then pass back again into the larger society. If this flow is to be compatible with a steady state, the number of unapprehended deviants must not be so great as to disorganize the society, and the number in the charge of the agencies of control must not be beyond their capacity. A decrease in either group would do no harm. But a change which makes it easier for criminals to escape detection and increases the number of unapprehended, or an overcrowding of penal institutions which lessens their influence, would upset the steady state. A dynamic process of problem-solving, to be discussed in later chapters, would then be required.

Our conceptual separation between the maintenance of a given steady state and the transition to a new one is in reality a mere construct. In modern life, any so-called steady state is changing in minor ways, and every transition preserves many features of what went before. This shading of one into the other can be illustrated with the procedures of moral reinforcement. Suppose a society has gone through a time of internal adjustment marked by a low rate of moral deviation. Suppose further that, because of slow migration into the society of alien elements and the ensuing maladjustments, there comes a slight rise in the rate of deviation. This might require no more than that the existing machinery of control be somewhat strengthened without being changed in character. If this is done, and the result is the leveling off of the rate of deviation at a higher level, has there been a change of the steady state? Obviously, there can be no cut-and-dried answer. What matters is whether the new rate is manageable. Generally speaking, we prefer to regard changes in quantity of control alone as carrying on the old steady state. Changes in quality of control would represent a transition to a new steady state.

According to our theory, a deviant individual is one who does not follow the prescriptions of moral norms or institutions that are derived from the societal common values. Only to the degree that those who run afoul of the law are at the same time deviants in our sense are we interested in them. For instance, if an autocratic monarch hands down edicts that do not reflect the moral judgment of the society he dominates, law-breakers may not be moral deviants. The same would be true if a legislature acted against the will of a great majority of the population. Finally, if a judge or jury were corrupt in the application of law that is itself morally valid, one would have to seek other evidence before labeling as deviant the conduct they condemned.

And yet modern societies cannot do without the law. Primitive societies can operate chiefly with informal controls because their deviants cannot escape the ubiquitous moral web woven close around everyone by the intimacy of a small community. But, under modern conditions, the web of informal controls needs to be strengthened with the steel mail of the law. Rules must be made definite and clear. Specialized social roles must be fashioned to administer the rules—police, sheriff, prosecutor, judge. Although the proportion of people who are intentionally deviating from accepted norms is small, the difficulty of detecting their deviation and bringing them to justice is such as to require a far-flung and costly apparatus. Even though law in action often fails to reflect the true moral orientation of the society, it is something the moral order cannot do without. In complex societies a high level of moral integration does not mean abandoning the law—that is anarchy—but binding it closely to the moral norms and institutions it is supposed to realize and supplement.

An instructive example of how the decisions of chiefs of primitive tribes may be rendered consonant with the moral consensus of the people is given by Raymond Firth. In Tikopia, he relates that there is a high-ranking person called a *maru* under each chief. If the sanctions imposed by the chief seem severe to the public the *maru* can mitigate them. He forbids the offender to carry out the sentence on himself. The offender then makes a gift to the chief. "It is witness to the power of the common people that even the chiefs accept the convention that the *maru* represents the views of the people, and also accepts his check on their pronouncements." In ancient Athens, the assembled citizens had the right to remit penalties, and in modern democratic states the executive frequently has the power to pardon as a sort of check on an overzealous judiciary.

While the connection with moral norms is most obvious for constitutional and criminal law, the rules of civil law are equally related to the common values of the society. Actions concerned with private property, contracts, or torts, though not initiated on behalf of the public, are still settled by laws believed to be compatible with the public conscience. It would be untrue to say that the public approves the details of civil law—it does not and cannot know its technical intricacies. But the general principles of civil law, by a process of selection over a long period of time, can be presumed to have a close relation to the moral web of the society.

Llewellyn and Hoebel in *The Cheyenne Way* (Chap. 9) point out an interesting difference between law and moral norms. Though both prescribe what right conduct is, only the law prescribes how breaches in the moral order shall be healed. Informal social controls are hardly suited to an exact specification of what steps are necessary to restore the moral order—this requires the sort of careful determination by experts which a legal system provides. The contrast is seen in the penalties for incest in a primitive and in a civilized society. Though incest is often condoned in the Trobriand Islands if no one makes public objection, Malinowski relates, once the guilty male is accused in public he feels tribal pressure so strongly that he commits suicide. Moral indignation in a modern society might be just as great, but generally the penalty for such an offense is something to be weighed and meted out by constituted authority. Indeed, so powerful has the law become that even if there should be a discrepancy between the sanction imposed by the law and that which public consensus fixes upon, the law would in the short run prevail.

In imposing sanctions, modern societies make a distinction between juvenile offender and adult. There are three general reasons for this. First, the child is thought to be less responsible for his conduct because he is under the tutelage of his elders and may have been misled by them. Second, the child is thought to be more responsive to correctional treatment because deviant norms and groups have not had so much time to fasten their influence on him. He is penalized less severely because he can be reformed more easily. Finally, the child seems less likely than an adult to commit the most heinous offenses. Hence, he can be dealt with more leniently without jeopardizing public security.

In adopting this less rigorous policy for children, societies are running the risk that the deterrent effect which more severe penalties might produce in potential child offenders will be lost. It seems likely that this possibility has been considered and judged to be of less significance than the probably brutalizing effects of severe punishment on the delinquent himself.

Despite the more thoughtful approach to juvenile delinquency which has developed in the past century, statistics show that the problem has in no wise been alleviated. This has led public-spirited citizens to sponsor programs intended to supplement traditional punitive approaches. In particular, there has been the attempt to diagnose the potential delinquent, so that his tendencies might be reoriented before they express themselves in deviant conduct. Teachers have been encouraged to detect problem children as early as possible. In addition to regular social work agencies, two special programs have developed for providing expert assistance in treatment. In larger urban centers child guidance clinics have been set up to which the schools, parents, social agencies and the juvenile court may refer children. Staffed with competent medical, psychological and social work personnel, these clinics attempt to obtain a complete view of the child's difficulties, and to make a recommendation to the interested groups for his reformation. Another approach which has a similar aim but requires less-trained personnel is the visiting teacher movement. Visiting teachers have the responsibility of consulting with the parents of problem children and with community agencies in an effort to work out a plan of co-operative action for the child's better development. Though these approaches to the delinquency problem seem promising they have not been widely adopted.

We noted earlier that most agencies which try to build child character, such as Y.M.C.A., Y.W.C.A., Boy Scouts and Girl Scouts, rarely appeal to those who are most exposed and susceptible to degenerative influences—the children of the deteriorated areas of large cities. These organizations are considered "soft" by those whose feet are already set upon the path to delinquency. The arrest of deviant tendencies by drawing potentially delinquent children to character-building institutions will therefore remain rare until these children look upon them as part of the normal way of life of their neighborhoods. This implies greatly increased stability and the removal of underworld influences. We come back to the old truism that fundamental defects can be cured only by fundamental remedies.

It should be said parenthetically, however, that these character-building agencies undoubtedly do perform a great service in keeping powerful moral influences focussed upon children who would otherwise slip into delinquency. We have no notion how many more juvenile delinquents we might have were it not for the devoted efforts of the agencies I have mentioned.

Preliminary to our discussion of the reformation of deviants we should note that modern societies, in their penal strategy, give relatively more weight to reformation than to deterrence. There are probably two reasons. First, deterrence has been tried and failed. Even very severe penalties do not seem to have had much deterrent effect. It is said that the London police never had more trouble with pickpockets than in the crowds that witnessed the hanging of pickpockets. Second, as life becomes more and more complex, the public knows less and less about what happens to apprehended violators. The extent of deterrence cannot be proportional to the severity of the penalty simply because most potential offenders do not learn what the sentence is.

In connection with both deterrence and reformation, social scientists generally believe that certainty of punishment is much more important than severity. Obviously the criminal himself is not likely to be reformed if he is not caught; and others like him are much more impressed with a high ratio of conviction to crime than with an occasional though severe sentence. Isolation from normal society for a time is in itself a considerable penalty. If it were seen as inevitable by every adult tempted to commit a serious offense, severity would be relatively unimportant.

Certainty of punishment implies a race between the increasing anonymity of modern life and improving police methods. During the period of rapid growth of cities following the industrial revolution, many criminals found that they could escape detection by hiding out in one of the transient areas of a metropolis. More and more crimes were committed without subsequent arrest. In addition, the very disorganization of city life that made escape easy also made for corruption among the police and on the bench. Arrests of guilty persons were often not followed by conviction. In large American cities the ratio of convictions to crimes committed has for a quarter of a century been in the neighborhood of 12 per cent. So far at least, the forces of law and order seem to be losing the race to the forces of disorganization and anonymity.

If and when a sound program of remedial action is formulated, it will almost certainly lay chief emphasis on prevention rather than rehabilitation. Better internalization of values and norms, more vital connections with societal institutions, and the reorienting of potentially deviant groups are the key problems. But a vital, though secondary, part of such a program must deal with individual treatment once serious deviation has occurred.

The quality of the performance of police and criminal courts is mostly a question of integrity and competence of personnel and of efficiency of procedures. More of the deviants will be brought to justice if the police force is well-selected, well-trained, well-paid and well-led, and if prosecutors and judges have the character to resist pressures from the underworld, and the knowledge and human understanding to deal discriminatingly with offenders.

Roughly four kinds of punishment can be distinguished in the practice of modern societies: (1) Return to normal life with some supervision after admonition; (2) commitment to institutions with a strongly educational orientation; (3) commitment to custodial institutions for long periods and under unpleasant conditions in the hope of making the individual an expedient adherent after release; (4) the removal of the culprit from normal society, by permanent confinement or death.

The first three anticipate the return of the deviant to his society, but each of them attempts moral regeneration in a different manner. In discussing these types of punishment from the viewpoint of maintaining a steady state of society, we shall assume that integration in terms of the existing common values is desirable. From that viewpoint, and from that viewpoint only, it is proper to speak of certain measures as good and others as bad, to say that there is a need here and a weakness there.

Return to normal life after admonition and with supervision is very common for juveniles, and not uncommon for adults whose offense is minor. In many cases of infractions by children, the culprits are handled informally by probation officers and not taken before the juvenile judge at all. In the cases reaching the juvenile courts, the judges usually consult with parents, school authorities and other interested parties before agreeing to return the deviant to his normal family relationships or, if the family is deemed unsuitable, to a foster home. Courts that deal with adult offenders usually put them on probation only after careful study of the conditions to which they will return, and of the possibilities for arranging adequate supervision either by private agencies or by probation officers. This disposition assumes that the normal life pattern can be strengthened sufficiently by the supervisory measures taken to keep the individual from further deviation. The hold of societal institutions on him is thought to be such that this strengthening will rehabilitate him. The degree to which this theory works out in practice differs from place to place, and from time to time. For success, the court's estimate must be correct, and the supervision adequate. Perhaps in the majority of cases the method is successful, but there is always a large minority of cases in which it is not.

The second line of action, commitment to what are often called training schools, is followed for juveniles and young adults who are not suited for immediate return to normal life but for whom there is hope after a period of care in such schools. The atmosphere in the training schools is expected to be more conducive to normal personality development than that in a jail or prison. Juveniles and adult first offenders are thus kept away from the pernicious influence of hardened criminals; and the approach of the training personnel is meant to be one of sympathetic concern for the person's future welfare. Despite hopes and intentions of making training schools humane and reformative in their influence, it is well known that the inmates most experienced in crime tend to become the heroes and leaders of the rest, and the institutions to become in fact the "schools of crime" they wish so ardently not to be.

The reformatories for young adults in the United States were originally intended to exemplify this second type of punishment. Because of the great wave of criminality among youths between eighteen and twenty-one, however, reformatories have become so large and prison-like as to offer little but regimentation. If it is true that character is molded most successfully in small, intimate groups, these reformatories almost inevitably belie their name. For instance, the Gluecks found that four-fifths of those released from a Massachusetts reformatory became again offenders within five years. Even though there is the attempt to classify prisoners and to keep the less hardened away from the more hardened, it is usually impractical to prevent their mingling in the recreational periods. Besides, inmates are rarely kept sufficiently busy. Though commendable efforts are made to give them both academic and vocational training, it is difficult to arrange for work experience that will be reformative. There is only a limited number of types of work that can be performed without incurring the wrath of business enterprises which feel that competition from penal offenders is unfair. Further, men can rarely be strongly motivated unless they are earning substantial amounts by their labor.

There is strong evidence that a different type of institution would have greater success. Pioneering work has been carried on in Great Britain, especially in the so-called Borstal institutions. These are small reformatories for youths between sixteen and twenty-three. All sentences are for four years—from six to thirty-six months in the institution itself, the rest of the time on parole. The institutions are usually colonies of separate "houses" in which the inmates live with the supervisory personnel. Staff members wear civilian clothes, and the inmates work seven to eight hours a day for small but consequential wages and can by good behavior win ratings and privileges. Most of the work is challenging outdoor labor, frequently joined in by the house masters. Considerable loyalty to the various houses seems to develop. Against the 80 per cent recidivism within five years of those discharged from the Massachusetts reformatory, the Borstal institutions show rates varying from 40 per cent to 55 per cent. Although this result is still not good, it perhaps points the direction in which greater accomplishments may be sought. The New Jersey reformatory at Annandale was the first American institution to incorporate successfully most of the features of the Borstal system.

Following the adoption in 1941 of legislation modeled after the Youth Correction Authority Act put forward by the American Law Institute, California developed new institutions for youthful offenders. By having a number of small institutions it is able to differentiate them to suit the needs of particular age groups and treatment categories. Some of the units, such as the forestry camps, are remarkable for their success in handling youths with bad records under "open" conditions and with a minimum of discipline. Evidence from a Michigan prison camp suggests that one of the reasons for success may be that, where treatment rather than custody is paramount, the natural leaders among the prisoners develop favorable attitudes toward the staff and the program and influence their fellows to co-operate. It is too soon to be sure, but to all appearances the California institutions have a lower rate of recidivism than even the Borstal institutions.

If the procedures for handling juvenile and youthful offenders were more successful, countries like the United States would not have such tremendous numbers of adults in prison. Criminal tendencies that might have been cured early in life become so set later on that they lead over and over again to confinement. Though it is probably true that a certain proportion of the prison population—perhaps 25 per cent—is well-nigh incorrigible, most prisoners even at the adult stage can be reformed if proper methods are employed.

There has been much research in the field of penology, especially on the factors in the inmates' history that make for success on parole. But there have been very few controlled studies of the comparative effectiveness of various methods of treatment. The currently accepted doctrines are therefore largely a product of the gradual accumulation of experience and the sort of informal analysis which occurs when practitioners exchange views.

Adult criminals who relapse are almost always committed to a maximum-security type of institution where they are subject to long incarceration and strict discipline. This has been traditionally justified in terms of protection to the society, and of deterrence of other potential offenders. There has been a belief, too, that severe punishment would make the criminal conform to society's moral code after his release, if not for reasons of conscience, at least for reasons of expediency. All authorities agree that adult criminals, like younger offenders, should be carefully classified. The procedure is well understood and is already carried out on paper in many penal institutions. The main difficulty is that the physical layout of most prisons makes the effective application of classification impossible. The prisons are usually very large—housing anywhere from 1,000 to more than 5,000—and are not easily broken up into separate units. Men of different classifications inevitably mingle in the mess hall and during the recreation period. It is a practical impossibility to establish anything like the "house" plan which has been described in the most progressive systems for younger offenders.

Obviously, a more differentiated system of institutions is needed. For the incorrigible, the men who have become professional criminals and are serving long sentences, a maximum-security type of institution is indicated. Here the protection of the public against further depredations becomes the main concern. But for the majority for whom there is still hope, a much less rigorous type of treatment is desirable. The consensus among experts is that the closer prison routine is to normal life, the better. At least three elements are thought to be decisive. Prisoners must be kept busy at productive labor and at training for their release. They must be housed in units small enough so that a group spirit can develop under the leadership of the prison staff. The staff itself must be oriented to treatment rather than punishment.

If character development were the only consideration, these desiderata could probably best be realized by institutions placed in the open country where the inmates could work as farmers or foresters. The trouble is that these forms of work will not prepare many prisoners for their release. The great majority will probably have to earn their livings in urban surroundings. This makes it desirable to have available in prison other types of work that will lead to later employment. An interesting example of what can be done is the airplane mechanics schools in the Federal reformatory at Chillicothe, Ohio. It is certified by the Civil Aeronautics Administration both as a training facility and as a repair shop for aircraft. Another institution which seems to have had great success is at Chino in California. Although mainly a farm, it also has equipment for shop training. Selected men from the custodial prisons have been transferred there to finish out their terms under minimum security conditions. The number of attempted escapes has been low, as has the rate of recidivism.

One of the perennial problems in the employment of prisoners is the objection from business concerns and unions that goods made in prisons by unpaid or poorly paid labor subject both capital and labor to unfair competition. Efforts have been made to avoid this criticism by making products that can be used by the state government itself. Nevertheless objections have often been so strong that prison employment has been curtailed and prisoners left to a corroding idleness.

One solution would be, of course, to pay standard wages to prisoners. This solution has not appealed to the public because it would add to the cost of running the prisons, though everybody agrees that some opportunity to earn while confined is an integral part of a constructive program of reformation. The solution that seems most in favor is to set up a number of prison industries. There are three advantages. Any one of the industries would supply only a minute percentage of the market for that product, thus reducing the objection of unfair competition. The prisoners would have more diversified job training. And each industrial unit could become the focus of a small penal institution. This plan has the great initial disadvantage that it would require the decentralization of large prisons and the loss of the capital invested in them. Though better results would in the long run almost certainly justify the seeming waste of resources, it would take a great program of public enlightenment to persuade legislatures to expend the necessary funds.

Lloyd E. Ohlin, a sociologist well-qualified in penology, recently suggested that there are two clashing ideologies among the staff in most correctional institutions, but that the situation calls for a different point of view, more scientific than either of them. One of the existing orientations is the authoritarian attitude of the old-line custodial personnel. To the extent that it prevails there is vast social distance between custodians and prisoners, and a strong tendency for the inmate culture to be anti-societal. Leadership among prisoners tends to gravitate to those who have spent most time in confinement and have been convicted of serious crimes. Clarence Schrag's research on the subject was limited to one prison, but his results are striking: His statement, "Prison culture is organized around the values of its most persistent and least improvable members. . . . Socialization in prison means, for many inmates, the acquisition of the skills and attitudes of the habitual criminal," is discouraging.

The other point of view is represented by professionally trained staff members who have in recent years become attached to correctional institutions in increasing numbers. Most of them have a psychological, psychiatric, or social work background. They are accustomed to think in terms of the personality as a system and to regard each criminal as a case to be dealt with separately. One of the results of this orientation is that, to the degree that they are successful in their reform efforts, individual criminals tend to become detached from the anti-societally oriented majority. This subjects them to suspicion that they are informers and they become stigmatized as "rats." This stigma few prisoners have courage enough to contemplate, since it means not only ostracism but frequently physical violence as well.

Attempts to circumvent this problem by setting up programs of group psychotherapy have not always been successful. Ohlin suggests that this is so because the groups are made up of volunteers and not the "natural" informal groups prisoners have formed. When a prisoner returns from a group psychotherapy session to his own informal group, he runs the risk of being regarded as disloyal, going over to the other side. Rehabilitation would be much more likely if the informal group could be induced as a group to undergo therapy.

These considerations lead to the third point of view—one which has been rarely acted upon in the maximum security institutions but which has been practiced in institutions for juvenile offenders. The theory, well stated by Marshall Clinard, is that men will reform only if they are given group support during the process of moral transition. This is implicit in the "house plan" of the Borstal institutions. To put such a program into effect in the large prisons would call for very accurate classification procedures, and for the complete separation of groups according to their capacity for reform. This would mean more staff members trained in group work, and the physical decentralization of the prison population in a manner that would be very costly. Those who believe that in this direction lies progress are certain, however, that ultimate costs would be greatly reduced because rates of recidivism would be sharply lowered.

Once started, a program of this kind should be accompanied by careful operational research. We do not know enough to be sure what the most favorable conditions are. Donald R. Cressey has tried to codify our knowledge in this field and has come up with one most interesting result. The most effective reformatory situation, he says, exists when criminals must join with noncriminals to reform other criminals. This effort on the part of the first set of criminals reforms them even if it doesn't reform their subjects. He calls this retroflexive reformation.

Whether the deviant has been committed to a training school or a prison, much planning and effort must be given to the situation which he faces after his release. Experience indicates that success depends upon the care with which that situation is planned. Both he and his mentors need to concern themselves with this problem from the very beginning of his confinement. All aspects of his training and re-education should be appropriate to the conditions under which he will probably take up normal life again. Indeterminate sentences are useful because they give a parole board some latitude with respect to the date of release. Unless both the prisoner and his mentors feel that his reformation has progressed sufficiently to make him a good risk, he should not be returned to normal life. To grant parole only on the basis of good behavior in the institution is a mistake. Such behavior is no certain sign of ability to adjust to the outside world. The system of gradual release appears to have worked well wherever it has been tried. Under this plan the men about to be paroled are assigned to a special group that has the privilege of making visits to home and friends during the last months of confinement. They thus get used to normal society before they are sent out to sink or swim.

If it is important that the prisoner be prepared for his release, it is perhaps even more essential that the outside world be prepared to receive him. Institutional connections should be waiting for him. This requires preparation long before he leaves prison. First of all, his family must make plans for his reincorporation into the group. This is a matter which the man himself, his wife and children, and his future parole officer can discuss together and work out. Second, a suitable job should be sought into which he can step almost immediately. There are employers who are willing to give an ex-convict a chance, but they are all too few. More understanding and helpfulness among the public would pay large dividends here. Many men who are released try to go straight but lose hope when they are discharged because of their criminal record.

Parenthetically, one should note that the unwillingness of employers to give ex-convicts jobs is a natural result of society's necessary feeling of indignation at the crimes they have committed. It is asking a great deal of the public to be so discriminating that they clearly understand both the need for indignation at the time of the offense and the need for sympathetic help at the time of release. This difficulty underlines once more that it is preferable to concentrate on prevention rather than on rehabilitation.

From the moment of release and until he has become thoroughly accustomed to a moral pattern of life, the ex-convict needs the help of his family and friends, his employer, his church if he has one, such neighborhood institutions as have something to offer, and the parole officer. The world into which he goes is full of temptations. He usually returns to the same surroundings from which he went to prison. Old associations that are morally hazardous beckon. He must be protected so far as humanly possible from falling back into old ruts. Strong institutional connections are the best guarantee.

Careful supervision means so much that it has been suggested the law should make possible the placing of men on parole even though they have served their full sentences. The reason the parole board has not paroled them is usually that they have been considered bad risks; all the more reason that they should be given help after their release.

We have so far passed over a subject that has concerned sociologists for twenty years or more: so-called white-collar crime. Edwin Sutherland is to be credited with important pioneering contributions to criminology at this point. He contended that attention has centered on the sort of crimes that are associated with police enforcement—murder, rape, robbery, burglary, theft—and not on the sort that involve the investigations of administrative agencies—misrepresentation in financial statements of corporations or advertising or salesmanship; commercial bribery and bribery of public officials to secure favorable contracts and legislation; misapplication of funds in receiverships and bankruptcies; manipulation in stock exchanges; misgrading of commodities; and the like. These are just as much against the law as the former and, in money terms, much more costly to the public—but they are not stigmatized to the same degree. Part of the reason is that many of the judgments are passed not in criminal courts but in administrative tribunals. Sutherland believed it another part of the explanation that the people who commit such crimes move in higher social circles, and often are business and professional men of considerable social status. Outwardly respectable and the object of emulation, the public is reluctant to class them with thieves and rapists.

At least two other factors appear to make for differential stigma. First, most white-collar crimes are too sophisticated for many laymen to comprehend adequately. The intricacies of the worlds of finance and distribution are beyond their grasp, and their moral norms in these areas therefore are somewhat hazy and weak. Where the issue is readily understandable, as in embezzlement, the consensus is strong. But such clarity is the exception in white collar crime. Secondly, the business world since the end of the Middle Ages has traditionally been regarded as an area where controls should be minimized. "Let the buyer beware," has been accepted as sound doctrine in many situations in which it has become morally unsound. Many moderns expect sharp practice in the business world, and believe that a man who takes advertising claims seriously deserves to be made a fool of.

An interesting difference between most white collar criminals and the more conventional type is that the former do not learn in the school of juvenile delinquency. They learn after they are adults, from business and professional colleagues. This fact led Sutherland to propound the general theory that criminal behavior, whether of lower or middle-class persons, springs from differential association. Criminals learn crime from their close associates.

It is evident that whereas ordinary crime stems in large measure from the moral "uncovering" of the lower socio-economic groups in modern society, white collar crime is more closely connected with that other aspect of the new scale of life, nucleation of social structure. White collar criminals are men who use their positions in economic and political hierarchies to take advantage of complex relationships that are hard to keep under moral surveillance.

Part of the blame for white collar crime, as for all crime, must be laid to a failure in the internalization of values and norms in youth, and to weaknesses in the institutions that guide youth. But the principal blame falls on the social structure within which middle and upper-class adults move. There is a diffuse, cancerous growth throughout this structure. Nothing less than the professionalization of all the occupations that wield economic and political power would seem able to cure the blight. Control by law is so difficult that it needs strong support from within the groups involved. It is interesting that one as distrustful of big business as Adolf Berle was in the '30's should now suggest in his *The Twentieth Century Capitalist Revolution* that there are growing signs of conscience in the large corporation. But even if the industrial giants are beginning to realize their responsibility to the society they so nearly dominate, it will take many decades for real professional ethics to filter through the various levels of business and reach into the marginal areas where rackets of one kind and another abound.

Our discussion of punishing and retraining the deviant has rested on the wisdom of those who have had practical experience with these problems, and on the insights of social scientists who have studied them. If modern societies are to do a better job, many careful investigations are needed at two points: the etiology of delinquency and crime, and the etiology of reformation. Although the former will contribute chiefly to the processes of prevention, it will contribute also to the processes of reformation. The first step toward curing a deviant is to know how he became one. This is only a first step, however—we cannot go back and remedy the conditions at fault, we must go on to a positive solution, working with the instruments at hand.

Civilized democratic societies differ markedly in the success of their programs of punishment and reformation. Some European countries, like Sweden and England, show a creditable record. On the other hand, American society—with its high proportion of deviants who escape all penalties and its widespread failure to reform those penalized—can perhaps not even be said to be in a steady state at all. Although our civil order has not broken down entirely, it may well be questioned whether delinquency and crime have not passed a threshold beyond which there waits disaster unless fundamental measures are taken. Such measures cannot be a mere extension of those already in force—the problem seems to demand something new and radical. Experts in the fields of criminology and penology have offered many promising ideas, some of which have been validated by trial. The great shortcoming of the present situation is the unconcern of the public and its political representatives. So far the problem has not entered the area of public discussion to the extent that makes possible the consensus which must precede positive action.

CHAPTER 8

Societal Resistance to External Pressure

Up to this point we have spoken only of threats to a steady state of the moral order that may arise from within modern democratic societies whose moral web is adequate for its task. We have dealt with the acceptance of common values and moral norms, the maintenance of institutions, the reorientation of deviant groups, and the punishment and retraining of individual deviants as so many ways to repel such internal threats. From the internal threats we now turn to external ones.

In the world of the physicist, steady-state analysis falls nicely into statics and dynamics. If the system is able to cope with changing stimuli around it the processes which occur are called statics. If those factors in some way overpower the system, a threshold is crossed and readjustive processes take place which are called dynamics. The operation of the solar system is a good example of the statics of a steady state. But if another giant star were to appear close to the solar system a period of rapid readjustment would occur. Some of the outer planets, like Pluto and Neptune, might be torn away from the sun and start circling the newcomer; the orbits of other planets would be disturbed. These processes would be called dynamics. They, too, are orderly. Astrophysicists, given the size and position of the new star, could predict what would happen. Transitions from one steady state to another are, then, not beyond scientific generalization.

This same clear-cut dichotomy can be observed in the social realm when there is sharp separation between the autonomy of a particular societal system and the forces that bear upon it from without. If the society is strong enough to resist the external pressure without changing its character, the existing steady state continues. But if it is not strong enough to resist without internal reorganization, a dynamic process must ensue.

The subject of this chapter is an intermediate process, not wholly static nor yet exactly dynamic. This is because the boundary line between what is controlled by the societal web, and what is not, is blurred. When there is cultural contact and the prospect of cultural borrowing, man lives in two worlds. First, there is the sphere of interaction within society, where conduct must be nicely adjusted if all the members are to share a common way of life. Second, there is the sphere of the known, most of which lies within the first sphere, some of which lies beyond. In this outer envelope are the ways of other societies of which we have knowledge: a great realm of conduct and idea that is not actual but potential. The relation between the larger sphere of what is known and the smaller one of societal interaction is what blurs the distinction between statics and dynamics. A society is capable to an extent of selecting from the sphere of mere knowledge what it will allow to come into the sphere of societal interaction. If it does so with a view to maintaining its own way of life while allowing minor changes, is such selection a feature of statics or of dynamics? It is neither and both.

To appreciate the full reach of the problems here raised, let us range systematically from the most static to the most dynamic situations. To begin with we visualize an operating society in Western Europe which knows nothing of an important event in some other society, say the invention of gunpowder in China. The steady state of the European society is then in no way affected. Next, we suppose the event is observed by some traveler like Marco Polo and is reported to Europe, but is given no weight by the European society because the only known use of gunpowder is for fireworks, and the European society has no culture complexes to which fireworks appear relevant. Presumably the report of gunpowder would not be long remembered in Europe under such circumstances.

The situation is quite different, however, once the practice known to exist in another society is seen as potentially relevant to one's own. Three possibilities now open up. First, the trait may be perfectly compatible with the existing moral web, so that no problems are raised to hinder its incorporation. In other words, the new trait is an acceptable new means which fits existing ends and values; simple items of material culture, such as shovels, or brushes, or fountain pens are examples. That even such simple implements may raise problems, however, is shown by the case of steel axe heads coming into Yir Yaront society. The stone axe, Lauriston Sharp recounts, had been a totem of one of the clans. When the steel axe spread through the society after contact with missionaries, great confusion was caused in the tribe's ideological system. We here discern a principle: when the trait that is being replaced in the receiving culture has a sacred quality, the replacing trait will make for serious strain.

Often, however, new cultural items are adopted and the existing steady state is maintained without widespread repercussions. Such items may even come in, be used for a while, and then drop out again without giving rise to moral problem-solving. Faddish games like Mah-jong, Monopoly, and Canasta illustrate the possibility.

Second, the alien culture trait may be perceived as in some degree dangerous to the moral web. This situation gives rise to the processes to be discussed in the present chapter. There must be problem-solving of a sort, though not the kind discussed in later chapters, for the problem is potential, not real in the sphere of societal interaction. What happens is more than just statics, since changes in structure occur to meet the threat. But it is not the usual dynamic case, because the problem-solving, if successful, results in the preservation of the old steady state, not the creation of a new one. We shall call it anticipatory rejection.

Third, the external practice or idea, though attractive to some members of the society, may prove to have repercussions that upset the existing moral order when it is brought within the sphere of interaction. At this stage, anticipatory rejection can no longer be effective. The matter has become an internal problem and must be solved as such. Chapters 9, 10, and 11 will be devoted to such situations. If the practice is in the end accepted, in pure or modified form, it becomes part of a new steady state. If finally rejected, it will have caused the original steady state to become unsteady temporarily.

We are concerned here only with active rejection, not with apathy. Most peoples do not reject other people's languages as a means of communication. It simply never occurs to a Frenchman that English might be his language. For many generations, Europeans knew of primitive art in Africa and were not influenced by it. It simply did not interest them—not until the *fauves* became enamored of it. Perhaps the matter can be generalized by saying that the more dependent a culture trait is on symbolic meaning, the more likely it is that people of other cultures will not be interested in it. In *The Study of Man* (p. 339) Linton gives a revealing instance of the difficulty of understanding abstract concepts in another culture: "There is a story of an educated Japanese who was trying to understand the nature of the Trinity and after a long discussion with a European friend burst out with: 'Oh, I see now. It is a committee.' Such a remark shocks a good Christian. The Trinity is certainly not a committee, but it may bring the point home to the reader if he pictures himself trying to explain to this Japanese student just how and why he was in error."

Our task here, then, is to examine how a society resists an idea or practice without going through the elaborate process of partial acceptance and trial. It is unfortunate from our viewpoint that anthropological accounts and theory have been much more concerned with the acceptance of new traits—what is called acculturation—than with their rejection. Two of the few theorists who have explicitly dealt with rejection are Linton and Nadel. They seem agreed that, short of the actual residence of some representatives of the giving culture among the potential receivers, three qualities are important to the acceptance of a trait: its utility, its compatibility with other culture elements in the receiving society, and the fact that it is carried by a group enjoying favorable status with the recipients. Rejection is likely in case of lack of perceived utility, incompatibility, and bearers with low status. To these three we should add the general trait of closed-mindedness in the receiving society.

Closed-mindedness appears to be the psychological manifestation of a cultural structure with few receptors. A society that has solved most of its problems may turn in upon itself, so as to offer no points of purchase to new ideas. Complex societies, accordingly, tend to be more open than simple ones. Their very differentiation means that there are more exposed elements to which external events can offer stimulation. The distinction stated by John Embree, between loosely structured and tightly structured societies, is also relevant here. This distinction, elaborated by Ryan and Straus, has to do with the range of alternative channels of conformity to norms, the degree of toleration of unstable behavior, and the degree to which associations are ill-defined and unstable because they are subordinated to the individual ends of participants. A loosely-structured society is marked by alternatives, by toleration, and by indeterminate associations. On the theory that ambiguity should make for easy entry of new traits, one would expect loosely structured societies to be less closed-minded than tightly structured ones. In a later work, Linton seems to agree: "In closely integrated cultures the introduction of any new culture element immediately sets in train a series of obvious dislocations. Other things being equal, the closer the integration, the more extensive and immediate the dislocations. These changes give a preview of the social and psychological consequences of incorporating the new element into the culture. They become obvious before the new thing has been fully accepted and often are disconcerting enough to result in its rejection." Linton cites the Rio Grande Pueblos and the Guatemalan Indians as examples of societies that have had bitter experiences with change and now invariably reject all of it.

Of the four factors that tend to keep alien traits from being adopted, only incompatibility for moral reasons is closely related to the preservation of a steady state. Perceived lack of utility does work to maintain the existing order, but the motive involved is purely one of technical or organizational efficiency. It simply does not appear expedient to members of the society to import a way of doing things which has no relation to their problems or, if it has, is inferior to their own solution.

The refusal to consider the adoption of traits because their bearers are looked down upon stems no doubt from the need to maintain a secure collective image, rather than from concern for the maintenance of a way of life expressive of common values. A trait which is rejected for this reason might have had integrating consequences from the standpoint of moral order. A religious ceremonial, for instance, could be well suited to the whole value system of a particular tribe, and yet it might not be borrowed because those who practice it are thought inferior.

Finally, rejection by reason of pure closed-mindedness—what might be called an introverted culture—says nothing about moral order. What is probably at work here is a mere structural incapacity.

A society that has had a history of relative isolation, through which it has maintained both the simplicity and the rigidity of the social organization, is likely to be closed-minded. It has few growing points where new ideas could take hold.

If simple and isolated societies borrow only with difficulty, civilized, exposed societies seem to have equal difficulty in rejecting traits without trial. Not that they have any fewer common values or moral norms or institutions with which the new items might be incompatible, but their moral webs are not so firmly knit. There are always some categories of the population, or some groups, that do not share in the societal consensus. These may be attracted to elements of culture observed abroad which to most of the society seem clearly incompatible with the established moral order. But those who are attracted may actually try to introduce such traits into the everyday life of their society, causing an internal problem that must be met dynamically.

In view of all this, when does a civilized, democratic society resist cultural pressures that might be disrupting? The answer seems to be threefold. First, it resists if its members believe that outsiders are trying to impose their culture on them. The extreme example is a military attack that threatens invasion. December 7, 1941 brought the American people a sharp fear that their way of life was endangered by the Japanese.

The other two occasions of resistance are not easy to distinguish in practice, though significantly different in theory. They relate to Weber's distinction, discussed in Chapter 2, between an ethic of ultimate ends and an ethic of responsibility. If a foreign idea that on its face appears to be incompatible with essential elements of the value core of a society is brought to the attention of the society's members, it will be rejected almost blindly even if there is no attempt to force its acceptance. The rejection springs from conviction, not from calculation of consequences. The idea is repugnant to the common values, and so discarded. This is active rejection, and not a case of apathy.

The ethic of responsibility operates when a new idea, though not itself immediately repugnant, is rejected because of its foreseen repugnant consequences. In this situation, the society usually realizes that the new idea or practice will be attractive to some of its members, and that they are likely to adopt it. Because of their limited vision or perhaps irresponsibility, the remote consequences do not prompt them to reject the trait immediately; but the more perceptive members of the society feel that they must marshal public opinion to counteract the temptation.

It is not easy to decide which of these two processes is in fact operative in a particular instance. Amish and Mennonite communities in the United States, for instance, rejected the automobile, but it is not clear whether they did so because they believed that automobiles are sinful in and of themselves, or that the indirect consequences of automobile riding, especially among young people, would be deplorable.

In a broad sense, impinging culture traits can be put on a continuum of increasing distance from the value core. Those that are closest will tend to be rejected out of conviction, while some of those lying farther out may be rejected out of a sense of responsibility. Whereas in the latter case, only the elite is likely to have the foresight necessary, in the former case both the elite and the masses of the society will reject the trait: the ordinary persons who accept the societal common values will feel their standards threatened quite as much as do leaders of institutions. There are many examples in history. Once the Reformation had been consolidated every attempt by Catholics to bring the Protestants back into the fold of the Roman Church found vigorous resistance not only among the rulers and the clergy but among the peoples themselves. The Thirty Years' War could hardly have been so long and bitter otherwise. Indeed, religious wars throughout history have always been relentless simply because the inmost selves of all believers are ardently involved. The dread of the Mohammedan peoples, which is still alive among European Christians and which goes back to the Ottoman conquests between 1453 and 1683, shows how deeply influential the experience of religious threat can be.

The culture trait that is rejected need not be specifically religious as long as it poses a direct threat to the central value core. A fascinating instance is the rejection of the canoe by the Yir Yaront of Australia. We do not know historically how this happened, but the interpretation of the situation given by Lauriston Sharp suggests that it must have been a decision that was broadly shared.

The Yir Yaront are an Australian tribe living on the west side of Cape York Peninsula. Before European contacts were established, their northern neighbors possessed the canoe, and this was well known to the Yir Yaront. Yet they did not adopt it, despite the fact that they had the material with which to make it. The reason seems to have been that they had projected their present way of life back on their ancestors, and regarded it as sacred in terms of their clan totems. They could not accept the canoe without a myth about the canoe which would establish it as a totem of one of the clans. They were thus caught in the vicious circle of their self-contained culture. "The Yir Yaront have not made the adjustment and in this case we can only say that ideas have for the time being at least won out over very real pressures for technical change."

Although Sharp does not know for certain, he believes that the Yir Yaront must have been sorely tempted to adopt the canoe. They must have appreciated the great advantages in fishing their neighbors possessed. Only the strongest of motives could have caused them to shun the thought of changing their ways. Their totemic ideologies, which explain the universe as fixed since the beginning of time, must have proved more powerful than secular advantage.

A very similar case is reported by Loeb in *Sumatra, Its History and People* (p. 167). The Mentawei Islanders are said not to have borrowed rice cultivation because it is incompatible with religious devotions that require work to cease for months at a time.

In an important recent work Fred Cottrell has suggested that the ancient Egyptians refused to use the sailboat because of its probable ill effects: "Ships would be useful only if considerable trade were permitted. To turn to trade meant the introduction into Egypt of variables which might upset relationships between groups, individuals, and regions which had proven in the past to be very fruitful. To turn to trade meant the introduction of goods not produced under the sanctions of Egyptian law, religion, and morals. To turn to trade, then, was also to increase the power and prestige of the traders; to encourage men who would reduce objects with artistic, religious, social and moral connotations to a neutral denominator, price; and, more dangerously, to set up a group which might bid for the loyalty and arms of those who found no satisfaction in the existing order of things." The last clause (as befits an absolute monarchy) emphasizes considerations of power, but the rest of the quotation suggests anticipatory rejection on moral grounds.

Turning to modern societies, one may wonder whether considerations of essentially the same sort do not account for the almost complete rejection by German society of the so-called progressive education movement stemming from the philosophy of John Dewey in the United States. The strong authoritarian strains in traditional German culture might find such ideas repugnant, not for their ultimate consequences but intrinsically.

A conclusive illustration of how even a modern, democratic community may ward off influences that threaten its social system—but this time somewhat further along the continuum toward concern for consequences—is furnished by a recent attempt at mental health education in a Canadian town. The attempt proved a complete failure. The people of the town not only did not change their attitudes toward mental illness, but they grew increasingly hostile to the efforts to educate them. The mental health workers from outside came to the conclusion that the town had developed its own way of handling mental illness—to deny its existence as long as possible and then to place the ill person in an institution—and that it regarded any education implying a change in that method as a threat to the community. Their way of handling a difficult problem was being questioned, and a diffuse anxiety or perhaps even guilt feelings were aroused. One finishes reading the account completely baffled, wondering whether it is even wise to attempt such educational campaigns on matters close to the value core.

The more remote the relation of the item of foreign culture is to the value core of a society, the more its threat, if any, is likely to be perceived only by leaders. The threat here consists not in the immediate effect of the new item but in its delayed or indirect effects. The man in the street is not likely to appreciate such secondary connections as well as do the better informed leaders, and may see no harm in adopting the trait. The leaders, who do appreciate the seriousness of the threat, usually try to ward it off before the masses are exposed to its seductiveness. To do so successfully, they must act firmly but quietly—otherwise dissident elements will almost certainly spring up.

A good example is the way in which Roman Catholic countries

fend off the intrusion of physical or chemical contraceptives. The religious leaders, in accordance with the doctrine laid down by the Vatican, interpret the use of such materials as a sin because they are thought to be an "unnatural" interference with conception and the birth of children, which is the natural culmination of the holy estate of matrimony. The great mass of the people, many of whom may be desperately poor and some of whom may want to better their class position, are likely to be tempted to use contraceptives. In countries where the Roman Catholic Church is the established church its leaders therefore consistently bring the power of the state to bear in warding off, without general discussion, the importation of contraceptives.

There are many instances, of course, where particular business groups try to keep a foreign product out of their home market simply because importation would jeopardize their livelihood. In doing so they usually seek to make their action appear as a defense of fundamental values. A fascinating example has been the post-World War II campaign of the French wine industry to exclude American soft drinks from France. The French populace had been introduced to American cola drinks by U. S. soldiers, and the sales were beginning to mount. The threat to the wine industry was taken so seriously that a bitter campaign against the sale of cola drinks was waged all the way to the Chamber of Deputies. The term "coca-colonization" was coined as an epithet to damn American business, which was painted as trying to displace the refinements of wine drinking with a somehow materialistic American habit. It was even argued that the soft drinks contained so much caffeine as to endanger health.

A problem not unique to our times but certainly more acute today than ever before is the defense of a society's secular values against attempts by members of other societies to undermine them. Modern means of communication and propaganda reach across national boundaries, and can try to shake the confidence of the masses of another country in their own beliefs. The policies of Communism since the Russian Revolution have highlighted this process. Something of the same sort took place after the French Revolution, and the fascist states of Italy and Germany during the troubled '30's followed an identical policy.

An authoritarian society can deal with such intrusion by authoritarian methods. It can censor publications, "jam" radio broadcasts, imprison those suspected of disloyalty. A democratic society, however, must discriminate between attempted subversion by agents of a foreign state and the legitimate desires for change of loyal citizens. The would-be subverting power knows this limitation and makes skillful use of it. "Front" organizations with innocuous names are formed into which loyal citizens are drawn. Their policies are manipulated by a hard core of subversives. These organizations are then used to plant the seeds of disillusion about the societal moral order, and to encourage the acceptance of a different set of values.

Because social science has given little study to the various ways of dealing with this problem in democracies, little can be said on the subject. It is clearly difficult to preserve the democratic norms of free thought and free discussion while preventing a sort of indoctrination that short-circuits these freedoms. The usual and perhaps natural reaction has been to become so incensed over the tactics used as to adopt sweeping measures that violate fundamental civil liberties. This sort of reaction has become known in the United States as "McCarthyism." The sanest discussion of the totalitarian threat and how to counter it that has yet appeared is that of Philip Selznick, in his book *The Organizational Weapon*. He shows (in Chap. 8) that social science knowledge leads to an appreciation of the need for a differentiated policy, one that deals with specific institutions and specific classes of people in accordance with their special functions and position in the social order. To take one example, it may be necessary to exercise a degree of surveillance over a labor union, because of its power in an area affecting national security, which would be quite inappropriate over a liberal arts college. Since the latter makes no decisions of immediate consequence to national survival, there need be no encroachments on its freedom of thought and discussion.

Practices with respect to anticipatory rejection are bound to vary among modern democratic societies, depending upon the degree to which the elite is trusted to act on behalf of the citizenry at large. The only excuse for anticipatory rejection by leaders is that it saves the society confusion and travail. The assumption is that in the end the people themselves would reach the same conclusion. Because the masses are not so well equipped to foresee the indirect effects of some new cultural trait and its threat to the value core, leaders are trusted to short-cut the long process of popular consideration and rejection. In proportion as they do so judiciously and effectively, their society is likely to acquiesce. But if fundamental liberties are ignored in the process, or if selfish use of power becomes manifest, the citizens will withdraw their trust.

No matter how wise the elite's anticipatory rejection may be, it may fail for lack of control over the channels of entry. The new trait may creep in despite the attempted rejection. The people will then have to face the problems foreseen by the elite, consider the alternatives, and arrive at a consensus. If they decide to reject the trait, they will have gone through what we call learning in the hard school of experience. If they decide to accept it, they may do so grudgingly or willingly. If the trait has obtained so strong a hold as to make the consequences of rejection seem more disruptive than those of acceptance, the trait will grudgingly be allowed to remain. If, on the other hand, the consequences are found not to be so dire as predicted by the elite, the trait may be accepted with good grace. Many Northerners in the United States believe that this is what will happen in the South as the desegregation of the races in schools takes place. They believe that as young whites begin to associate with young Negroes the regional value system will gradually be undermined. What appeared to their elders wholly repugnant will appear to them more or less acceptable.

Looked at in broadest perspective, the process we have been discussing is part of a functionalist view of society. Every operating system needs mechanisms to protect its way of life. One of them, to reach out and ward off threatening forces, is particularly difficult to adopt in complex, democratic societies because it requires a symbolic problem-solving scarcely compatible with mass participation. In fact, it is quite rarely used, but it is important none the less because it shields the very heart of a society, its value core.

CHAPTER 9

The Process of Readjustment

When the moral web of a society loses in some degree its fitness to the situation, a process of readjustment, of seeking a new steady state, sets in. As Thomas and Znaniecki put it: "[The pre-existing] equilibrium is disturbed when processes of disorganization can no longer be checked by any attempts to reinforce existing rules. A period of prevalent disorganization follows, which may lead to a complete dissolution of the group. More usually, however, it is counteracted and stopped before it reaches this limit by a new process of reorganization which in this case does not consist in a mere reinforcement of the decaying organization, but in a production of new schemes of behavior and new institutions better adapted to the changed demands of the group; we call this production of new schemes and institutions *social reconstruction*." Institutions and moral norms must grow and change until they can again mediate satisfactorily between the common values of the society and the conditions under which it operates. The ability to do this is the mark of any vital social system. Like the body which generates new tissue to heal a wound, the society spins a new section of moral web to replace that which has been weakened or torn. The French have a saying "The more things change, the more they are the same" to express the paradox.

It is important to study the method of transition from one steady state to another because in times of change such as ours a low level of moral integration may be due not so much to the original unfitness of the moral web as to the slow and fumbling process of readjustment. If we can discover the optimum processes for complex societies built on democratic values, the way is open to more intelligent and less costly societal change.

How societies make such transitions becomes clearer if we understand why they make them. Most writers, following the biological analogy, have assumed that societies change in order to survive. This is true provided it is understood that, for a society, survival implies survival of the cherished common values as well as of the people. The way savage tribes have fought to the last man in preference to submitting to an alien way of life is testimony enough. The transition to a new steady state will involve modifications of institutions or moral norms—of parts of the moral web, in short—but it will not involve much change in the common values themselves, because these are what makes life worth living.

Pieris has offered a theory to account for the fact that some tribes lose interest in life when conditions seem to be forcing upon them a change in their moral webs. He attributes it to the fact that what he calls their ideal and behavioral patterns of conduct have traditionally been completely integrated—in our terms, the common values are completely identified with the existing moral web. The two have been in mutual adjustment so long that all experience of change has been forgotten. If, then, some outside force is applied which requires a change, the people lose interest in living and their rate of reproduction declines. This, Pieris says, is what happened to the Tasmanians when they found Western civilization engulfing them, and to the Melanesian natives discussed by Rivers when the British forbade head-hunting. Although head-hunting was only a means to the realization of ultimate values, it was so closely identified with those values that only the natives who were won over to Christianity found a substitute in terms of which they wished to go on living. Pitt-Rivers reports that the Maori of New Zealand were so outraged by the way in which missionaries forced them to violate their traditional taboos that they too lost interest in life.

This loss of the will to live, Pieris believes, does not occur when change is threatened in civilized societies, because in their cultures the moral web is never an altogether adequate embodiment of the common values. They have therefore, always a certain degree of cultural tolerance which makes adjustment to outside forces relatively easy.

When a society believes its old steady state outmoded it will generally move forward to a new one in order to stave off disorganization. It will not do so, however, if its common values cannot be carried over into the new pattern or if it regards its old moral web as the only possible implementation of its common values.

There are two sorts of transition from one steady state to another. One is so gradual and unnoticed as to constitute a moving equilibrium. The other is episodic: there is a break in equilibrium and a recovery. Because the recovery follows from the detection of a problem and its solution, we call this process problem-solving. Both sorts of transition are analogous to the process of learning in the individual. They represent the addition and rearrangement of elements which enable the society, like the person, to achieve its goals more effectively.

There seem to be two components to a moving equilibrium: structural drift and a strain for consistency. The first supplies the dynamic element, the second the steadiness.

Structural drift means that small changes occur so slowly as to be imperceptible to the members of the society. An illustration would be the gradual reinterpretation of moral norms as conditions change; another, the gradual redefinition of roles within an institution. In his *Folkways* (pp. 5–6, 39) Sumner identified the strain for consistency among cultural elements. He pointed out that mores, which correspond to our moral norms, tend to evolve in such a way that they remain adjusted to one another. Hence, if in a given society structural drift occurs in family relations, for instance, norms in the field of economic relations will tend to change slowly to fit.

Cooley was keenly aware of these processes, and particularly interested in the relation between the conscious and the unconscious elements in them. In *Social Process* (p. 21) he says, "The principle of unintentional adaptation is at work in human life, and we need to be reminded of it because the place of the will at the center of our personal consciousness leads us to exaggerate the sphere of its activity. The social processes, though they result in a structure which seems rational, perhaps, when it is perceived, are for the most part not planned at all. Consciousness is at work in them, but seldom consciousness of anything more than some immediate object, some detail that contributes to the whole without the actor being aware of the fact. Generally speaking, social organisms feel their way without explicit consciousness of where they want to go or how they are to get there, even though to the eye of an observer after the fact their proceedings may have an appearance of rational prevision."

A moving equilibrium is most likely in a loosely structured nonliterate society. In all nonliterate societies, social change is slow because of their relative isolation from other cultures. If the society is loosely structured in addition, there is more free play for structural drift. Things can start moving without causing maladjustments that would attract attention and bring on problem-solving. Modern urban societies also are loosely structured, but here social change is so rapid that one part of the culture gets far out of step with another. Hence the strain for consistency cannot operate unconsciously.

Clear examples of a moving equilibrium are not easy to obtain from historical literature, for the very reason that the fact is imperceptible to contemporary observers, and later historians find no records to document the process. Perhaps a simple hypothetical example will illustrate what probably takes place.

Let us assume an American Indian tribe living between the Mississippi River and the Great Plains during the period from 1650 to 1750. Such a tribe would not have felt directly the pressure of the white man, but would have felt it indirectly through the gradual westward drift of other Indian tribes displaced by the colonists. We can picture a gradual increase in the pressure for hunting grounds, and a mounting hostility toward other tribes. This development may well have taken place over several generations so that it was scarcely noticed by the participants. The changes would tend to make the male secret societies more and more concerned with defense and preparations for warfare. This in turn might affect the obligations of the young braves toward their wives and children, perhaps shifting more of the burden of household duties to the wife. If all this can be imagined as happening very slowly, it is conceivable that quite different moral norms and institutional arrangements would arise without the members being conscious of the shift. The steady state would have evolved.

A moving equilibrium is superior to problem-solving in that there are no periods of maladjustment through which the society has to pass. It therefore becomes important to ask whether modern democratic societies can do anything to make a moving equilibrium more likely and so to reduce the necessary amount of problem-solving. This is a question to which sociologists have devoted little study. In general, the answer would seem that the better the web of connections among the parts of the society, the more the readjustment of any one part will have immediate influence upon other parts. Thus if schools, churches, families, and industrial enterprises are in effective interaction, an interaction dominated by common acceptance of a set of values, a moving equilibrium should be possible and even likely. Isolation of one institution from the others, or rigidities within institutions that retard their readjustment, produce lags which then become problems. The social engineer who would facilitate moving equilibria should thus attempt to open up effective channels of communication, and to break down tendencies toward formalism and red tape in important societal bodies.

A sort of half-way house between a moving equilibrium and societal problem-solving is diffuse problem-solving through institutional groups like families or schools. It would be effective only if the leading figures in these groups could be counted upon to keep the societal interest uppermost in their decisions, to act as responsible agents of the larger society. This makes much greater demands on them than did Adam Smith's principle that the general interest would be served if everyone looked after his own interest. That principle may have been adequate for a simple society where there were strong norms of proper action and where power was relatively equal—but under modern conditions it is clearly inadequate. Where differences of power are great it takes real attachment to the societal common values and intelligent judgment on how best to implement them for institutional groups to act in terms of their responsibilities. This is much more than enlightened self-interest; it is enlightened societal interest. Although, as we have indicated earlier, it was Whitehead's hope that modern civilization could move in this direction, there are many obstacles. The family seems to be a particularly weak link in the chain. Many parents seem not to realize they have an obligation to the wider society to inculcate its values and norms in their children. Many more who do realize it are ill equipped to meet the obligation. The prospect is brighter with institutional groups led by members of professions—schools, hospitals, churches, and the like.

Here even a slightly higher level of moral integration in the society might make possible a wide delegation of responsibility for problem-solving.

This brings us to the main concern of this chapter—societal problem-solving. It does not take place automatically, like a moving equilibrium, but requires intelligent effort. Here is where social scientists can make a contribution to curing the moral malaise of contemporary societies.

Societal problem-solving is often a wrenching experience. Groups become intensely partisan over alternative solutions to problems and deep hostilities spring up. Devotion to common values is of course the main guarantee against a splitting of the society over how best to solve a problem. Especially important is the subsumption of these values under a national loyalty or "we" feeling. Common memories, the national heroes, the flag and other symbols, all help to give a solidarity that can withstand the divisive consequences of partisan approaches to current problems.

But there is another element that is important. It is the ecological interdependence of the population. Those who depend upon one another for their daily living cannot afford to wreck the system that sustains them all. In his *American Society* (Chap. 14) Robin Williams calls this phenomenon "factual cohesion." One aspect he emphasizes is that not everyone needs to be dependent upon everyone else. Modern life is formed of overlapping circles of interdependence—A and B are interdependent in one relation, B and C in another, and C and D in a third. Thus there is much diversity but at the same time a sort of unity. If modern societies did not have this "factual cohesion" they would be even more handicapped in mending their moral webs than they are. They would have greater difficulty in marshaling their resources, in reacting as wholes. They might yield to pressure instead of solving their problems. There would not be transitions from one steady state to another because there would be no adequate steady state to begin with.

An integrated society resorts to problem-solving when in the face of some change a moving equilibrium has not been achieved. The old moral web begins to appear unsuitable for keeping behavior tolerably in line with common values. The inadequacies or incompatibilities in the moral web worry responsible people. They may find themselves confused as to what is right under the circumstances, or in conflict with one another over it. They realize that some force has carried the situation across a threshold beyond which the old steady state cannot be re-established. Hence their effort to modify existing institutions or develop new norms.

The problems of a society are not always solved. Societies have been known to disintegrate and disappear from the face of the earth. But usually difficulties are surmounted, and the society persists by a transition from the outworn steady state to a new one. Can this be done through any predetermined set of steps? Can any generalizations be made about the process? Or is it just a matter of trial and error in each instance?

There is certainly much in a society's problem-solving that is hesitant and tentative. Each case is in some way unique. On the other hand, men and societies have learned from experience. They have accumulated knowledge about how to meet critical problems and passed it on to their successors. Social science has slowly and fitfully been gathering such knowledge. We shall try to put this knowledge as it relates to modern democratic societies into organized form.

A preliminary but important question is whether data drawn from societies other than modern democracies can be of any service in our task. Much information is available about primitive, and some about modern authoritarian, societies. Is it completely valueless to us here?

In the first chapter we indicated that whether the central values of a culture are democratic or authoritarian makes a tremendous difference not only in the way in which problem-solving is undertaken but even in the way in which the acceptance of norms is secured and institutions are shaped. We shall not therefore canvass the data on authoritarian societies.

The case is different with nonliterate, democratic societies. (These have in general gathering, fishing or hunting economies; agricultural economies, because of the great role of real property, tend to be hierarchical.) Although primitive democracies do not possess the complex structure and far-flung communication networks of their modern counterparts, data from their problem-solving experience have relevance. They have had a kind of moral public opinion that did not have to wait for the development in history of modern democratic machinery. It is this that Cooley referred to in a striking passage of his *Social Organization* (p. 107): "In a life like that of the Teutonic tribes before they took on Roman civilization, the social medium was small, limited for most purposes to the family, clan or village group. Within this narrow circle there was a vivid interchange of thought and feeling, a sphere of moral unity, of sympathy, loyalty, honor and congenial intercourse. Here precious traditions were cherished, and here also was the field for an active public opinion, for suggestion and discussion, for leading and following, for conformity and dissent." Is there any reason to suppose that problem-solving in these small-scale, primitive, democratic societies would not be suggestive for our purposes?

Processes of problem-solving might be analyzed in several ways. One way would be to develop a series of temporal stages. A simple scheme might consist of three: realization of the problem, discussion of alternative solutions, development of consensus. Another would be an analysis in terms of the roles that need to be assumed in the process, such as the detector of the problem, the communicator, the diagnostician, the discussion leader, the organizer of consensus. We shall adopt neither of these but propose a third, based on the different functions that must be performed in a readjustment cycle. There appear to be six such functions: detection, communication, analysis, proposal or essay, evaluation, consensus.

It is difficult to discuss these six functions without seeming to adopt a very rationalistic position with respect to the readjustment cycle. Such a position is not here intended. Problem-solving does not require awareness at every point of what is taking place. Those who are performing one of the functions, say communication, need not always appreciate how their activity dovetails with other functions.

Since in modern societies there is always a great deal of deviation from norms, and since this always poses a problem of reinforcement, detection in the present context does not refer to the detection of any and all problems. It refers specifically to the detection of a lack of fit among elements of the moral web, or between such elements and either the common values on the one hand or the ecological web on the other. Someone must detect moral inadequacy or incompatibility somewhere.

One of the most common forms of unfitness detected is traditionalism in institutions. These role-structures either are attuned to common values which have been superseded, or are implementing accepted common values in ways that do not suit new conditions. A well-known example in the United States was the tardiness with which the institution of local government adjusted to the increasing complexities of life brought on by new developments like gas and electric services and the automobile. Communities had to cope with many problems for which their traditional forms of government were unsuited. Though the unfitness was detected quite promptly by reformers, it took something in the nature of a social movement before adaptive changes were made.

There are at least two forms of maladjustment in relation to moral norms that call for detection. One exists when the interpretations of a norm by different segments of the population become so divergent that one segment is criticized by another for deviation. This is usually a phenomenon of class differentiation. Thus, for instance, the meaning of orderly conduct on the street is probably much stricter for middle-class persons than for lower-class persons. Since they tend to live in separate areas this divergence does not cause a serious problem. But a similar difference in interpretation of norms of fair business dealings probably would.

Another source of norm difficulty is that conditions change so as to render an old norm inadequate. Here, adherence to the old norm usually leads to violations of common values because of the change of conditions. The advent of the automobile offers an illustration. The horse-and-buggy meant relatively little danger to life and limb, and no public nuisance so long as the vehicle kept to the right side of the road and the driver had his horses under control. Early automobiles were both speedier and noisier. Men driving them under full control and on the right side of the road could still cause havoc. Horses were so frightened that they bolted, the lives of unwary pedestrians were endangered, engines without mufflers were a nuisance. In other words, without violating horse-and-buggy norms, early automobile drivers were endangering the peace of mind, the lives, and the property of others. A set of norms had become inadequate to its task. It took no great perspicacity to realize that here was a new problem calling for new moral norms and legal implementation.

Situations of this kind are not always obvious, however, and detection of the problem often requires a creative act. It must have been difficult, for instance, to see the need for a principle of conduct to supplement in certain cases the principle of *caveat emptor*—"let the buyer beware." As long as things sold were simple commodities whose value could be checked by inspection, *caveat emptor* was a perfectly moral rule of trade. At some point, however, things became so complicated that if they had hidden defects the buyer could not easily discover them. Someone then must have detected the problem and started the moral readjustment which obliges the seller not to misrepresent his product.

A successful reformer is such a creative person. He senses a problem where most other people see none. He points out that practices which are generally accepted represent a falling away from the moral principles that the society at bottom accepts. Because it is the drift of events rather than any dramatic new factor which has brought about the condition he criticizes, he himself rather than any external cause is usually credited with the initiation of change. Indeed, Bogardus classifies him as an "intentional disturbance" which starts the public opinion process, in contrast to inventions, catastrophes, and wars, the "unintentional disturbances."

The function of communication must be performed at almost every stage of the readjustment process. Since the new steady state has to meet societal needs, it must represent general consensus. The problem itself must be shared; analyses of it must be shared; there must be discussion of various proposed solutions; convergence of view requires continuous interaction; and, finally, the new norm or institutional arrangement must become publicly known. From beginning to end there must be contact of mind with mind. Collective readjustment calls for collective wisdom.

Leaving for a moment our consideration of democratic societies, we may note that authoritarian societies too require communicative processes, though of a different pattern. Theirs operate through two networks: a very narrow one connecting the members of the elite who do the actual problem-solving with each other; and a very broad one whose function it is to keep the elite informed with respect to what is on the mind of the public, and to communicate back to the public in propagandistic fashion the decisions of the elite. Thus it is not true to say that the moral orientation of the people has no effect in authoritarian society. Rather, it has just as much effect as the elite group believes must be allowed in order to keep the society on an even keel, and them in power. Institutions and moral norms probably show to a considerable extent the influence of the experience of ordinary people. Laws, derivative in nature and backed by coercive sanctions, may reflect less.

So much has been written about the obstacles to accurate and effective communication in modern complex societies that it would be superfluous to enter into detail here. Suffice it to say that despite all the intricacies of modern point-to-point and mass communication the necessary information is frequently not supplied in a form understandable to those who need it. In the analysis stage of a problem, the experts may not learn the necessary detail about its nature. In the evaluation stage, the chief danger is that those who control the mass media will covertly introduce their own biases into the discussion. When this happens, consensus may proceed on a false basis.

Perhaps the function which differs most from primitive to urban societies is that of analysis. Only rarely in primitive life is it prospective, and thus societally problem-solving—usually it is simply rationalization after the fact. When an hereditary chieftainship is replaced by a chieftainship filled by the selection of the tribal elders, the change may be explained in terms of the displeasure of the gods with the old system, while in fact the reason may have been that the hereditary chieftainship had failed to produce the sort of military leadership that the tribe needed for survival. In modern societies, on the other hand, prospective analysis may be very full and the public may be influenced by scientific findings. When a lack of fit shows up in the moral order, social scientists may carefully probe the problem and conduct research specifically aimed at discovering not only the historical circumstances in which the maladjustment arose, but its causes as well. This process might be illustrated by what happened in the United States after the onset of the economic depression of the '30's. Economists investigated the causes. Their work was popularized by such agencies as the Brookings Institution so that public opinion became well-informed. The establishment of Social Security stemmed from this analysis.

Analyses need not be communicated to the whole democratic public, but they must be communicated to all those who may possibly be capable of putting forth fruitful suggestions. This involves all the professional specialists in the area of the problem, the political leaders, and the well-educated portion of the population generally.

Proposal or essay is the process by which solutions of the problem are tried. This is a necessary aspect of the larger readjustment process. We never know enough to move surely in a new direction; our steps are always tentative. Usually this function is first carried out symbolically by the proposal of changes in the moral structure. Suggestions may be few or many, and may arise in any class or any region. In a complex modern society it may be hard to find the persons who make the original proposals. Suggested solutions are so quickly communicated, and so often reshaped as they are discussed, that it is difficult if not impossible to give specific credit even for the one around which consensus ultimately forms.

Proposal passes over almost insensibly into essay. The more convinced a special segment of the population becomes that it has found the solution to a societal problem the more likely that the members will attempt to try it out. Thus the plight of the workers of Rochdale in the early days of the industrial revolution gave rise to the first attempt at consumer co-operation, and the evils of the city gave rise to the trial of "garden city" suburbs. Be it noted, however, that the more intertwined the various elements of life become the more difficult it is to try a plan without general societal consent. Thus essay is likely to occur only after consensus is well developed, leaving proposal as the form initiative takes in the early stages of the process.

There is much to be said for essays of an experimental sort, under conditions of relative isolation, before the widespread adoption of any new institutional program. The Tennessee Valley Authority is perhaps as good an example as can be cited of this possibility. One reason why such prior assessment is so necessary is that advanced planning tends to become so rational as to neglect feeling and sentiment. Trial in human terms will expose such weaknesses.

In modern societies, where the moral web must function over areas quite diverse in culture, moral norms and basic features of institutions are commonly incorporated into law. Hence, proposals for changes in norms and institutions become almost immediately proposals for changes in law. As soon as a suggestion gets out of the area of primary association where it was born into the area of public evaluation, it is recognized that legal issues are involved. From that point forward problem-solving seems to take place with reference to law, though actually it is moral norms and institutions that are being shaped too. This is demonstrated by the fact that a new law passed without support built up at more fundamental levels of moral structure cannot be enforced successfully. The difference between peasant and urban societies is not so much that the one solves its moral problems by norms and institutions, the other by law—the difference is rather that peasant societies need the added sanction of the law much less than do urban societies.

The evaluation of proposals and essays winnows the wheat from the chaff. It involves simple people as well as intellectuals, the neighborhood groups no less than the parliament itself. Discussion is the chief means of evaluation, for it is in the interaction with others that one sees all aspects of a problem. The solution often seems easy until someone brings up a difficulty that has been overlooked and that demands another line of approach.

It is almost impossible to describe the process of evaluation in a modern, complex society because it takes place in so diffuse a manner. The proposal to abandon segregation of races in school systems in the southern United States has been discussed in every conceivable forum—over back fences, in Parent Teacher Associations, in sewing circles and bridge clubs, in town councils and state legislatures.

Depending upon whether the subject of public discussion is a proposal or an actual essay, the discussion will be based upon experience differently. If proposals are being evaluated, the past experience of many sorts of persons in the public with situations similar to those now envisaged are brought into the discussion and examined. If, on the other hand, there has actually been a trial of the new program, then of course it is the experience of that trial which is closely scrutinized. Another source of evidence is a trial in another society. This is rightly regarded as of limited relevance to the indigenous problem since other circumstances are certain to vary.

Broadly speaking, there are two aspects to the evaluation process that correspond to the two types of ethic discussed in Chapter 3. One has to do with comparing a proposal or essay with the common values of the society and approving or condemning it according to its seeming compatibility or incompatibility with them. This is like an ethic of ultimate ends. One might, for instance, refuse to consider the adoption of a zoning system in a city because one felt it incompatible with the valued freedom of using one's real estate in any way one wanted. On the other hand, a proposal or essay can be judged in terms of its consequences. This corresponds to the ethic of responsibility. Thus one could oppose zoning because it might prove in the long run to constrict the natural development of the city.

These two kinds of evaluation are not really alternatives but usually two aspects of a single process. One thinks both of the common values and of the consequences; one judges the desirability of the probable consequences by their compatibility with cherished values.

The Dutch scholar Frederick L. Polak in a forthcoming book, *The Future Is Past Tense,* has called attention to one important force in the evaluation of alternatives in a dynamic society—what he calls the image of the future. It is his thesis that every society, like every person, tends to have a conception of its own future. In the United States the term "the American dream" has often been used to indicate this conception. Polak believes that such projections, once they are accepted by the majority of a society, tend to affect all choices in the readjustive process. This raises the old notion of the self-fulfilling prophecy to the status of a scientific law.

Leadership plays a great part in both proposal and evaluation. Once the masses realize that there is an important moral problem facing the society and have some understanding of its nature, they feel a great need for guidance in finding their way out of the difficulty. They may have a general orientation with respect to the direction in which it is desirable to move, but they are not well equipped to decide unaided on the exact route to take. It is the role of leaders of public opinion to frame clear alternatives of action and, through public discussion, to bring out their strong and weak points. What is needed is full objectivity with respect to means coupled with full devotion to common values. The sociology of knowledge teaches us that leaders are likely to have these characteristics only if they are a little withdrawn from the maelstrom of practical affairs. They should not be marginal to the society, because then their hold on common values would be weak, but neither should they be strongly identified with any particular segment of the society, because then they may lose their objectivity about means. Historically it has been the role of the intellectuals to supply this type of leadership.

Walter Lippmann has put forth a somewhat more aristocratic theory of democratic leadership in public opinion than that sketched here. In *The Phantom Public* (pp. 61–62) he says: "We must abandon the notion that the people govern. Instead we must adopt the theory that, by their occasional mobilizations of a majority, people support or oppose the individuals who actually govern. We must say that the popular will does not direct continuously but that it intervenes occasionally." He is speaking specifically of law, however, rather than moral norms and institutions. It is probable that he would admit a more continuous participation of the public in the gradual change in these other aspects of the moral web.

Leadership operates in the more restricted areas of the neighborhood, informal work-groups, and leisure-time associations as well as in the broader publics. A careful study of voting behavior comes to the conclusion that there are "opinion leaders" at all socio-economic levels and that their influence is great. They form a link between the wider life of the society and the intimate associations of primary groups. They reinterpret issues for their friends and colleagues. The consensus thus brought about in primary groups proves powerful when one of their members is wavering in his evaluation of the proposed course of action.

In a large and complex society, no consensus on a moral issue is ever complete. But no moral readjustment is possible without a convergence of sentiment and opinion after a problem has been detected, analyzed, and new paths have been explored. So long as the process of convergence goes far enough to give dominant influence to the newly evolved standard, a new steady state will be created.

The term consensus is apt for what we wish to denote because, where values are motivating the development, sentiment is quite as important as thought. The members of the society must almost literally feel their way together toward readjustment. This process may have its ups and downs, its unfulfilled promise, its sudden and dramatic closure. Surely no more fascinating history was ever written than that of the slow and painful process by which the United States reached consensus on the problem of Negro slavery.

Consensus is achieved by many means. Louis Wirth has listed persuasion, discussion, debate, education, negotiation, parliamentary procedure, diplomacy, bargaining, adjudication, contractual relations, and compromise. This list is rather heavily weighted in the direction of formal methods. It reflects the rational, differentiated character of modern urban life. Such terms as negotiation and bargaining suggest the fact that opposed points of view on public questions frequently give rise to organizations to express them. These may, like the abolitionist societies in New England or the Anti-Saloon League, concern themselves with only a single reform; or they may, like labor unions, concern themselves with many problems in which their members, because of their class interest, have a stake. The modern tendency to press for legal change as a means of building the necessary underlying moral structure has emphasized the strategic advantage of organization.

It would be wrong, however, to assume that in the modern world the more informal processes of reaching consensus are not also important. After proposals have been evaluated by leaders there is a great deal of interchange among the common people. Basic sentiments come into play to lend support to one solution or another. Sometimes strong factions do not develop, and the enlargement of consensus is more like the growth of a rolling snowball. Once the initial momentum has been acquired it carries all before it. This seems to have been the case with the plan for insuring bank deposits by the United States government which was adopted during the New Deal of President Franklin D. Roosevelt.

There has been much discussion of the extent to which the masses in modern societies can be manipulated in the formation of public opinion. Hitler was tragically successful in this regard. Sociological literature gives different answers, perhaps depending upon the experience and observations of the authors.

Cooley held that the masses live closer to the springs of human sentiment than do elites, and that they therefore are not easily misled on moral issues, guidance for which is furnished by primary-group experience. Cooley was writing out of a knowledge of American society in the late nineteenth century with its predominance of small towns and the intimacy of its neighborhood life. In such a society, he felt, moral issues were simple enough and well enough understood by the masses so that these could be trusted to give general direction to the emerging consensus. Cooley would certainly have been surprised, for instance, when Hitler was able to get many German adults to accept a system in which children spied upon their parents. Conversely, he would not have been surprised when the U. S. Congress waited to see how the public wind was blowing before taking any action on President Roosevelt's proposal to enlarge the Supreme Court in order to obtain a majority sympathetic to New Deal legislation. This he would have thought showed good judgment on the part of Congress.

Selznick, on the other hand, writing in the nineteen-fifties suggests that the creative elites have been the preservers of a society's ethos; that urbanization and bureaucratization, by lessening the hold of primary groups and increasing the access of the masses to cultural institutions, have introduced a leveling that makes it impossible for the elites to carry out their traditional function. In the absence of creative leadership, the masses are easily led by power-oriented politicians into stereotyped thinking. This, he believes, is the tendency in democratic as well as authoritarian societies. Selznick emphasizes the power of the mass media in organizing thought.

A recent piece of evidence bearing on this question is a study by Stouffer on attitudes toward civil liberties in the United States. He found that in cities between 10,000 and 150,000, persons who occupied fourteen designated positions such as mayor, president of the local Chamber of Commerce, chairman of the Community Chest, president of the largest labor union local, and publisher of the largest local newspaper—in short, community leaders—were consistently more tolerant of ideological nonconformity than was the general populace. Since at the time of his study there had been a strong movement led by Senator McCarthy to stigmatize all radicals as subversives, the results would indicate that this sort of grass-roots elite has a greater understanding of the critical importance of civil liberties than do the masses. This would seem to cast doubt on the views of both Cooley and Selznick. Cooley's high opinion of the masses' moral insight is not confirmed—but neither is Selznick's view that urbanization leads to lack of moral leadership. Whether or not the so-called creative elites are still functioning as moral leaders—and Stouffer's study gives no evidence here—there has developed a leadership at the local level that seems awake to the dangers of stereotyped thinking and witch-hunting.

It appears that there has been a shift in these matters that corresponds to the increasing scope of functional co-ordination outlined at the end of Chapter 3. The nucleation of social structure and the "moral uncovering" of the urban lower class have made the masses less able than they once were to evaluate specific proposals. When most issues were local in character, primary group experience gave a good basis for moral judgment. Now that social problems grow out of the complexities of far-reaching structures of which the masses understand little, the common people are less sound as moral guides.

It would be foolish to assert that crude power does not enter into the achievement of consensus. In the short run, at least, it certainly may. Often the communication of the problem and of its analysis to the people is arbitrarily limited by a ruling group. Often this same group puts forth its own proposal and checks the development of others. Often the discussion process is controlled so as to lead to a quick consensus. All that can be said is that any such consensus might soon melt away. It is most unlikely that the moral web that is approved will be the same as that which would have been approved had there been no power interference. As time passes and experience accumulates under the new moral web, more and more people will realize that they have been misled into sanctioning something which is not consonant with their own deepest convictions.

In all probability, the difficulties of obtaining moral consensus in a complex, modern society will give rise to new social structures. There appears to be a great gap between the discussions of societal problems at the legislative level and at the level of small neighborhood groups, a gap very inadequately filled by the activities of the special-interest groups that lie between. Community Self-Surveys, State Corrections Associations, and the like may be harbingers of a new kind of social unit that will consider moral problems more thoroughly than can neighborhood groups, but under fewer political pressures than plague legislatures. Thus public opinion and public sentiment may be formed on the basis of a richer store of experience so that the moral web will be more wisely fashioned.

Consensus on new elements in the moral web sufficient to bring about a new steady state bears in itself no guarantee that it will last. For one thing, group expectations may be disappointed; there may have been miscalculation of the need or the effectiveness of the innovation. If conditions change still further, even a recently developed structure may have to be altered. It now appears that segregated schools for Negroes in the South will disappear after almost a century of existence. The consensus on educational segregation, reached with great difficulty after the Civil War—a consensus shared by many Negroes as well as the whites—has been gradually undermined by the march of events until now there has been a reinterpretation of the Fourteenth Amendment and the abolition in principle of segregated education.

In connection with the instability of consensus, the question has often been raised whether the premature passage of a law on a moral issue may not contribute to the instability. It is certain that much more than 51 per cent of a democratic public must support a norm to make a law embodying that norm work satisfactorily. Robin Williams in *American Society* (Chap. 10) has pointed out that what he calls "patterned evasion" is an almost certain result of a law passed without adequate consensus. Those who oppose it are a large enough segment of the population to prevent, by systematic deviation, its enforcement. Gambling is often a case in point. In such instances the old steady state has been forsaken but a new steady state has not been achieved.

On the other hand there are always people who are undecided on the issue or who, though persuaded of the rightness of the new norm, yield easily to temptation. Such people are influenced by the pressures that a law can bring. Hadley Cantril has estimated that when opinion on an issue is not solidly structured, the passage of a law on the subject gains it immediate acceptance by about 10 per cent of the population. If this is so and if something like 85 per cent consensus is necessary to successful enforcement, then the time for the enactment of legislation has come when 75 per cent consensus is achieved.

Gunnar Myrdal, in his great work *An American Dilemma* (Appendix 3), has called the phenomenon just discussed the principle of cumulation. This principle states that, when the interrelated parts of a whole are in equilibrium and then one of them is moved in a certain direction, there will be a tendency for the others to move in the same direction because of their interrelations. One of the parts of the moral web is the law. When it is moved in a new moral direction there is a pull that tends to bring normative attitudes along.

This result is not foreordained, however. If the opposition is nucleated rather than diffuse, if the opponents have particular prestige and power, or if the problems of enforcement are particularly difficult, the principle of cumulation may not work. Then Williams' patterned evasion will ensue.

Investigators of small group process have isolated a problem-solving function that needs to be performed in addition to the six we have specified. This is the maintenance of solidarity during the process. Bales, as we saw in Chapter 5, has noted that small groups usually need a leading figure to keep the group functioning together, as well as a leader to initiate ideas and guide their discussion. But in our study of how a complex society accomplishes changes in its moral web we need not single out this function since the maintenance of equilibrium during moral problem-solving is achieved by all the thousands of other customary activities not currently affected. Only in the most violent transitions, such as revolutions, would this function be of crucial importance.

The whole trend of modern life is toward the development of societal institutions that are prepared to deal with change effectively. Anthropologists have drawn the conclusion from primitive life that only rather loosely structured societies can readjust promptly and creatively to change, because only these societies are used to a certain degree of free play. Their members are not shocked by the prospect of altering institutional arrangements. Although many sociologists might not agree, I believe that the tight structuring of a society is no handicap to readjustment, *provided the moral web has built-in mechanisms for change.* Since moral norms are held diffusely in the population and therefore not subject to quick readjustment, it is the institutions of the society which must afford these mechanisms. The best known and most frequently used such mechanism is the legislature. Others are the judicial interpretation of legislation, courts of equity, and a whole host of regulatory commissions and administrative tribunals which, though operating under general law, almost always have broad powers of interpretation.

What is known broadly as social planning is also being more and more institutionalized in modern democracies. In so far as this planning has to do with the allocation of land uses and the regulation of resource exploitation, it may seem a far cry from the moral order. Such problems of relation to the habitat are not usually seen as moral problems, though frequently they involve moral elements. But when it comes to development of residential plans, the extension and co-ordination of health and welfare services, and the provision of recreational areas, there can be no doubt of the moral implications. To the degree that such readjustments are being studied long in advance by institutionally employed experts, are being carefully planned, and are being presented to the public for discussion and approval, to that degree we may be said to have societal self-control through institutions.

We have spoken as if every case of problem-solving in relation to the moral web were clear cut, as if there were always a well-defined pre-existing equilibrium that is upset by some change in conditions, and as if always a process with characteristic features ensued, leading to a new equilibrium. Actually matters are rarely so plain. In civilized societies particularly so much change is going on and so many problems are being solved simultaneously that the aspects of the process in relation to any one feature of the moral web do not stand out clearly. Equilibria are not society-wide, but only problem-wide. The automobile may have dissolved equilibria in several fields successively. It may have caused problems in parent-child relations earlier than in the tracking down of criminal offenders, for instance. Perhaps the first problem was well on its way to solution before the second one became a problem at all. Thus the sequence of events from one steady state to another is an abstraction that applies to aspects of the moral web but not to the moral web as a whole.

Like most other processes of life, successful problem-solving is a matter of balance. If matters move too fast, hasty and ill-informed judgments will be made and the moral web altered in ways that will not last. On the other hand, if the process is unnecessarily slow, the society is detained in an unsteady state, with all this implies by way of confusion and deviation. The more institutional machinery can be devised to foresee change and guide it, the better.

CHAPTER 10

Changes in Conditions and the Moral Order

A society, at any particular moment in its life, can be thought of as functioning in terms of certain conditions. Some of them, like climate and topography, are given by nature. Others, like technology, population distribution, and the presence of neighboring societies, are the products of man's own past development. To both classes of conditions the present generation adjusts. Both are, for practical purposes, given.

To understand how changes in conditions operate we recall our statement in Chapter 3 that the moral web and the ecological web are in a mediating position between the common values and the conditions. Changes in conditions affect the ecological web and may disturb its adjustment with the moral web. It is then that the moral problems considered in this chapter occur, at the point of contact between the two webs.

Changes in conditions, however, do not necessarily give rise to new problems. The existing moral web may remain adequate. Improvements in technology, for instance, do not always have marked effects on the relations among people and cause maladjustments. Better knives, spades, or cooking utensils have no noticeable effects except to make work somewhat more efficient. However, when the change is focal—e.g., the automobile replacing horse and buggy—then all sorts of other changes follow, many of them in human relations. Some of them are likely to raise moral questions. The old moral web may now be inadequate to control behavior in accordance with common values. This is what initiates the readjustment of moral norms and institutions.

The first sign in the individual of this kind of inadequacy in the moral web is confusion. Because the new situation creates problems that do not find an obvious solution under existing norms and institutions, the individual no longer knows the right line of conduct. Something like this seems to have occurred when white men first began trading whisky, "fire-water," to the American Indians. The Indians had not known strong alcoholic drinks before, and had not fashioned normative controls for the situation. In such an event, members of a society are thrown back for guidance on common values. But the meaning of these values under the new conditions is usually not clear, and hence different individuals give them different interpretations. Behavior in the new area of conduct then tends to diverge—the average person is confused. Note that if all members were wholly devoted to the common values of the society, and if they were gifted with omniscience, this confusion would not occur. They all would see eye to eye on what changes in the moral web are necessary; a new steady state would quickly be achieved.

To those who think of technology as wholly instrumental and always subordinate to ultimate ends and values, it may seem puzzling that technological change should raise moral issues. They may be inclined to suppose that a change which is compatible with the society's common values can be readily accepted; if it runs counter to them, it will be rejected. The point is, however, that whether or not it is compatible is not always obvious. It takes time for all its effects to become apparent. By the time they do, the use of the new technology has become well established. It is by then a very complex problem to determine how far the new trait can be reconciled with the existing moral web, and how far changes will be needed.

To a Marxist the whole matter looks quite different. Technological change is to him the principal cause of all social change—the only problem is to complete the social reorganization logically implicit in the new technology. Moral norms are to him only rationalizations after the fact, made by the group in power.

It is very difficult—and perhaps unnecessary—to give a logical and exhaustive classification of changes in conditions. The principal types of change can surely be placed in one of the following categories: changes in the habitat because of natural forces, such as shifts in climate, normal erosion, earthquakes, and the redistribution of plants and animals; depletion of natural resources, whether inanimate, plant, or animal, because of man's own activities; population growth or decline, and redistribution; invention and discovery in the realm of material objects and processes within the society; introduction of material objects and processes into the society from other societies; the opening up of new trade areas; shifts in the attitude of other societies.

The effects of changing natural forces in the habitat have not meant a serious problem for civilized societies. Such natural changes normally occur so slowly that adjustment can be made through a moving equilibrium rather than through societal problem-solving. And even if the natural force operates swiftly—a cataclysmic earthquake or a hurricane—civilized societies have built up cultural protection in the form of assistance from outside the affected area, so that only short-term moral problems spring up. These we have considered under the reinforcement of institutions, in Chapter 5 above.

Man's use of natural resources, on the other hand, often disrupts the existing order and thus creates problems that call for readjustment. A primitive society, for instance, may exhaust its traditional supply of game. If it finds another area in which it can continue its old way of life, it may migrate there and carry on with its traditional moral web. On the other hand, it may become more warlike in order to bring under its control a larger area. Then its norms with respect to conduct toward its neighbors may change sharply. An interesting case in point is that of the Navajo Indians in the United States' Southwest in the '30's. Severe overgrazing of their pasture lands had begun to cut down the food supply for their growing flocks of sheep. So bleak was the outlook that the Federal government stepped in and compelled the Indians to sell 40 per cent of the sheep, thus reducing the number to what the grazing lands could support. As a result many Navajos had to become wage workers, on railroads or elsewhere. An unforeseen further effect was that the traditional reciprocities among members of the same clan, such as making presents of sheep, diminished. The lessening of reciprocities affected the sense of loyalty to the clan. The overgrazing of the land had in the end produced a change in the moral order. It is difficult to find so striking a case in a modern urban culture because here the effects of the misuse of a natural resource are cushioned in many ways. Yet the suffering of the migrants from the "dust bowl" in Western Oklahoma and Kansas during the '30's could perhaps be regarded as partly responsible for the adoption of a social security plan in the United States.

Population growth or decline and redistribution, like changes in the habitat by natural forces, usually occur so slowly as to induce a moving equilibrium rather than moral problem-solving. The city man's relative coldness to his fellow, his feeling that he is not in any immediate sense his brother's keeper, probably developed very slowly as communities grew bigger and bigger and it became more and more impossible to take a warm interest in all those with whom one came in contact.

A challenging theory linking the character type of members of a society to stages in population growth has been set forth by David Riesman in *The Lonely Crowd*. He offers three hypotheses: one, that a traditional type of morality accompanies the situation of high birth and death rates which is typical of primitive and peasant societies; two, that what he calls inner-direction—a conscience firmly established in childhood by somewhat authoritative primary-group indoctrination and capable of dealing with new situations successfully—corresponds to the period of rapid expansion in population when death rates fall and birth rates remain high; and three, that other-direction, or an inclination to fit one's conscience to the current situation as indicated by what one's peers are thinking, is produced by the slowing down of population increase as the birth rate falls to meet the death rate and the emphasis in the society shifts from production to consumption. Riesman explores these hypotheses with great imagination and cites much interesting evidence, particularly concerning the third stage, that of other-direction.

Two principal criticisms may be made. First, Riesman almost certainly overstates the degree to which men are of one character type at any period in history. One might admit that there has been a statistical shift in the preponderance of one or another type, but one would be inclined to doubt that the shifts are of the magnitude Riesman claims. Second, even assuming that the facts of character tend to show the historical sequence set forth by Riesman, it seems less likely that the population cycle is the cause of the moral types, and more likely that both of them are effects of a more basic cause— the evolution of technology and the ecological web based upon it. The three stages would then appear as: (1) small-scale social order, (2) transition to a large-scale social order, and (3) large-scale or bureaucratic social order. In the first stage, mores are traditional because poor communication makes for little cultural diffusion and hence little change. In the second stage, an era of rapid social change renders traditional mores outmoded, but community life is still intimate enough to foster more abstract common values that can cope with new problems when internalized by strong primary groups. It must be noted, however—though Riesman makes little of this—that there is much disorganization and deviant behavior during this period too, since not all primary groups are strong. The other-direction of the third stage would then represent a first groping attempt to adjust to the elaborate social structure of a bureaucratic society. It is a stage in which consciences have superficial breadth but little depth. This analysis seems to preserve what appears valid in Riesman's theory while eliminating the very dubious dependence of social character on stages in the population cycle.

Population changes, even when they cause moral shifts, do not always act in terms of a moving equilibrium. Occasionally thresholds are passed, and the public confronts new types of problems that require quick, even dramatic solutions. Perhaps the simplest example is that of population pressing on the natural resource base. Contemporary Japan is a case in point. Her very rapid population increase since the middle of the last century, capped by the loss, after 1945, of overseas territory into which population might be drained off, alarmed the body politic. It became generally appreciated that the population must be stabilized at all costs. Some argued that the best solution would be the general approval of the practice of contraception, but what happened was the approval of abortion for economic reasons. Thus moral norms shifted to meet the problem of overpopulation. Recent indications are that this stage is passing and that contraception is being widely adopted in Japan.

By far the most frequent kinds of changes in conditions are those involving new instruments or processes. Invention and discovery within a society, and diffusion into it from other societies are the forms such changes take. Though man-made, these changes are seen as conditions of the social structure, not because they cannot possibly be avoided—they are at times rejected—but because they are usually adopted gradually and secure a firm foothold before their ramified effects are seen. By the time these begin to raise moral problems, the new technology is so widely accepted that it is thought of as part of the natural environment. Railroads, automobiles, and airplanes no longer appear to Western man as things that could be eliminated. If they create problems, it is the moral web which is inadequate and must be readjusted. Thus, not the situation itself but rather the society's definition of the situation is what makes norms and institutions inadequate in the face of invention, discovery, and incoming diffusion.

Problems of the inadequacy of the moral web in this sense are much more characteristic of civilized than of primitive societies. This is because nonliterates live so close to the margin of subsistence that they fear any kind of change—their societies tend to be static even when loosely-structured. In societies that have reached a level of living which allays this fear a more experimental attitude is possible. Modern Western nations represent an extreme in this regard. They have become used to a rapid rate of change, and have adopted a secular attitude toward it. New elements of material culture easily take hold if they seem to promise an increase in efficiency. The frequent result is that problems arise as new technology begins to influence the relations among people.

It is this general tendency to accept material change, and later to attempt solving any problems thus created, that gave rise to Ogburn's famous hypothesis of cultural lag. This hypothesis states that there is a tendency for technical elements in a culture to change first, while what he calls the adjustive elements of culture—institutional behavior—lag behind. This, in his view, is the reason that social problems occur. Ogburn's hypothesis receives a great deal of support from the history of Western nations in the nineteenth and twentieth centuries. Doubtless the successive adoption of steam power for industry and transportation, electricity for light, heat and power, the internal combustion engine for land, sea, and air transportation, and now atomic power, has brought many dislocations with which societies have struggled.

Yet there is a weakness in Ogburn's theory. It is implicitly indicated in a recent work by Frankel, *The Economic Impact on Under-developed Societies* (pp. 21–23). Using the example of an attempt to increase the productivity of an African community which has had a subsistence, cattle-owning economy, Frankel points out that the production of butter and cheese for commercial markets presupposes basic alterations in the structure of the society—its land ownership, its forms of employment, stability of village life, political structure, and so on. Indeed, large butter and cheese production could not be successfully carried out until many of these changes had already occurred.

It would appear, then, that Ogburn's hypothesis of cultural lag is valid only under special circumstances. Technological change is likely to run well ahead of social readjustments only when a society is already so complex as to contain many varieties of social structure. Then a technological innovation can take hold because the structure will at some point be adapted to its exploitation. The innovation can then show its worth sufficiently to be widely adopted, even though considerable social maladjustment may ensue. The period of maladjustment constitutes the period of what Ogburn calls cultural lag.

Many inventions, discoveries and importations leave no lasting impression. The principal reason is that they do not meet a permanent need. They are killed by apathy. A minor reason, already noted, is that societies reject those inventions, discoveries and importations which after careful consideration or trial seem incompatible with the way of life the people wish to follow.

Even when a society is inclined to reject an innovation on moral grounds it may gradually curb this inclination if rejection threatens to cause desertions from its ranks. Hutterite communities in the United States are an illustration. Their leaders maintain the traditional customs intact as long as possible, but when deviation—mostly on the part of young people—rises sharply, they may announce a new and more liberal rule. Eaton has called this process "controlled acculturation." He suggests that it works only because of the recognized authority of the religious leaders.

It has frequently been noted that borrowing from one culture to another is highly selective. In part this is because some items are consistent with notions of propriety in the receiving society, some are not. It has not so often been remarked, however, that a single item may be selectively used in accordance with the same principle. Stout recounts that the San Blas Cuna now use guns instead of bows and arrows for hunting, but do not use them in the ceremony of scaring off the demon that is devouring the sun during an eclipse. Presumably the gun is too secular a weapon to be employed in magical rites.

Interesting as such cases of selective acceptance are, they do not constitute the type of problem-solving that is here our concern. In so far as the existing moral web successfully controls incipient changes of conditions, no problem of readjustment arises. Real problems are posed only when changes of conditions bring about activities in the ecological web that are incompatible with accepted common values. The precise way this happens seems to be the following:

A new ecological element is introduced into the culture—say the airplane. It brings with it altogether new types of hazards, very inadequately covered by existing moral norms and laws. If the society allows the operation of airplanes with no restrictions other than those that apply to surface vehicles, common values soon are threatened. An airplane flies too low over a city, the motor fails, and lives and property are destroyed. While driving norms for automobiles and trucks had given protection to householders from this kind of catastrophe, the lack of flying norms has exposed them to it. Although there are common values regarding the sacredness of life and the privacy of property, they are not protected from violation by low-flying airplanes until the rules for aircraft are specifically spelled out. It is the spelling out of new elements of the moral web that constitutes problem-solving, that moves the society from an outworn steady state to a new one.

It would be highly desirable if conclusions about the optimum methods of problem-solving could be based upon a systematic accumulation of scientific evidence. If sociological literature allowed us to compare cases in which readjustment was quick and lasting with others in which it was not, we could come to firm and significant conclusions. Unfortunately the literature affords us no such opportunity. The relevant material is most often anecdotal and discursive, and seldom are cases closely comparable. The conditions under which problem-solving takes place are so various that it is hard to assign a definite degree of efficacy to this or the other method or agency. In the absence of such systematic analysis we shall have to be content with somewhat impressionistic generalizations, drawn from reading about many instances of problem-solving, and from reflection thereon. These generalizations are at best hypotheses.

At first glance, it might seem that the problem-solving process is different when a steady state is upset by a change of condition originating outside the culture rather than within it. There is a likelihood that a technical trait received by diffusion is associated with alien value elements, and is therefore more incompatible with existing traits than one developed within the culture. Greater incompatibility would presumably make the problem-solving more difficult.

But information on actual instances makes us doubt whether the difference between the two situations is as great as expected. From the moment of entry, a diffusing trait undergoes a process of "stripping," so that by the time it is established well enough to have possible maladjustive repercussions it is little more upsetting than as if it had originated within the culture. A rather amusing instance is reported by Redfield from Yucatan. In the native culture there, special significance attaches to the number three, so that classification tends to be in triads. An outside physician gave a lecture on the benefits of vitamins to the people of a small village. A year later these people were saying that vitamins are "three little beings who inhabit the body, one to make flesh, another bone, and the third blood."

This "stripping" may even be done projectively. When commercial television was proposed in Great Britain, there was much fear that all its shortcomings as they had developed in the United States would be repeated. The prospect was so dismaying that great precautions were taken to ban blatant commercials and be sure that programs shown during the children's hours of viewing did not emphasize violence. Commercial television was stripped of two objectionable features before it entered British society at all.

So far as we know, there have been no untoward repercussions in the two cases just cited. The diffused trait was fitted successfully into the existing culture.

But even when there are repercussions, there is little evidence that they are more serious than when the new trait is indigenous. A famous case of societal problem-solving will illustrate the point. The

Tanala are a tribe in Madagascar whose whole way of life was made over by the change from a dry-rice to a wet-rice culture. The dry-rice method of cultivation consisted of cutting and burning the jungle to obtain space for planting. The land could not be used for more than ten years in succession. Each year joint families were assigned tracts adjoining a village. Inequities because of differential fertility were corrected the next year. When the soil gave out, the whole village moved elsewhere and started over. The original land became reforested and suitable for cultivation again after twenty-five years. Since the cutting and burning required co-operative work, there was no individual ownership of the soil or of the crop. The head of the joint family saw to it that the distribution was equitable among its households.

Then wet-rice culture was borrowed from a neighboring tribe, the Betsileo. At first it was auxiliary to the cultivation of dry rice, and was practiced by those households that had easy access to swampy land. It did not require much preparation of the land, and could therefore be done separately by each household. Since wet-rice cultivation went on throughout the year and did not exhaust the soil, the land did not revert to the village. It now was not necessary to move on periodically. As a result, those households which had good opportunities to grow wet rice did not want to move when the dry-rice cultivators had to do so. The villages and even the joint families split. Since the wet-rice cultivation was the more productive system, the households that had to move tended to settle where they too could take up the new method. Thus the co-operative production by joint families died out and the life of the villages became sedentary. Their permanent settlement gave rise to more elaborate fortifications. Warfare became a stalemate. Strong central authority took the place of the earlier democracy among the joint families. The life of the tribe had been transformed not only economically but in terms of its moral web.

The change in Tanala life happens to have been started by the borrowing of a trait from the neighboring Betsileo. But it does not seem likely that the pressure would have been very different, or the problem-solving either, if wet-rice cultivation had been discovered by the Tanala themselves. The pressure on the existing moral web did not begin at once. It was only after a good many households had learned to cultivate wet rice to the extent that they no longer needed to move periodically, that the habits of co-operation were impaired. The decline of loyalty to the joint family was a natural consequence.

The Tanala case beautifully illustrates a fact of basic importance in all cases of change in conditions: the ultimate effects are not seen at first—indeed they are very difficult to see—and thus the moral problem-solving is delayed until the change has had wide repercussions on the social structure.

Another aspect of the matter, apparent only when many cases are reviewed, is that the ecological web is not passive clay molded by changes in conditions. It has its own characteristics and thus tends to accept the influence of change selectively. One could almost predict the directions in which it is and those in which it is not modifiable.

Somewhat different from the cases considered thus far are changes due to crises like a declaration of war or the onset of a severe depression, which may lead to conquest or internal disintegration. Such crises not merely introduce a new factor into the ecological web, they threaten the very functioning of the whole ecological system. They will both be fought by means of readjustments in the moral meb, but, since their nature is very different, the processes involved are unlike those we have considered so far.

A war poses a clear problem. Military manpower must be multiplied; production of "luxury" items must be curtailed, of weapons greatly increased; national life must be ordered to produce maximum effectiveness in making war. These tasks call for intelligent planning, good communication, and discipline at all levels of the population. It is relatively easy to see what is needed and why persons are enrolled in the armed forces or are shifted from one type of industry to another. New institutional arrangements and new norms may be called into being, but their necessity is not hard to understand and on the whole people accept them with good grace. The process of strengthening the moral web is pursued in a straightforward manner because of the great need, popular acquiescence, and the clarity of the goal. Oftentimes the tightening of controls is carried to an unnecessary extreme and in a manner to jeopardize democratic values. This happened in the United States during and after World

War I and again with the outbreak of the Korean War in 1950. In both cases, however, democratic values reasserted themselves after a few years.

The onset of a depression is more gradual, and the demands of the situation are less clear. Whereas during a war the basic character of the moral web is retained because it is the way of life that is being defended, in a depression the way of life itself is faltering. It may have to be reorganized in quite fundamental ways. Neither the degree nor the manner of this reorganization is ever obvious. It often takes considerable experimentation before a new, satisfactory moral web is fashioned. The New Deal of the '30's in the United States was such a time of experimentation.

The detection of a problem for the moral web resulting from change in conditions obviously requires an awareness of the changing pattern in the ecological web and a sensitivity to the demands of norms and institutions. Detection means the perception, from the moral perspective of the society, of a shortcoming in the emerging factual situation. If the ecological processes are allowed to develop without critical appraisal until the problem has become acute, detection is of course simple. Anyone may then be the detector. Something like this happened with the automobile. Its use grew by leaps and bounds, and no one seemed to think much about some of the societal problems it might raise—such as its use by criminals— until serious maladjustments actually occurred. This procedure is very wasteful. The earlier detection takes place the better. If, for instance, State Police systems had been set up in the United States before World War I, the organization of bootlegging gangs in the '20's might have been prevented.

Problem-solving, then, can proceed most effectively if detection is anticipatory—if the problem is seen before it becomes serious. This seems to call for two kinds of skills.

On the one hand, the trends in the ecological web must be understood well enough to forecast probable developments. This is facilitated by the realization that ecological change does not occur capriciously but selectively and according to the existing properties of the social system. The introduction of the auto truck, for instance, into a society possessing an elaborate railroad network has very different effects from its introduction into a society that has no railroads. In a simple society, forecasting trends can be done by anyone with intelligence and a thorough grasp of the life around him. In complex societies, the training of social scientists comes to be more and more essential for such forecasting.

The other skill needed for anticipatory detection is the ability to appraise the moral situation after the ecological developments have taken place. Someone must be sensitive enough to the values of the society to estimate whether the existing moral norms and institutions will be adequate to implement the societal common values in the emerging situation. Again, in simple societies this function can be performed by anyone steeped in the moral tradition and with a knowledge of the current working of the control mechanisms. In modern urbanized societies it may call for the special insights of the novelist, social psychologist, ethical theorist and religious thinker.

In our day there is a great need for the mating of these two skills. If future stages in the chain of social effects can be anticipated, problem-solving can be undertaken before the problem actually arises. But such mating has rarely happened. Perhaps one illustration of it is the manner in which those who planned the Tennessee Valley Authority foresaw that the necessary bureaucratic developments there might seriously violate American democratic values unless specific efforts were made to protect them. Steps were taken to bring the people of the area into the planning and the actual operation of the various projects. This so-called "grass roots" approach gave local organizations and institutions an opportunity to share in the making of decisions. Having detected the problem in advance, the planners took steps to solve it before it arose.

There is nothing in the nature of problems due to a change in conditions that makes the communicative aspect of the problem-solving unique. The population must be widely aware of the problem, there must be easy interchange of views regarding its causes and possible solutions, and there must be a common process of evaluating proposals so that consensus can gradually be achieved.

Anticipatory detection of a moral problem indicates that the process of analysis has already begun. The TVA planners who foresaw the inadequacy of existing democratic norms and institutions to take care of the inevitable bureaucracy of that great undertaking understood full well why bureaucratic processes were bound to develop and why new democratic machinery would have to be created if American common values were to be given full expression.

The vital role of communication in problem-solving stands out at this point. If the anticipatory detection and analysis cannot be shared by the general public, it will have no awareness of the problem, no interest in it, and no basis for the development of consensus regarding its solution. The whole problem-solving process will bog down for lack of effective public participation. This is strikingly illustrated by the events following upon President Roosevelt's decision to develop the atomic bomb. Some of the scientists, it now appears, had moral qualms from the very beginning. They foresaw that a weapon of such destructive power might offend the consciences not only of other peoples, but of Americans as well. Here was the detection of a problem, and some analysis too, but military secrecy made it impossible to communicate the matter to the public. Hence general awareness, full-scale analysis, and a discussion of proposals for solution were forestalled until after the first bomb was dropped. Since then, however, some of the world's best minds have attempted to see the problem from all sides in order to deal with it. Religious leaders, philosophers, social scientists, statesmen, and writers have contributed their analyses. Among those most concerned have been nuclear physicists.

The essential function of analysis is that of giving the right direction to proposals for solving the problem. Since such proposals will have to do with new or improved normative controls, analysis must produce the raw material out of which these controls can be fashioned. Two sorts of findings are needed. First, it is most helpful to know why the ecological web does evolve in the way it does. Unless we understand the causal nexus behind a phenomenon it is difficult to design controls for it. The layman who read about the Hiroshima bombing might detect the moral problem but he is unlikely to understand the complicated historical forces which were expressing themselves in that explosion. Yet it is exactly these historical forces that must be appreciated if effective proposals for the control of atomic warfare are to emerge. Second, the moral web must be analyzed to discover what elements in it might apply to the problem that has been detected. Though the very existence of the problem means that the moral web is not adequate, there are always norms and institutions that could, by extension, be brought to bear upon the problem. Analysis must discover these possibilities. In the case of atomic bombs, for instance, international law was searched for precedents dealing with analogous weapons, such as poison gas, and international institutions were assessed for their ability to make a contribution to control.

The analysis of a moral problem in a complex society need not be carried out by a single person or group. But all those who contribute to it will need to be very well informed. Industrialized societies are so complex that only those who understand the relations clearly can be of much help in identifying the causes or seeing what might be relevant to a cure. Analysis is a much more demanding process than detection—it demands both a knowledge of the past and a penetration into the present.

The fourth aspect of problem-solving is proposal or essay. It flows naturally from analysis. Since we are assuming that there is enough free play to allow adjusting the conditions and the societal common values to each other, a change in conditions requires only a new working relationship between the ecological and the moral web that lie between these poles. Tentative solutions, then, take the form of modifications in the moral web which do not altogether deny the new developments in the ecological web but keep them under control. One can predict, for instance, that when the population of a country like India begins to grow rapidly because of a lowered death rate, and to press upon the sustenance base, modifications of established norms to permit birth control will be suggested, but in a form consonant with established common values. Another example is furnished by early nineteenth-century England. There the norms about work, relief, and the mobility of workers changed drastically and quickly before the need for men in factories. Outdoor relief was practically abolished in the effort to recruit workers for the mills of Lancashire.

Proposal or essay is not always a highly rational process. Although in modern societies only attempts based on analysis are likely to prove successful, many proposals not so based may be put forward. Most of them will have a common-sense character, some will be harebrained. Besides there will be essays that are not purposefully instituted at all but merely represent the sort of event that life is constantly throwing up. Examples can be imagined in regard to crime and horror comic books in American society. A highly rational proposal would be to carry out widespread, careful research as a basis for drawing up a code to be enforced by law on the publishers. A common-sense proposal might be to let the local police destroy any comic books they consider undesirable. Some crackpot might suggest that the publishers be visited by vigilantes. Finally, a denial to the publishers of adequate paper stocks because of a national emergency might render the comic book business unprofitable, thus solving the problem inadvertently while dealing with another.

Effective problem-solving is furthered by having many good alternatives to choose from. It is particularly desirable that proposals and essays be made which draw upon the experience of different classes in the society. This will ensure that the moral innovations on which consensus is ultimately achieved will be influenced by the new condition as it is felt throughout the population, and should prevent the instability that derives from the later protest of those who were not consulted in the solution.

Like analysis, evaluation of proposals and essays calls for contributions of the best minds. Two difficult judgments are needed. The first is whether the proposal is workable. Will it in fact meet the problem? Will it bring conduct and relationships up to the standard required by the common values? Secondly, will it have other, unintended results that are objectionable? Will it cure the immediate problem only to produce effects in other fields which run counter to common values? The role of informed, practical men like skilled politicians in making these judgments is clear. Perhaps less clear is the role of social science.

One of the best examples of this role that can be given is Madison's contribution to *The Federalist* on the separation of governmental powers, written at the time the adoption of the U. S. Constitution was being considered. Functioning as a political scientist, he scanned the experience of many governments in an effort to predict what provisions would work well, what ill, under the circumstances of American society. He tried to foresee not only the immediate effects of various provisions but their incidental effects as well. He was astonishingly successful. A more recent example is Keynesian economic theory as applied to limiting the amplitude of the swings in the business cycle.

The evaluations of proposals by the practical leader and the theoretician need to be well informed concerning the sentiments of the populace among whom new elements in the moral web will operate. It is the essence of democracy that solutions to problems are supported by the masses. This is why leaders and theoreticians need to keep in close touch with life at all social levels.

Despite all attempts to consider the acceptability of proposed solutions to various segments of the population, the evaluations of people in particular classes are bound to be influenced strongly by their own experience. And this is true even though the problem, being one of inadequacy in the moral web, is one on which they are not likely to have strong preferences. It is simply that there is enough variation in subcultural background to make it seem much more of a problem to some than to others, or a different kind of a problem. Let us take, for example, the viewing of crime stories on television by children—a matter for concern in the United States because of its possible relation to the rise of juvenile delinquency in the last decade. Lower-class parents appear to be much less concerned about this matter than middle-class parents. Several explanations suggest themselves. First, the behavior patterns of the lower classes are probably more violent than those of the middle class, and the adults therefore not so easily shocked. Second, the television fare may appear preferable to the neighborhood influences to which lower-class children, though not middle-class children, would be exposed if they were on the street. Finally, the lower classes probably do not think in terms of social causation as readily as does the middle class. It may not occur to members of the lower class that crime and horror programs might stimulate anti-social behavior. None of these suggestions indicates any less concern among lower-class parents for the welfare of their children. But they do account for a differential opinion regarding the need for television controls and show why specific proposals might be evaluated differently.

In one of the few studies of the problem-solving process, Fuller and Myers, dealing with residence trailers in Detroit, found that evaluation of different proposals went forward in three areas of discussion: among neighbors and in unorganized groups, by pressure groups such as real estate organizations and parent-teacher associations, and among governmental and specialist personnel such as members of police and health departments and social workers. Both the question of ends—what role should the residence trailer have in a metropolitan community—and the question of means—how arrange to have it play that role—were earnestly debated. The general public was thus helped to see the problem from all sides.

The proposals of some persons or groups will carry more weight than others. No society is so equalitarian as to be without prestige differentials. In many instances the proposals that really fight it out for supremacy are those of two sets of prestige figures. In the United States, for instance, there has been struggle between traditionally-oriented medical practitioners and public health specialists over the desirability of government-sponsored programs in the health field. Even a person with great prestige may fail, however, in his advocacy of some new idea. In his *Innovation* (p. 320) Barnett recalls the example of Ikhnaton, who almost but not quite succeeded in having the Egyptian people accept monotheism as early as the fourteenth century B.C.

Evaluation is already the beginning of consensus. Communications passing back and forth among the public, including both leaders and led, illuminate the problem from many angles. Weaknesses and strengths are brought to light, and a foundation is laid for a gradual convergence of viewpoints. That convergence comes more easily in cases of inadequacy in the moral web such as are discussed in this chapter than in cases of incompatibility which we shall discuss in the next.

The moral issue raised by the proposed use of atomic energy for nonmilitary purposes in the United States provides an illustration. Should the government become the sole user of this form of energy, or should it be made available to private enterprise? We had not developed norms to guide us here. The only way to do this has been to relate American common values to the facts of the situation and evolve a way of dealing with the problem that seems best under the circumstances. Some have felt that fissionable materials should become commodities like any other, subject to the ordinary rules of private property. Others have taken the position that the dangerous character of these materials, and the fact that all the developmental work on them was done by the government, call for a new property conception.

The very fact that a change in conditions working through the ecological web confronts a society rather suddenly with a new moral problem tends toward rationality of solution. The sudden gap in the moral web invites quick objective action. Of course some will try to build out bridges of analogy from one side of the gap, some from another, but the protagonists are not likely to be wedded to traditional attitudes *on this subject,* for the very reason that it is so new. Perhaps this is why new norms and new institutional arrangements in such cases are likely to be worked out through the legislative process. Law generates mores. The great mass of the people do not have developed views on the subject and are therefore willing to follow the leaders.

An interesting example of the power of pre-existing law as a source of consensus in a new situation is found in the history of Negro slavery in Latin America. Spanish and Portuguese law, rooted in the Stoics and the Christian fathers, had given recognition to the moral personality of Moorish slaves. When African slaves were first imported into Latin America, their master was accorded rights over the body of the slave but not over his soul. Slavery was seen as a misfortune of human rather than divine origin. The church early worked for manumission and obtained acceptance, at least in Brazil, Cuba, and Mexico, of the principle that slaves could force their masters to accept payment for freedom. Since there had been no history of slavery in England since the Conquest, the common law in force in the North American colonies had no traditional way of dealing with slaves. If men were not fully men, they could only be chattels, subject to the norms which govern the use of chattels.

It would be a mistake to assume that, once a new trait has become established in the ecological web and has created a problem, problem-solving will necessarily be carried through to a consensus. Sometimes the process fails, usually because of differences in the interests of segments of the population. Or there may be legal enactment without really solid moral support. This has happened in predominantly rural areas when the minimum age for automobile driving has been set in terms of the needs of the urban situation. Most city-dwellers are not anxious to have their children drive before the age of sixteen, because of the accidents they may have and the temptations that the new-found mobility may bring in its train. Rural parents, on the other hand, often want their children able to fetch supplies from town and aid in the work of the farm, and so may favor a lower age limit for driving. The different rural and urban attitudes on such an issue are not always easy to reconcile. Usually it is impractical to have different rules for the two sets of children. Almost the only way in which consensus can emerge is for each side gradually to come to understand the other's problem. Then the enactment of some kind of compromise into law gradually works to crystallize a general moral norm.

Failure to achieve consensus usually means a discrepancy between social contacts at the ecological level and at the socio-psychological level. Relations are close enough to call for an overall rule, but not close enough to bring about a coalescence of views. In our example, a solution would be much easier if there were many organizations in which rural and urban people met and mingled—which there usually are not. Such social differentiation as the source of moral problems will be discussed fully in the next chapter.

Even after consensus has been achieved there is no guarantee that it will persist. Actually the evaluations that have led to it may have been based upon false information or false inference, and the moral web so created is not in fact capable of solving the problem. This will soon become apparent. Thus a new problem, though not perhaps as baffling as the original one, arises and has to be solved. The behavior of a society is sometimes not unlike that of a ship which in changing course swings too far. It has to be brought back again, but this time through a smaller arc.

Nonliterate societies accepting some elements of Western technology furnish many examples of readjustments that do not last. It is so common as almost to be the rule that unforeseen consequences of the new technology are unsuited to their traditional moral web, and a revulsion takes place. Nativistic movements like the Ghost Dance among the Plains Indians testify to the dream of either recapturing the old way of life or quickly finding a new synthesis. Such movements succeed rarely if ever in reversing the trend of events—the new technological features have become too deeply embedded. They do testify, however, to the difficulty of finding the right social adjustment at once, and to the strength of old attitudes that must somehow be modified to fit the new techniques.

CHAPTER 11

Incompatibility in the Moral Order

In the last chapter, we have dealt with problems created in the moral web by changes in conditions that induce changes in the ecological web. In such cases the existing moral norms and institutions prove in some way inadequate and have to be modified in order to foster orientation and stability in place of confusion. The old steady state is no longer workable, and a new one has yet to be found.

The present chapter is focussed on disharmony among the elements of the moral order itself. Such disharmony may exist either among the common values of the society and its moral web, or within the moral web.

Incompatibility in the moral order is perhaps harder to judge than inadequacy. Neither common values nor moral norms nor institutions are as tangible as are the changes, usually of a physical nature, that take place in the ecological order. In situations of inadequacy, at least one side of the problem, so to speak, is tangible; in situations of incompatibility, neither side is.

We shall distinguish five types of incompatibility, according to the causes giving rise to the problem: (1) that stemming from the evolution of common values, as when a new creed like Christianity develops in an old society; (2) that which occurs when new evidence shows that old norms are not in fact the best instruments to carry out societal common values; (3) that resulting from immigration of groups with different values, norms, and institutions; (4) that which accompanies the interpenetration of regional subcultures of the same society; and finally (5) that following upon differentiation of population elements within a society.

As suggested in Chapter 3, common societal values are neither necessarily static, nor are their changes necessarily determined by influences coming from the ecological level: religious prophets no less than secular thinkers have stirred men's minds to new orientations and new aspirations. The rise of Christianity in a remote Roman province in Asia Minor and its spread to other societies of different social structure argue for at least a partial autonomy of the value elements. New values are of course subject to selective processes as they enter a society, but the tolerance is rather wide. One cannot infer the common values of a society from the ecological conditions in which it operates.

When new values enter and conflict with the established common values, the analysis through the problem-solving process described in the preceding chapters is not appropriate. If there are no settled principles in accordance with which a judgment between them is possible, there is no real basis for consensus. There is no rational way to determine whether new values knocking at the door should be allowed to enter. To say that they must be compatible with the existing values is to condemn the society to dead uncreativeness. On the other hand, to take the position that a society should always adopt values which a large part of its members think better than the traditional ones, opens the possibility of ill-considered change that will later be regretted. Even if there were some scientific way to prove that one of two sets of values would have more favorable results for the society in this world, there is no arguing with those who believe that the other set would be more acceptable in the eyes of God. Convictions are not subject to any test and hence cannot be treated in a problem-solving manner.

When new value elements creep into a culture there is, then, a struggle between the old and the new. Among the factors that determine the outcome are of course the ecological ones of economic productiveness and security. But factors such as religious beliefs may be influential too. Here the sociologist cannot take his usual stance and say, "If A is the society's goal, then my observation of life suggests that X is the best route to take," because the goal itself is undetermined—that is just what the society is trying to work out.

The sociologist might, of course, assume the role of adviser to any of the groups supporting different values, pointing out to them the most effective way to wage the struggle. But this is not a societal function. His only societal function is to stand on the sidelines and tell both parties what the social implications of the two value positions are, what consequences are likely to flow from the adoption of either. If, knowing these implications, both parties wish to fight it out, there is nothing the social scientist can do, no matter how much he may want to save his society from travail.

It is not always easy to say whether a conflict is one of ultimate values or merely of different interpretations of the same values. The struggle over the teaching of evolution is such an instance. This particular problem was dramatized in 1925 when William Jennings Bryan and Clarence Darrow, two great trial lawyers, represented opposite points of view on it in the Scopes case in Tennessee. Was it the ultimate values of religious fundamentalists and religious modernists that were really different, or was it merely that the same ultimate values could be so differently interpreted as to lead one group to a literal interpretation of the Bible and the other to a more figurative one? Whichever explanation we accept, there can be no doubt that the struggle was bitter.

Incompatibility may follow upon change in common values, or accompany the change itself. Even after the movement for women's rights had won the day in Western countries, there was still room for differences of interpretation concerning the fields to which the emancipation applied. Were women free to smoke? On the streets as well as in the home? Cigars as well as cigarettes? Such questions can become serious moral issues. The opponents in the struggle are not necessarily classes or other easily identified sociological categories. It seems likely that those who would give the broadest interpretation to the new common value would be they who had fought for its acceptance; while those who only acquiesced in what seemed a general desire would tend to limit its application. If this is true, the problem-solving process is once again inappropriate, since the difference is in fact merely one of definition of the new common value. There is as yet no common objective. Until there is, means cannot be selected rationally.

Such situations tend to cure themselves in time through a gradual process of communication and interaction. The emancipation of women tends to take on more and more specific meaning, as experience clarifies what is concordant with other common values and other aspects of the social structure.

A slightly different process seems to be occurring in South and Southeast Asia. One writer alleges that the individualistic Western pattern of values has there been supplanting the previous pattern centered on kinship, as it supplemented feudalism centuries ago in Europe; but that because of overpopulation and other handicaps, the individualistic value system now has less chance of success than in the days when the Western world was expanding. Disillusion and discouragement are the result. If this diagnosis is correct, what is happening is that new norms and institutions based upon the new common values are being found inappropriate to the conditions of life within which the South Asian societies operate. Their situation seems to be rare in human history—probably because a society does not usually adopt a new set of common values without much preliminary experimentation to determine whether they will work under the existing conditions. Only the great prestige of the industrial West among Asian natives, accentuated by contacts during World War II, can account for the situation.

An even more striking case, but this time a successful one, is that of the Hawaiians cited by Kroeber in *Anthropology* (pp. 403–05). Their king, in close contact with Western culture, realizing its technical superiority and believing that their traditional religion was limiting his people in various ways, overthrew that religion in one stroke and adopted Christianity. His prestige was such that he was able to carry his people along with him. This is perhaps the most dramatic case on record of a sharp change in the moral order. It can be squared with sociological theory only by concluding that, in spite of a striking change in religious and other norms, the shift at the level of common values was not great.

A form of incompatibility hitherto rare because dependent upon new scientific knowledge is our second type. Here the common values do not change, but suddenly it is discovered that the old norms which have been fashioned to implement some value do not in fact do so as well as would some other norms. The society may believe, for instance, that a norm compelling uncongenial parents to stay together until their children are grown up helps the character development of the children, while research may prove that this is frequently not so. As long as knowledge of the incompatibility is confined to a few experts there is no problem. But as soon as it begins to be disseminated to the public, the old norm will begin to decline in favor. It may take a long time for a new norm, adequate to the situation and compatible with the rest of the moral web, to develop, but the process of readjustment is a straightforward one.

A clear illustration is the problem, mentioned in Chapter 9, of the desegregation of whites and Negroes in American schools. For at least seventy-five years Americans thought that their common value of equal opportunity was well enough implemented by an educational system in which the avowed aim was "separate but equal" facilities. Not until social psychologists began research on the attitudes of white and Negro children was it discovered that separate facilities cannot give equal opportunity so long as one race holds a dominant position in the society. The findings of such research were marshaled to prove, in a series of court cases, that the common value of equal opportunity demanded a change in the institutional pattern. This change was called for by the famous decision of the U. S. Supreme Court of May 17, 1954. It will probably take a long time to develop societal consensus from this decision. A proposal has been officially evaluated in a favorable manner. But the problem-solving process still has far to go.

The third type of incompatibility results from the influx of immigrants with a different normative orientation. If the influx is small and if the immigrants scatter, there is really no problem of societal readjustment. The immigrants appear as somewhat deviant individuals who have to be brought into line with the existing moral norms and institutions. This matter of acceptance of norms, spreading of institutional influence, and rehabilitation of deviants has been treated in earlier chapters.

But if the immigrants are numerous, and particularly if they settle in large colonies, a problem of a different sort is posed. They are then subgroups with considerable solidity capable of exercising social influence as well as receiving it. Immigrant enclaves not only possess their common values, they bring with them their own moral web.

Old-country norms come into operation, old-country institutions are copied if not reproduced. A different way of life is carried on in the midst of the receiving society.

In cases of this kind the nature of what now takes place depends upon the common values of the society. If these are both ethnocentric and authoritarian, the immigrants will be treated as groups to be assimilated by coercive means, and the moral web will be reinforced to do the job. The situation will not be seen as one requiring any readjustment of that web. The less ethnocentric and authoritarian the common values, however, the more the immigrants will be regarded as having human dignity, and the greater the likelihood that their cultural ways will be treated with respect. This is especially true if their society of origin has high prestige. Since there are no existing societies that are completely democratic and completely without ethnocentrism, the readjustment that ensues is usually one in which the native culture plays the dominant role.

What occurs in fact in most contemporary Western societies is a process of accommodation. The immigrant norms and institutions are modified very radically, the native moral web only a little. It is apparent, for instance, that Scandinavian immigrants to the United States have not succeeded in giving the consumers' co-operative movement the central place in the new culture that it had in their home cultures. Yet the movement has gained a marginal place in the American capitalist economy.

Sociological research indicates clearly that the rate at which accommodation of this kind takes place is linked to the extent of social participation across the ethnic barriers. If there are many groups that bring natives and immigrants together to follow common interests or to solve common problems, the rate will be rapid. Appreciation of the other man's point of view and an understanding of the worth of his values, norms, and institutions will be fostered. Mutual acculturation is then almost inevitable.

The native culture will be the predominant partner in any such acculturation, not only because it is more widespread and powerful, but also because it is closely adjusted to local conditions. Immigrant cultures, developed in other places under different circumstances, will probably have only a limited fitness to the new situation. But it would be a mistake to assume that the immigrant culture will not affect matters at all. Human life has its universal as well as its specific aspects, and many an imported culture has broadened the vision of a receiving society. Greek slaves brought many of the finer aspects of Grecian culture to the capturing Romans.

The problem of readjusting the moral order of a society to accommodate large numbers of immigrants is solved not so much by processes of public opinion in the ordinary sense as by a multiplication of contacts and groupings across ethnic lines. Here again there is clear framework within which problem-solving can be conducted. So long as there is some principle of human dignity in the dominant culture, the immigrant normative systems will affect the result. The only scientific advice that can be given is that frictions can be eased, and an accommodated situation be reached more quickly, if social participation is stimulated and encouraged.

A different but related problem is that of the society which, because of conquest, has not one center of gravity but two. Here the old moral order of the conquered is in conflict with the new moral order of the conquerors. Over a very long period of time an accommodation usually takes place, though the Polish people furnish a good example of how resistant to the orientations of the conquerors a people can be. Poland was partitioned among Russia, Austria, and Germany for more than a hundred years without losing its distinctive national way of life. In terms of our scheme of analysis the only way to deal with this phenomenon is to say that in such cases two societies interpenetrate, with a clash of moral orientations.

The fourth situation causing incompatibility is the interpenetration of regional cultures of the same society. Modern communication is usually the proximate cause here. In large societies, such as the German, the Russian, or the American, distinctive regional subcultures developed in the period before the advent of railroad, automobile, and airplane. These subcultures could have distinctive normative elements so long as these did not conflict with the degree of interdependence that existed at that time. Isolation conferred a certain autonomy. With the coming of modern communication and transportation, the isolation and with it the autonomy has gradually given way. One of the best examples we have already cited—the norms concerning Negro-white relations in the United States. So long as South and North were largely separate social worlds, Southern customs of segregation in transportation, in recreation, and in education could without great friction remain different from Northern customs. But with the development of industry in the South and the migration of Northern whites into the area, and with the return to the South of Negroes who had become used to non-segregation in their military service or through employment in the North, the situation became intolerable. The two sets of mores which formerly existed side by side now clashed head-on. A serious social problem arose which could be cured only by the acceptance of some nation-wide moral standard.

The very factors that create such problems tend to solve them. The more the people of different regions meet and mingle, the more alike their experiences will be, and the more their interpretations of the societal values will coincide. If the differences have deep historical roots, like the contrast in Negro-white norms between North and South, many years of common experience will be needed to harmonize the regional mores. But under modern conditions of communication it seems unlikely that friction can build up, as it did a hundred years ago, to the point of civil war.

The fifth and for our purposes most important type of incompatibility is that which follows upon differentiation of population elements from within a society. Here the problem-solving analysis described in the last two chapters is appropriate, because here the common values of the society are not in question. They afford a criterion in terms of which a solution can be sought.

Class or caste differentiation is the most common cause of this type of incompatibility. Not every differentiation, however, gives rise to moral problems. If certain accounts of the development of the feudal system, for instance, can be trusted, that system seems to have caused a minimum of strain. The Germanic tribes were moving across Europe, pillaging and destroying. The Roman Empire was no more. The small landowners were glad to come under the protection of the bigger ones, who could provide rude military protection. All parties wanted a peaceful, productive life under the wing of the Christian church, on the territory of their ancestors. Feudal society was a system of institutional arrangements and differentiated norms that suited their common objective.

Since the process of differentiation does not always produce incompatibility, the mere existence of differentiation does not imply it. Even the traditional caste system of India, one of the most differentiated social structures in the history of mankind, does not seem to have experienced much moral incompatibility. Each caste accepted its place in the scheme of things and recognized both its own responsibilities and those of other castes.

In the modern West, however, the process of class differentiation has usually torn the moral web in one way or another. More responsible than any other factor has been the Industrial Revolution. In country after country the societal norms and institutions that had once been accepted came to seem to the working class less and less expressive of societal common values. Though history has refuted the Marxist theory that the moral standards of a class are solely determined by its relation to the means of production, there can be no doubt that Marx rightly judged the great influence of differential life situations on moral interpretations. Sometimes the problems so created have been dealt with intelligently, and a reform accomplished by a problem-solving process. Sometimes they have been neglected, and revolution has followed.

We are here concerned with peaceful methods of problem-solving. Revolution, though it is of course one way of getting from one steady state of the moral order to another, will not be considered. It typically occurs when problems pile up with which an inept ruling class seems unable to grapple effectively. The situation that produces revolution may be glimpsed by contrast with Brinton's description of its opposite (in *The Anatomy of Revolution*, p. 39): "All we can expect of what we may call a healthy society is . . . that most people should behave as if they felt that, with all its faults, the society were a going concern." When a large segment of the population feels that society is not a going concern, and sees no possibility of making it so by legitimate means, it may begin to plot a revolution. Any ideology from whatever source that seems to offer a theory of reconstruction will then, of course, exercise a strong influence on the revolutionaries.

The drifting apart of classes does not have to involve the proletariat. The most plausible interpretation of the National Socialist movement in Germany is that the lower middle class, ruined by the inflation of the '20's and the depression of the early '30's, became alienated from the machinery of bourgeois democracy and sought to give traditional German values a different implementation.

A less striking but more general form of differentiation is that which occurs when urban people begin to multiply in what was formerly a rural society. Then the split is not so much between the moral views of two classes as between the moral norms and institutions suitable to a simple type of life, in which primary groups set the pattern, and those suitable to a more complicated and impersonal way of living. In a degenerating society like the late Roman Empire, a similar conflict can occur, this time between the cynical and materialistic elements of the population who have lost their moral roots in primary groups, and the "better" elements that still have a strong sense of moral responsibility.

The usual case, however, is that the upper and middle classes tend to rest satisfied with the traditional norms and the institutional forms inherited from a simpler economy, whereas the workers feel that these no longer represent a fair and adequate expression of the society's common values. A clear example is the struggle in the United States during the depression of the '30's over federal enforcement of collective bargaining. There were no essential differences in the common values of the contending parties. The dignity of the person and the democratic way of life were equally cherished by both sides. The difference was that those who were in the weakest economic position felt that these values could not be adequately safeguarded without collective bargaining, while those who were less subject to the uncertainties of the economy felt that such bargaining would jeopardize individual initiative and personal freedom. The difference in viewpoint was the result of a long period in which capitalist enterprises had been becoming larger. The perspective of the wage earners had been diverging more and more from that which was embodied in the traditional moral web and still held by most employers.

Another facet of the same process is that wage-earners in democratic societies may come to regard the traditional prerogatives of the employing classes as incompatible with the society's common values. The degree of control which seemed proper enough when relations between owner and workers were face-to-face in a small shop seems arbitrary when the factory is large, the manager a distant and unknown figure, and the workers feel themselves to be merely faceless robots in a giant mechanism. They begin to wonder whether it is not more in keeping with the dignity of the person that they have a voice in the control of shop practices such as the speed of the assembly line with which their work is synchronized.

In putting so much emphasis on the Industrial Revolution we may seem to be subsuming the process of differentiation under the subject of changes in conditions discussed in the preceding chapter. This is not our intention. But since the distinction between the two subjects is a fine one, we had better clarify the matter. In Chapter 10, our concern was with problems for the moral web posed by new developments coming up through the ecological web. Here, we are concerned with incompatibilities in the moral web itself. These, it is true, are usually indirect results of ecological change, but the process has gone so much further that the results are different in kind. It is not the repercussions of a new development like the automobile that pose the problem, but changes in the social structure itself.

It must be stressed again that we are not here concerned with differentiation in the *ultimate* orientations of social classes. If conflict arises because all common orientation is lost, little can be done except to fight it out. So long as there is some consensus on ultimate common values, however, the process of readjustment may be peaceful. By an appeal to those ultimate common values, by gaining insight into each other's position, and by a sense of justice and a willingness to compromise, things can be worked out.

Perhaps the greatest work on this subject is Dicey's *Law and Public Opinion in England During the Nineteenth Century*. Dicey pictures for us first the previous "steady state"—what he calls the period of Old Toryism; then its breakdown between 1800 and 1830 because of the differentiation within the society of an urban proletariat; and finally the gradual evolution of new moral norms, new institutions, and new laws as the process of public discussion produced strands of consensus.

Exactly what constitutes the breakdown of a steady state of the moral web? How do differentiated interpretations get started? Much has been written on the subject from many points of view but there seems to be no accepted general theory.

Perhaps the first sign is restlessness. Blumer says: "When people have impulses, desires, or dispositions which cannot be satisfied by the existing forms of living they are in a state of unrest. Their feeling is one of feeling an urge to act but of being balked from doing so; consequently the experience is one of discomfort, frustration, insecurity, and usually of alienation or loneliness." Presumably the principal reason for the balking experienced is the existence of frustrating norms and institutions. Perhaps a worker recently entering a cotton mill finds the experience galling, though he may not be aware that his restlessness is due to the factory regime. He does not realize that he is upset by the change from the putting-out system where he had more control over his hours of labor. In this example there has been no change in the common values of the society. The worker has merely entered a situation where norms different from those he has been used to have been derived from the same common values. Even when he enters into circular interaction with his fellow workers and a state of social unrest develops there may still be no awareness of the causal factors. Blumer believes this is shown by a random character of behavior. "People are likely to move around in an erratic or aimless way, as if seeking to find or avoid something, but without knowing what it is that they are trying to find or avoid." Under modern conditions this period of aimlessness is, however, likely to be short. Quick detection of the problem is rendered probable by rationalistic habits of thought and the growing public appreciation of the influence of social factors on attitudes and conduct.

Detection does not carry the society far toward a solution unless it is accompanied by quick communication to many elements of the public. So long as large segments of the society do not see the problem, there may be protests but there will not be real problem-solving. This happens frequently in occupational hierarchies. The lower strata are so isolated from the upper that their belief that old norms are obsolete is not effectively communicated to the higher strata. Matters get worse before they get better.

Once the problem has been detected and communicated to others, two things may happen. A specific reform may be proposed, evaluated favorably, adopted, and become part of the way of life. This happens when the objectionable norm or institutional arrangement does not constitute a serious vested interest of some other element of the population; hence the analysis can be accepted by all. There is then no concerted social resistance—only inertia opposes the change. A case in point is the adoption of safety standards for factories. The norm which prevailed in the earlier days of factory work was that it was the responsibility of the operative to safeguard himself in the presence of dangerous machinery. The mounting number of industrial accidents gave rise to resentment on the part of the employees. When their complaints began to mount and became concerted, the more discerning employers, for reasons of production as well as humanitarianism, felt that it would be the part of wisdom to accept safety codes. They saw that the situation was in fact anachronistic, and that the lack of safety regulations reflected the situation of a former day when machinery was simpler and less dangerous.

If the norm or institution that is thought to be outmoded does represent a strong vested interest, the situation is different. A vested interest means consolidated power. The particular element of moral structure complained of will prove to be interwoven with other cultural elements. An attack at the point of objection will meet resistance on a broader front. The only strategy that can here succeed is to seek more inclusive changes, to strive for a more fundamental restructuring. To carry through such a strategy requires long, well-organized, and persistent effort—in short, a social movement.

The kind of movement appropriate to the peaceful problem-solving process is what Blumer calls a reform movement. It differs from a revolutionary movement in that it accepts the basic values of the existing order and attempts to correct some institutional defect. "The reform movement starts with the prevailing code of ethics, and derives much of its support because it is so well-grounded on the ethical side. . . . By contrast, a revolutionary movement always challenges the existing mores and proposes a new scheme of moral values."

The ultimate aim of a reform movement is a change in moral norms or institutions through the processes of public opinion. By analysis of the existing situation, and by the proposal and favorable evalution of its program, the movement hopes to persuade the public. The ideology of the movement usually includes both a positive justification for what it is attempting and negative evaluation of present conditions. As Blumer points out, a successful movement must also arouse feelings and impulses through agitation, develop *esprit de corps*, obtain real conviction among its sympathizers, and perfect a set of tactics for gaining and holding adherents and reaching objectives. Only if it is thus fortified will it grow in power and have a chance to overcome the resistance of the vested interest opposing it. Though usually working on behalf of a distressed group, a reform movement, unlike a revolutionary one, "tries to enlist the allegiance of a middle-class public on the outside and to awaken within them a vicarious sympathy for the oppressed group. Hence, generally it is infrequent that the leadership or membership of a reform movement comes exclusively from the group whose rights are being espoused."

Not all reform groups, however, can be said to have the aim of aiding a distressed group. The prohibition movement in the United States, for instance, was aimed at the evils of drinking in all classes. Before the Anti-Saloon League, it had not been thought necessary to implement the values of hard work and personal morality by a norm against the saloon and drinking. The aim of the League was to persuade the public that these values required such a norm. It succeeded in getting the idea recognized in law, first locally, then statewide, and finally nationally.

Heberle contrasts social movements with both political parties and pressure groups. The contrast with political parties is clear: they must take a position on many issues, whereas the social movement has a limited set of objectives. The contrast with pressure groups is less evident. Heberle says that the latter are more limited in their goals, and more formal in their organization, than social movements. The point about formality is well taken, but it does not seem that pressure groups are always more limited in their goals. One might rather argue that the contrast here is one of maturity of process. A social movement is evolving; it is fighting for the recognition of a viewpoint. A pressure group has arrived, so to speak; the pressure it is maintaining is for an interest which has already achieved some recognition.

In advancing the solution of problems of moral incompatibility, then, social movements are fitter instruments than either political parties or pressure groups: each movement is *specifically* relevant to an *emerging* problem. But a social movement does not in itself solve the problem—it only contributes to the solution. It brings the matter forcefully into the arena of public discussion and compels the old order to justify itself if it can.

Social movements are, of course, opposed not only by inertia but by the concerted efforts of those who feel themselves threatened. If these efforts are merely to maintain the status quo, they may be exerted through political parties or through pressure groups. But if the social movement which is feared is making headway, the conservatives may foster a social movement of their own to redress the balance. After the French Revolution, there were conservative movements both in France and England.

There are of course many instruments of power available to the upper and middle classes in a struggle against social movements with lower class support. The more privileged classes usually control the churches, the schools, and the press and can to some extent at least manipulate them so as to affect public opinion. In at least one American city, according to the Lynds' *Middletown in Transition* (Chap. 2), new normative instrumentalities were successfully fought off by such manipulation. Until 1935, Middletown resisted the groundswell affecting all the industrial areas of the United States in favor of industrial unions as a means of promoting the security of the workers.

Those who are dissatisfied with the traditional moral structure of their own society are likely to look to other societies for hints or suggestions. This is why social movements are likely to be contagious if there is a basic similarity in social structures. It is also the reason why conservatives can so often cry "foreign ideologies" or "alien doctrines" when faced with a social movement. There has indeed been frequent borrowing from foreign thought or foreign practice. But this does not alter the fact that the problem is real, and indigenous.

An illustration of what we have in mind is the history of the Industrial Workers of the World in the United States in the early twentieth century. They espoused a revolutionary and syndicalist viewpoint which was quite out of harmony with the main currents of American thought and which clearly derived from continental European sources. Was this a case where moral incompatibility was implanted from abroad? No serious student of the movement thinks so. The I.W.W. was composed of American workers, reacting to American conditions of the time. They used some foreign ideas for their protest, but the differentiation had already occurred and was not produced by the ideology. The point was that they saw conditions in American commerce and industry which seemed to them incompatible with the dignity of man. They believed that a fundamental re-structuring was needed.

An interesting case of influence from abroad is "the return of the native" with a new moral perspective. He may have been sensitized to the moral strain in his society before his departure, and thereby made receptive to new normative orientations abroad. He must of course find strong support among his stay-at-home contemporaries before a real incompatibility develops. Jefferson's stay in France may have affected him in some such way and upon his return made him a leader of an opposition party to the Federalists. But a probably more valid interpretation of the situation is that the United States had suffered a conservative drift in his absence so that he, coming back with essentially the same view as when he left, appealed to those who were dissatisfied with the trend of the times.

In whatever manner foreign ideas reach a society, it is evident that they will strike no root unless the soil is already prepared. It is the drifting apart of elements of the society's own population that brings about the moral divergence. Those discontent with the traditional moral web cast about for help in analyzing the situation, and for guidance in improving it. If they find that men in other countries have wrestled with similar problems and come up with answers that seem attractive, they will pay these answers careful heed, and perhaps espouse them. But the fact that the source is alien is of minor importance. The process that needs to be studied is at home.

We have discussed class differentiation in the moral web. There is another kind, that which results from differential rates of change. It is illustrated by the incompatibilities that develop in the moral norms and institutions of urban and rural people even within the same region. A simple example is afforded by the differing attitudes toward the implementation of the American value of humanitarianism on the farms and in the cities. Rural people have believed that most families can take care of themselves if they work hard and live simply; that if disaster or crippling illness strikes, the neighbors should pitch in and help until things are back to normal or relatives can take over. City people, accustomed to the impersonality and rationality of urban existence in the twentieth century, feel that private charities or publicly supported programs should take care of families in need. Because of the heavy toll taken by urban unemployment in the '30's the country as a whole tended to accept the city's view of the situation and new tax-supported arrangements were set up. This trend was generally resisted by rural people who felt that it was not the proper way to handle such problems.

Incompatibility does not always arise as a result of gradual differentiation of moral interpretations. A crisis may beget incompatibility very quickly. There came a time in the Great Depression in the United States—about 1932—when unemployment was so great that the resources of both private charities and local governments for helping the needy were exhausted. Many families had become desperate. Youths left home and "knocked around" the country in order to relieve their families of the obligation of feeding them. This social calamity brought about a sharp change of moral orientation among those in distress. Many a man who had always believed in norms of hard work and scrupulous honesty found his moral view suddenly so changed that begging and even stealing became right as means of relieving his family's need. Such views were naturally not shared by most of those who still had jobs, nor by the law enforcement agencies. The incompatibility in the moral web which was thus produced remained acute for several years until the works programs of the federal government, the institution of unemployment insurance, and the improvement of business conditions made possible a new steady state incorporating changes in institutions and norms. While begging and stealing were not given moral approval, the moral web was so altered as to obviate their principal causes.

In most instances of incompatibility stemming from social differentiation, the analyses of the parties themselves are biased. The very drifting apart that caused the moral split will in all probability cause the differentiated groups to analyze the roots of the problem differently. The Marxist proletarian sees the causes of poverty in exploitation by selfish capitalists, while to the capitalist it flows from lack of productivity on the part of the worker. Under such circumstances the proposals of one side are not likely to appeal to the other. The whole matter must be thrown into the arena of public opinion for the long and thorough discussion that is necessary before anything like consensus can be achieved.

From the stage of analysis on until consensus is finally reached, it is most advantageous to have on either side of the moral split some individuals who understand the position of their opponents and can sympathize with it at least to some degree. This should tend to produce some objective analyses, reasonable proposals, and fair evaluations.

One might suppose that movement up and down the scale of social classes would tend to bring about such a result. Since a person carries through life memories of his previous situations, he should be able to understand the viewpoint of his former fellows. It is interesting that the mere prospect of upward movement at least seems to have as much if not more effect than actual movement itself. Those who foresee that they are going to ascend the social ladder find it quite natural to identify themselves with persons higher up, and try to adjust themselves in advance. But since they also have to cope with the present reality, they are good mediators between class viewpoints.

Once movement in either direction has taken place, however, sympathy with one's former fellows may vanish. The man who has risen may want to prove to his new associates that he is completely one of them, may want to validate this position. This may lead him to the adoption of attitudes which show no trace of his former membership in a lower class. Similarly, a person who has fallen in status may be so embittered by the experience that he completely rejects either the viewpoint of the class from which he came or that of the class to which he has descended. It must be admitted, nevertheless, that the mobile person often serves to bring together people from different classes. Usually some of his new associates will meet at least his parents whom he has left behind. In general, we can perhaps say that vertical mobility gives the opportunity for cross-class appreciation—an opportunity sometimes realized, often disappointed.

Moral consensus arises from similarity of experience, either firsthand or communicated. In modern societies the opportunities for different socio-economic groups to have the same experiences are very limited, so that most incompatibilities caused by social differentiation have to be cured by a symbolic sharing of experience. Thus it is that only those in the same communication networks can have much hope of seeing issues alike—and even they do not necessarily do so. But otherwise there is no possibility of obtaining the same perspective, bridging the gap, and reaching consensus. Striking confirmation of this principle has recently come from a study of a small town. There it was found that the persons who had high rates of communication with their fellows about community problems were much more realistic in their appraisal of the class forces at work than were the "low communicators." The former, no matter what their class, had taken the first step toward solving community difficulties—they had a similar grasp of the facts.

The process of convergence is much more difficult in the case of incompatibility than of inadequacy. Incompatibility implies that consciences are in conflict, that people's very selves are involved. It is not just a matter of agreeing on a way to extend the moral web to cover some new problem raised by technological change. It is a question of altering viewpoints to which individuals are morally committed.

Very often, as Lowell pointed out in *Conflicts of Principle*, it is not that different interpretations are made of the same principle but that there are two principles competing for control of the area of conduct at stake. Both principles are legitimate enough in some areas of life. The disagreement arises over where one should leave off and the other begin: the range of their coverage is in dispute. One class, for instance the capitalists, would extend the idea of free enterprise very far. Another class, say the workers, want governmental regulation to extend over some of the same territory. Lowell also cites the liquor question, where the principles of personal freedom and those of social responsibility come into conflict. This is not a class-based incompatibility, but the conflict over the limits of applicability of two principles is the same.

In all such cases, there is a middle ground of experience which one group believes should be covered by one of the principles, the other by the other. These beliefs represent different priorities in fundamental values; consciences are deeply involved. The processes by which such conflicts are resolved cannot therefore be transient or superficial. The moral ground must be deeply ploughed before consensus is possible.

Although members of different classes in modern societies are in many of the same networks of communication, they are rarely in a position to obtain full understanding of one another's position. The mass media present the common issue on which consensus is needed, but they do not help much to foster the consensus. In the first place, most persons select their newspapers, their radio programs, and their television programs so as to confirm their own beliefs; and even when they do not, they remember what is compatible with their beliefs, and forget what is not. This is largely because, as they attend to the unwelcome stimuli, they are constantly marshaling arguments in defense of their own positions. They make little effort to put themselves in the other person's shoes. The fact that persons from the two sides are in the same network of mass communication, therefore, rarely does much to create consensus.

But it cannot be denied that exposure to the same mass media, supplying people of different social classes with noncontroversial topics of conversation, may contribute to an atmosphere in which consensus on controversial matters might develop. Thus interest in popular sports, television programs, or comic strips may serve as an entering wedge for people thrown together on buses, in stores, in barber shops, and the like. Such casual acquaintances may ripen into the sort of friendship which contributes to consensus on moral issues.

That something beyond casual acquaintance is necessary is suggested by Park's distinction of "knowledge about" from "acquaintance with." The Germans make this distinction between *wissen* and *kennen*, the French with *savoir* and *connaitre*. The first expression in each pair has the significance of objective, rational knowledge; the second connotes some degree of sharing or fellow-feeling. What is the difference in experience which results in acquaintance rather than mere knowledge? It seems to be that of the full-rounded view as against the partial or segmental one. A physicist knows a cat from one viewpoint, a psychologist from another, a physiologist from a third; but the fond child who plays with the cat daily is really acquainted with her. Thus it is that the other man's moral position has little appeal to us unless we see it from all sides as he does, unless we feel a little of the pull it has for him. We are not likely to appreciate his view in this way unless we have come to know him intimately.

There are few opportunities in industrialized societies for members of different classes to come to know each other well. Most cliques and fellowship groups do not bridge the social gap between classes, and there are relatively few formal organizations of a sociable type that do. In the United States, small town churches may perform this function, and the Catholic church even in larger communities is said to do so. The tendency, however, in metropolitan centers is for the churches to become differentiated by social class, so that no one of them finds a very broad segment of the status spectrum in its membership. Much the same can be said of schools. High schools with their larger size are likely to be less class-bound than elementary schools. But no school is a very powerful influence toward consensus because the children are little concerned with the society's moral problems. Veterans' groups constitute another type of organization which sometimes enrolls men of very different social status. But whether they meet often enough and intimately enough to further consensus on moral issues where classes divide is doubtful.

Two types of experience of some duration seem somewhat promising. The first is compulsory military service. In armed forces fed by conscription young men from all walks of life live in close contact with one another for long periods. Undoubtedly there is a tendency for the status differences of the outside world to affect the formation of cliques, but a certain amount of intimacy among men in the same tent or barracks is unavoidable. These contacts give a basis for the kind of acquaintance that conduces to moral consensus. The other type of experience is the mingling of college boys with working class members on summer jobs. Here many young men from business and professional or other white-collar families labor alongside of men from lower social strata. The contact is not so extended as in military service, but in return it is set in the normal surroundings of civilian life, so that the problems of the society are more immediate, the likelihood of discussing them greater. Many a college student has returned from a summer job with a greater respect for the point of view of the laboring man and a greater willingness to meet him half-way in overcoming moral incompatibilities.

A small but significant experiment was made recently when an English clergyman brought a group of inmates from a Borstal institution into a summer camp with a group of Oxford students. The report in *Time* (August 5, 1957) indicates that both groups broadened their perspectives: "The Borstal boys showed a surprising curiosity about university life, and equally surprising willingness to talk about their troubles. At nightly bull sessions, the Oxonians managed to offer sympathy and advice without seeming to patronize. Says an Oxonian: 'If we can give them some inkling of what the rest of the world is like, we will have done our job.'"

Although intimate acquaintance among members of different classes is probably the most powerful way to set the stage for the achievement of consensus, imaginative literature can also be influential. The emotional appeal of a great novel or play often inspires an appreciation of the viewpoints of other classes that no amount of rational argument could produce. The role of *Uncle Tom's Cabin* in converting people to the abolitionist cause is known. Steinbeck's *Grapes of Wrath* may have played a similar part in creating concern for the victims of the "dust bowl" in the '30's.

In a modern democratic society it is almost inevitable that long-term moral issues find their expression in novels, plays, or poetry. The more deep-running the issue, the more appropriate are these forms of communication. Only in the struggles of human character can the deepest issues be symbolized. One might almost prescribe for a society: "If you wish to have your moral incompatibilities settled in terms of fundamental analysis, encourage your creative writers to deal with them." The artist sees the issues in their living context in a way that no reporter nor social scientist can match.

An equally fundamental contribution to moral consensus is occasionally made by the philosopher. He transcends the problem as currently stated and offers a new frame of reference in which the moral incompatibilities find resolution. Dicey shows how Bentham performed this function for his generation. There were many obvious abuses in English society at the beginning of the nineteenth century —the treatment of prisoners, a poor law which seemed to perpetuate poverty, growing factories with intolerable working conditions, women chained to dissolute husbands, gross inequalities in parliamentary representation, and many more. Bentham concluded that all social institutions should be studied rationally and reformed in accordance with the formula "the greatest good to the greatest number." He believed that there was an exact science of morals and legislation based upon utilitarian principles. Although he never succeeded in creating that exact science, he did jar the thought of his age loose from traditional standpoints to such a degree that a fresh view was possible. He persuaded his contemporaries that a rational approach to social problems would enable the contending parties to find amicable solutions. In this sense he paved the way for the great series of reforms which began in 1832, the year of his death.

Although the works of creative writers and philosophers may plough the ground and plant the seeds of consensus, the seeds must still be nourished in a process of discussion and choice. The forums in which this occurs are both private and public.

The most striking example of private discussion that often ends in a resolution of moral incompatibilities is collective bargaining in industry. The recent agreements in the U. S. automobile industry to supplement government unemployment insurance are an illustration. They go far to reconcile formerly irreconcilable notions on the part of management and of unions about the responsibilities of the corporations for the economic security of their employees.

The great advantage of settlements reached in the private forum is that they are not compelled by government power, and are therefore more likely to be followed willingly. As we shall see, when the state settles a moral issue it does not necessarily mean that consensus has really been achieved. On the other hand, the weakness of settlements in the private forum is that they do not have as much influence on elements of the population not directly concerned as do settlements arrived in the public forum.

It is a great shortcoming of modern urban life that there are not more private forums. One bright spot is the promising movement toward community councils. These councils aim to bring together persons acquainted with the community from many points of view. Not only the main functional interests such as business, labor, education, social work, and the churches are represented, but various ethnic groups and perhaps even geographic areas of the community. Certainly such councils, active and well-led, should facilitate the development of moral consensus.

The two great forums of public argument and decision in modern societies are the court and the legislature. Though they function differently in dealing with moral incompatibility, their general relation to the process by which complex societies move from one steady moral state to another is quite similar.

We have seen that a modern society is hard put to it to deal with moral incompatibilities without resort to public institutions. Informal contacts are not likely to bring together opposing viewpoints, because the opponents do not move in the same circles. The ordinary means of mass communication do not involve the readers or listeners sufficiently to affect their attitudes. Only when special forms of groupings such as collective bargaining sessions or community councils are set up, do the proponents of different moral positions find themselves in personal contact. Under these circumstances the role of the court or the legislature is to provide an arena within which the struggle may be carried on and a conclusion reached. But this struggle and this conclusion are not the total moral process. Indeed, they are merely its middle term.

Recent history seems to indicate that an excellent way to resolve issues of moral incompatibility is to carry out a three stage process. It appears highly useful, if not always essential, first to get the issue before the public in general terms, so that discussion of it takes place and proposals are made from several quarters. During this period the weaknesses in the more outlandish suggestions for solution are brought out by the mass media, even though no strong tendency toward consensus develops. When the public has achieved some acquaintance with the problem it is time for the second stage, that involving the court or the legislature. Since the public is now aware of the problem and interested in it, the actions of the governmental organs will be followed closely. The relative validity of the arguments used by the parties can be assessed. When the decision is reached, a considerable section of the public will have been prepared for it and will understand on what considerations it is based. Then comes the third stage, that of achieving a public consensus which conforms to the legal position. It is by no means a foregone conclusion, however, that such consensus will occur.

The processes in the first stage are so multifarious in a complex society as to defy enumeration. Any and all forms of communication can help to stimulate discussion among various elements of the public.

In the second stage the two chief agencies of decision are courts and legislatures. Only a very small proportion of all the cases that come before courts involve the sort of judicial interpretation that is problem-solving in the moral sphere. Most cases turn on issues of fact rather than of law. This leaves those in which there is real doubt as to which line of precedents, which statute, or which constitutional provision affords the controlling principle in the matter at hand, or what the meaning of the applicable law is for the present situation. Of such cases, many have to do with minor technicalities of property or contracts that hardly concern the general public at all. It is rare indeed that issues like the rights and responsibilities of employers and employees, of spouses, of racial segments of the population, or of professional man and client come up for redefinition. But when they do, they may represent a moral struggle of the greatest importance. Two solutions to a problem may be vying for that legitimation which will set the accepted pattern for many years to come. Dramatic instances are the cases on racial desegregation in education, mentioned earlier, decided by the U. S. Supreme Court. The interpretation of the Constitution that was accepted will have a profound influence in moving a society toward a new steady state in the area of race relations.

In cases of this kind the briefs of the opposing counsel are proposals in the problem-solving process. Each suggests the line of precedents or the line of interpretation of statute or Constitution which, in the view of one party, should serve as the basis of consensus. Although the judges choose the alternative which seems to them to meet the situation in terms of existing law most effectively, they are in fact clarifying the law. They pick out those strands that appear suitable to the situation presented, and say that those strands shall govern. Suitability is probably decided, consciously or unconsciously, in terms of the common values of the society. In short, judges are organs of societal problem-solving.

Since legislation is the quickest and surest way in which to obtain an official pronouncement when two groups take incompatible positions on a moral issue, the courts are called upon only when the legislative avenue seems unpromising to one of the parties. Usually it is those of little power who thus seek a new judicial interpretation. Before suffrage became universal in Western democracies, for instance, the propertyless classes had to hope that their changing needs would be met through reinterpretation of the law, since they could expect little from legislatures for whose members they did not vote. Even in the middle of the twentieth century, the Negroes of the United States despaired of obtaining legislation favorable to educational desegregation, and so turned to the courts.

Since nonmoral power has a greater chance to influence law than to influence the moral consensus on which law is supposedly based, differentials in power are more likely to be mirrored in the evolution of the law than in the broader evolution of the moral web. Thus the law will often remain rigid while a traditional aristocracy holds the reins of power tight during a time of change, but it may also swing far to the other side when a new class finally overcomes the old. The history of revolutions is replete with such sudden shifts. Similarly, a lower stratum may violently object when a higher stratum changes legal prerogatives in ways that run counter to the accepted moral order.

It is a fascinating problem to determine the optimum conditions for achieving public consensus—our third stage—after a court or legislature has spoken. One important factor is certainly the prestige of the court or the legislature. A large section of the public often has no strong leanings one way or the other. If its members feel that a well-qualified body has carefully considered the matter, they are likely to accept its findings as valid. The principal element in the body's prestige will be its past record for wisdom and impartiality.

Perhaps still more important is the practical success which the new legal standard achieves. This was clearly illustrated during the Great Depression in the United States. Many of the New Deal measures of President Roosevelt were bitterly opposed by conservative elements for a number of years after their enactment. But the opposition died down gradually as experience under the new measures proved them not only not disastrous, but even in many respects salutary. The opposite situation is illustrated by the U. S. experience with national prohibition. Adopted during World War I, it proved unenforceable soon after peace was re-established. Bootlegging spawned so much illicit organization and gave rise to so many underworld activities that the people concluded the cure was worse than the original disease. In this case public consensus for prohibition never developed.

An interesting aspect of the matter is the role that symbolic elements may play in the development of consensus. In his book about the reconciliation of the North and the South after the American Civil War, *Road to Reunion* (Chap. 5), Paul H. Buck lays great emphasis on the decorating of the graves of soldiers of both sides by Union and Confederate veterans on Memorial Day. He also mentions the opportunities for reconciliation that were afforded by the several centennial celebrations of the founding of the republic held between 1875 and 1881. Confederate veterans came to the ceremony at Bunker Hill, for instance. The culmination was the joint celebration at Gettysburg in 1888. It might be argued, however, that these symbolic events were more significant in recreating a national loyalty than in producing consensus on the abolition of slavery.

If our view of the relation between the public and the lawgiver in modern society is correct, it is true that customary standards do not always precede law nor does law always precede moral standards. The process of consensus has typically started when the issue gets into the legal forum. It is furthered there, but it is not completed until there has been acceptance by the public after reference back to the societal forum.

We have spoken thus far as if the only possible solution to a situation of incompatibility in the moral web were a substantive consensus that somehow compromised or transcended the opposing positions. Very occasionally incompatibility is eliminated by a consensus to tolerate differences which formerly were thought to be intolerable. It was thus that the Treaty of Westphalia, which ended the Thirty Years' War, declared that Protestantism and Catholicism, in whose name countless thousands had been killed, were to exist side by side in mutual toleration.

Finally, a word about the role of the intelligentsia in overcoming moral incompatibilities. The men of literature, science and the arts, whether within or without universities, are less tied to particular class viewpoints than the rest of the population. By their very work they are withdrawn somewhat from mundane matters and can take a more objective view of events. Though they are not usually men of power and hence can rarely dominate the public forum, they have access to many channels of communication. Since they are likely to be the keenest analysts of the problem, their influence is felt in the preliminary discussions. They will be both fertile in proposals and shrewd in evaluation. If judges or legislatures produce law that is not approved by the intelligentsia, they can make the achievement of public acceptance extremely unlikely. All this they can accomplish if they become neither effete nor hirelings. If they do, the society is robbed of an almost indispensable source of guidance.

CHAPTER 12

The Integration of Democratic Societies

We peoples of the Western democracies are living in a time of troubles. Our very existence is in the balance. No doubt all societies tend to underestimate the difficulties that beset the peoples of other times and other lands and to overstate their own. But surely our problems are unusually worrisome. Seen from today the period just before World War I was a golden era, an Indian summer before the winter of the years ensuing.

In a time of troubles a society needs to be strong. It needs to be united in purpose and intelligent in action. As little as possible of its energy should be consumed in the punishment and retraining of deviants or in exploring blind alleys in the processes of societal readjustment. Yet exactly such a waste of effort is characteristic of contemporary democratic societies. They constantly have to bring up the laggards, and their leaders are often confused about the line of march. Better organization is the crying need.

It is one thing to recommend better organization, but quite another thing to achieve it. Certainly progress toward it will be marked by the tentativeness and the fitfulness which characterize all such efforts. Perhaps this study has made some contributions to a more systematic approach. These could be contributions of delineation, of knowledge, and of application.

Before we can deal with the problems of the moral order we must see it clearly. One of our aims has been to throw the moral order into bold relief by giving names to its principal features, and breathing the life of social content into the concepts thus labeled. The ideas with which we have worked throughout—common values, moral norms, institutions, adherence, deviation, anticipatory rejection, problem-solving and the like—have presumably given the reader some feeling for the reality of the moral order and some ability to see it as a system. Until these elements of social life are thus raised by conceptualization above the level of the complicated matrix in which they have their being, their systematic relationships to one another are difficult to grasp.

Our essential aim is the development of a certain kind of selective perception. Once we have become sensitized to the moral elements in society, they obtrude from the context and beg for analysis. As we said before, it is as if one were wearing a pair of glasses that screen out all the light rays except those of a single color, so that one sees in a great heap of objects only those of this particular hue. Then one can study their pattern intensively.

Knowledge has been our principal object throughout. The intention has been to digest and analyze what social science has to say about the processes and problems of moral order. It is evident that what it has to say is by no means clear and decisive. The system of thought that has been developed in this study is a mixture of plausible assumptions, broad generalizations, and researchable hypotheses. It shares in the inconclusiveness of any little tested theory.

The very cornerstone of the structure—that a society has a set of common values that are influential in shaping its way of life—is not an easily demonstrable proposition. A great many learned men who have studied the histories of all kinds of societies believe it to be true, but at least one school of thought—the Marxist—denies it. To the dialectical materialist a set of common values is merely a resultant of processes generated by the relations of production, and has no independent causal significance. One cannot say flatly that the Marxist is wrong but there does seem to be a good deal of evidence that societies often modify and sometimes reject new elements of technology because these threaten to undermine the value system.

Another current viewpoint—this one well represented among social scientists in democratic societies—holds that the way of life of a society is chiefly shaped by its controllers, or men of power. These are potent figures not only in the economic world, as Marx asserted, but in the civil government, the highly organized professions, and the military. From the standpoint of this theory the co-ordination of society is merely a means to the narrow ends of its controllers. What we call the moral web would then be the system of rules which they approve for the society. It is apparent that the theoretical difference between this viewpoint and the one developed in this study springs from a radical disagreement over the force that resides in common values carried in culture and accepted by the common man. Our contention would be that most of the activities of the power holders are controlled by moral norms and institutions which were there before they came on the scene and in terms of which they have achieved their power. The notion that the co-ordination of society springs from them and not from the cumulative experience of the society itself seems to us fallacious.

Once granted the scientific significance of common values, there is little doubt that they tend to be objectified in what we have termed the moral web—in institutions, moral norms, and law. A few might question the usefulness of the concept of moral norms on the ground that in modern industrialized societies institutions and law pretty well cover the field. The rejoinder of most sociologists and almost all anthropologists is that the moral norms, so obviously basic to the way of life of nonliterate peoples, are equally present in civilized life but are less obvious since they are overlaid by a structure of law enforced by the state.

If we look at the other end of our spectrum of theory, the relation between the physical conditions of the society's life and its ecological web, we find impressive unanimity. No social science discipline doubts that physical environment conditions the life of a society and even limits its development in certain directions. The Eskimos, for instance, can hardly become agriculturists, nor the Mongolians seafarers. More than that, all students acknowledge that the cumulative efforts of a society to wring sustenance from its habitat produce a complex of technological skills and equipment which profoundly affect the social structure. We have subsumed these relationships under the term the ecological web.

It is our contention—and it is one to which many sociologists would give assent—that societies work out what we have called steady states which represent a mutual adjustment of the ecological web on the one hand and the moral web on the other.

In discussing the maintenance of a steady state, we have dealt only with the processes as seen from the normative side. The equally important questions of stability seen from the ecological side are left to those who specialize in this type of analysis.

It is elementary, but terribly important, that the common values of a democratic society need to *control* the life of the whole, to discipline effectively the strivings of the participants. The danger is not so much from idiosyncratic values, since they will not have much power behind them, as from like values that are well established in the culture. American striving for pecuniary success is a case in point. Novels like *What Makes Sammy Run?* make us acutely aware of how uncontrolled by any sense of responsibility this striving often is, and how baleful are the consequences. There can be no such thing as a steady state of society if such values are not subordinated to common ones, so that they find a place within the moral web instead of rending it.

Under modern conditions the transmission of the common values and moral norms of the society is not automatic. Many children grow up in areas into which societal institutions reach but feebly and where deviant subcultures have developed. Such areas represent one of the disintegrative results of the increased scope of functional co-ordination in modern life. The nucleation of social structure has left them morally uncovered—societally-oriented leadership has been withdrawn. This very characteristic makes difficult the reorientation of the deviant groups which flourish there. Little that is sound enough to build a reform program on can there be found. And again, it is unlikely that individual delinquents and criminals, returning to such areas after having been dealt with by the law, will be successfully rehabilitated. There are too many influences in the direction of their former associations and activities.

In addition to the ineffectiveness of institutions in blighted areas, the maintenance of a steady state is handicapped by the tendency toward formalism in institutional groups and the incursions of crude or nonmoral power. The dangers of red tape in large organizations are perennial; but never have there been so many bureaucracies. By the same token, never have there been so many opportunities for the selfish use of power. Modern societies wage a running battle against these twin evils. Among their chief weapons are professionalization and public monitoring. When these prove inadequate, as they sometimes do, then the old steady state may have to be forsaken and new institutional forms developed capable of resisting these blights.

Penal institutions are a special case. Like all institutions, they implement common values, but they are focussed on those individuals who have violated normative controls. Crime is so prevalent in modern democracies that the penal institutions must constantly try to deal with more inmates than they can handle. Hence the steady state maintained through them is precarious in the extreme. For this reason, new experiments in penology are constantly being made.

Though interesting theoretically, anticipatory rejection of culture traits because of their probable repercussions is not often practiced in modern democratic societies. They are so loosely structured and so slow to mobilize their public will that they can rarely ward off influences in advance. Rather, they wait until a trait is diffused into the society and has begun to have effects. If these are judged bad, the dynamic process of problem-solving takes over.

The transition from one steady state to another is possible by means of a moving equilibrium, but under contemporary conditions this is extremely rare. Differential rates of social change make for strain, and strain makes for conscious problem-solving.

Problem-solving in a large democratic society is a very complicated business. It proceeds successfully only when: detection is reasonably prompt and accurate; the channels of communication are open and effectively used; experts are available to help in the analysis; proposals or trials are judiciously framed and widely communicated; these proposals are discussed and evaluated by all kinds of people in many forums; competent leaders guide the processes of interaction that lead to consensus.

One of the most frequent occasions for problem-solving is the impact of technological change. Often the indirect results of a trait that has been invented or has been borrowed from another culture are not foreseen, and sometimes they reveal inadequacies in the existing moral web. Then the problem is detected and societal processes are generated which lead to changes in institutions or norms such that the common values are more effectively carried out under the new technological circumstances.

Another critical situation requiring the achievement of a new steady state is incompatibility within the moral web. This usually stems from changes in social structure that make social classes put unlike interpretations on common values. Because these cleavages develop slowly, vested interests are likely to be at stake in the ensuing struggle. Hence problems of incompatibility are lastingly settled only when the classes at odds have come to understand thoroughly each other's point of view. Then compromises may be worked out.

On all these matters we have tried to bring to bear the results of relevant research. As is by now obvious, these results are modest and are not related to one another in a systematic fashion. In considerable part we have had to fall back on broad sociological theories which are the fruit of scholarly minds playing over their own experiences and over data informally assembled by travelers, journalists, social workers, even novelists. Such broad theories serve as a context into which the findings of particular investigations have been fitted. They constitute plausible bridges across the chasms of our ignorance. They are the best structures for thought about the moral order we have, but they need to be shored up by more verifiable knowledge. Indeed, this study will have served a useful purpose if it does no more than call attention to the great need for further research on this important aspect of life.

With respect to knowledge of the moral order, there has been one striking omission throughout: we have made no mention of the embryonic world moral order. All we have written has had the national society as its focus. We have assumed that what needs to be ordered is the life of a society and that the moral web is the mechanism for doing it. Some might infer that the relations between societies are not moral in character, but are motivated by power, expediency or indifference. There are many students of world affairs who would agree with this, pointing to the almost incessant wars between national societies and the current tensions in many parts of the world. They would assert that there are no common values which can serve as a basis of international institutions and international moral norms. This view is, however, not a necessary inference from our theory of moral order. It is true that most orderliness derives from the control over men exercised by national societies, but this is not to say that some slight influence is not being exerted from more inclusive social systems. The whole trend of history has been toward larger and larger units of social organization. There are many signs today that the relations among national states are gradually taking on a systematic character.

These processes have not gone far enough, however, for us to have a body of knowledge about them. They need to be studied to discover in what respects regional and world moral orders will be similar to and in what respects different from societal moral orders. Since it is axiomatic that law cannot operate successfully without a basis in moral community, and since only international law can guarantee peace, it becomes of the utmost consequence to learn what forces are generating or could generate these broader moral webs.

If strong regional or world moral orders were in existence, another chapter would have to be added to this book. It would deal with the processes by which a society adjusts its moral web to the requirements of the intersocietal one which forms its context. Such adjustments may not be far off, regionally. But it is probable that, at the world level, they will for a long time to come be minimal. The nations will not feel much constrained by the inclusive intersocietal web. There will continue to be many points of difference among their sets of common values. Yet these sets cannot remain completely discrete if there is to be peace. A few common threads will have to be woven through the moral webs of various national societies. The United States and the Soviet Union will have to agree on at least one principle, that of "live and let live."

The third contribution this study has attempted is to point the way for those who wish to increase the moral integration of their society. It is not necessary for the social scientist to be a social engineer, but there is no reason why he should not indicate what means are appropriate for reaching the goals that a particular society is seeking. Indeed, if the experience of the natural sciences is an indication, social scientists will be called upon more and more as consultants to policy makers.

In the twentieth century, one goal of all democratic societies is to strengthen their moral foundations. This is why we have ventured to indicate how concerted efforts applied at strategic points might maintain existing steady states or speed the transition to new ones. Here so-called "theories of the middle range" tend to be applicable.

Merton has described them as "theories intermediate to the minor working hypotheses evolved in abundance during the day-to-day routines of research, and the all-inclusive speculations comprising a master conceptual scheme from which it is hoped to derive a very large number of empirically observed uniformities of social behavior." We have not been concerned much with the specific working hypotheses Merton refers to, but we have been concerned a good deal with a master conceptual scheme—what might be called normative societal theory. The broadest ranges of this theory describe processes beyond the power of short-term effort to change. We will therefore content ourselves now with applications of theory relating to the organization of groups and the like, matters which are susceptible to influence if energy is applied intelligently.

One of the factors that in our analysis stands out as of the greatest importance is social stability. We found that instability interferes with the acceptance of common values and moral norms, and that it is the soil in which deviant subcultures flourish. The blighted areas of large cities particularly illustrate this condition. Moreover, instability greatly handicaps the readjustment process because there is no sufficiently stable context within which moral consensus can develop.

Although the instabilities of Western societies are in part responses to deep, underlying conditions such as the free labor market, the shift from rural to urban life that has accompanied industrialization, and the spread of modern means of communication, they are not totally beyond our power to control. Unemployment insurance, for instance, reduces residential mobility in periods of depression. Low-cost housing projects with play space for children make life in the metropolitan areas more attractive to members of the working class. Imaginative city planning can give all residents a greater joy in their community and a greater desire to remain a part of it.

A second and closely related precondition of a high level of moral integration is more effective leadership in those neighborhoods that are now handicapped by the concentration of the better educated in distant areas. It would appear that the most promising course is to work through institutional groups that are now present in the handicapped areas. Often the personnel assigned to such groups by superior authority is not of the highest caliber. School superintendents may send the weaker teachers, and denominational officials the weaker ministers, because these constituencies are powerless to make embarrassing protests. It is probably true also that the more competent teachers and ministers find working in depressed areas unpleasant and use their bargaining power to obtain other assignments. A higher level of professional responsibility and pride, however, would in large measure overcome these tendencies. If denominations and school systems regarded the blighted areas of our cities as the greatest challenge to the ability of their professionals, and gave such assignments the highest remuneration, the positive forces would be greatly strengthened. One of the most crucial tasks for the professionals would be the discovery and cultivation of embryonic leadership within the areas themselves. This is what the Chicago Area Project has tried to do.

A third worth-while line of effort is to increase the monitoring of institutional groups. This is difficult, because the differentiation of social structure makes many members of the public indifferent to groups of which they are not members, and perhaps renders them incompetent to judge their performance. The twin dangers of formalism and the selfish use of power, however, can both be lessened if the public is vigilant and prompt to act when abuse is discovered. Monitoring can be stimulated by training in the schools, by adult education, and by the policy of newspapers. A determined group of leaders in any democratic society could open channels of information to the public and set an example of the sort of constant critical assessment that is necessary. The institutional patterns which have evolved as the solution of the society's problems could thus be kept more vital.

It is doubtful, however, that increased monitoring will prove equal to the job of obtaining adequate institutional performance. The tendency toward nucleation in social structure has gone so far, and the power at the top of bureaucracies is so great, that the temptation to use high position selfishly is both hard to resist and hard to counter. It is probable therefore that a fourth desideratum would be the professionalization of more and more types of administrative roles. The conduct of large-scale business is beginning to be regarded as a professional task. So, too, is the performance of high-level governmental services. Is it foolish to suppose that the administration of giant labor unions will also some day be so regarded?

A fifth point is highly relevant to efforts for the reform of deviants. It is the principle that moral rehabilitation requires strongly supportive group influences. We have seen that the deviant, both during his period of correctional treatment and after his release, needs to be brought within the orbit of groups that share the moral orientation of the society. To establish this type of relationship is largely a responsibility of those in a position to make arrangements for him—judges, correctional officials, parole officers, social workers, and members of his family. As social research accumulates more knowledge about just what kinds of groups will have the most salutary influence, these mentors can be given guidance in their own task of guidance.

Readjustment in the moral web would be greatly simplified if the drifting apart of social classes could somehow be halted before it has produced different interpretations of common values and adherence to different norms. This sixth desideratum is indeed hampered by many of the underlying factors in contemporary life. The tide of social differentiation in all its aspects is running in the opposite direction. The means with which to combat it seem to be the formation of organizations that deliberately cut class lines, and the pursuit of policies that minimize class differences. Many people seem to believe that the media of mass communication can maintain similar interpretations of common values in all classes, but there is little support in research findings for this belief. The divergences during the Great Depression, for instance, as to what American values meant, developed in spite of a remarkable network of communication.

One can be only a little more optimistic about the possibility of establishing organizations that cut class lines. The chief ones that do so now are those that are linked directly with military service—the armed forces themselves, veterans' organizations, and institutions of higher education to which the government sends veterans for training. All studies of social classes show that there is a tendency for the members of most other organizations to be drawn from one status level or at the most two levels. Churches in small towns, and large Catholic churches in cities, are perhaps the chief exceptions. Even these do little to cross *racial* lines. But there are other possibilities here. One is to use the power of the state to bring about cross-class mingling, not only in the military service but through a scheme of labor service, as was done in Hitler Germany. There is much to be said on other scores for a period in which youths of both sexes serve their society at a minimum remuneration; but it is a particularly appealing program when it is undertaken in the attempt to mix young people of different classes and different regions. They can thus get a more adequate conception of how their fellow nationals live, and might make lasting friendships with persons far removed from them in social status. A second possibility is to set up a much larger program of scholarships for higher education than any of the democracies have yet established. This would broaden the class base of these institutions and make for similarity of perspective. Certainly these two proposals are worthy of serious consideration if all other attempts to arrest the drifting apart of classes fail.

Easier perhaps is a program for the reduction of class differences. In the United States the graduated income tax has already had much effect. Although earned income differentials are perhaps as great as ever, income differentials after taxes are now much less. The extension of public services has also operated to make standards of living less divergent. Add to this the similarity of stimuli that reach all the population through the modern media of mass communication, and one must conclude that the cultural difference between classes is being reduced.

A closely allied point, seventh, is the necessity of maintaining open networks of communication for carrying on the problem-solving process. The sixth proposition had to do with the prevention of incompatibilities based on class; this seventh deals with their solution after they have developed.

Here the great need is for forums of discussion intimate enough for the participants to understand one another's positions thoroughly. This the media of mass communication rarely accomplish. There are always unstated assumptions lying behind a protagonist's position which are difficult to draw out unless his antagonists can confront him to elicit them. But once they are elicited, and provided there is good will all around, the participants can begin to understand each other's preferences better. Then the road is open to modifications or proposals in the light of other views, and to the gradual achievement of consensus.

It is easy to state the need for such forums of discussion; it is very difficult to create them. The town meeting is no longer feasible under modern urban conditions. Neighborhood gatherings will not do the job because each neighborhood has too narrow a range of social classes in it. Possibly high schools and community colleges could foster public discussions of live issues that would bring together people from all sections of the community. Or it may be that television can make a contribution by arranging panel programs on important topics with panelists being drawn from various classes, nationality groups, and the like. This scheme would have a much greater chance of success if the television programs could be shown at specially arranged meetings of neighborhood groups which would thereupon continue to discuss the topic of the day after the program concluded. Ingenious methods of combining the resources of the mass media with the values of face-to-face discussion might pay large dividends.

Eighth, modern democracies would be saved much societal problem-solving if their institutions had built-in mechanisms for adapting intelligently to social change. So far the state is almost the only one that has such mechanisms—legislatures, judicial interpretation by courts and administrative tribunals, and planning bodies. In other institutions these might take the form of organs for continuous planning and for the training of imaginative leaders. The institutional mold would then be something with dynamic as well as static characteristics. Groups expressing institutions would be constrained not only to carry on their regular societal duties but to handle problems of change in the interests of the whole society. Institutions would become increasingly self-steering. If they failed to perform satisfactorily, the monitoring check from the wider society would operate to secure their readjustment.

A large part of the responsibility for bringing dynamic emphasis into institutional structure will rest with the universities. They are the trainers of the professional men who tend to become institutional leaders and it is such men who will be most influential in the development of new patterns of organization.

The last two points underline the possibility of an effective process of moral readjustment for societies. Such a process would afford an answer to those who believe that moral integration is a necessarily rigid concept—that if a society tries to increase its moral integration it will at the same time be less able to adapt itself to new situations. This view stems from the premise that men are creatures of habit, that once they have found an answer to a problem they cling to it long after it has ceased to be satisfactory. There is certainly ground for this view if one thinks of the moral web solely in terms of norms. Norms can and do become habitual, and no doubt people become traditionalists about them. The older generation may not be sufficiently sensitive to new experiences to initiate processes of change, and young people may accept their parents' norms before they are mature enough to see the problem. Perhaps one safeguard against rigidity is to keep the number of societal norms to a minimum, and to replace them by subcultural norms wherever possible. This will make for variety and an experimental orientation.

Institutions offer far greater opportunity for a society's moral self-control. They can embody problem-solving machinery in their structures and they are actualized in groups in which leadership can make itself felt. Thus they will be sensitive to change and alert to deal with it intelligently. Courts and legislatures and planning bodies already make indispensable contributions. As more and more institutional groups come under the influence of professionally trained persons who feel responsibility for the society's welfare, new organs of orderly change can come into being. Churches, universities, occupational associations, great corporations—all can participate in finding for their problems answers that are morally acceptable.

The good society, then, would be one in which leaders are working through many kinds of institutional groups to achieve the adjustments in the moral web that are both suitable to the conditions and consonant with common values. Thus could a dynamic and democratic society maintain a high level of moral integration even in this twentieth century.

Notes

Chapter 1

The nature of social science laws is discussed ably by Alan Gewirth in "Can Man Change Laws of Social Science?" *Philosophy of Science*, 21 (July 1954), 229–41.

Though the moral order is not often discussed by social scientists, Robert Redfield makes discerning use of the concept in *The Primitive World and its Transformations* (Ithaca: Cornell University Press, 1953), pp. 20–21. Florian Znaniecki uses another term, the axionormative order, for the same concept in *Cultural Sciences* (Urbana: University of Illinois Press, 1952), Chap. 11. A part of the moral order, the normative aspects of culture, has been labeled the "ethos" by William Graham Sumner. See *Folkways* (New York: Ginn, 1906), p. 36.

The trends of research in group dynamics are well exemplified in Dorwin Cartwright and Alvin Zander, Eds., *Group Dynamics* (Evanston: Row Peterson, 1953). The classic discussion of the importance and functions of primary groups is that of Charles Horton Cooley in *Social Organization* (New York: Scribners, 1908), Chaps. 3, 4 and 5.

Though we do not know much about the moral order in the U.S.S.R., excellent social research has been done on other aspects of that society. See Barrington Moore, *Soviet Politics* (Cambridge: Harvard University Press, 1950); Alex Inkeles, *Public Opinion in Soviet Russia* (Cambridge: Harvard University Press, 1950); A. A. Rostow, *The Dynamics of Soviet Society* (New York: Norton, 1953).

The value-free use of the term moral integration has been orthodox among social scientists for half a century. It has been challenged in a recent lecture by Morris Ginsberg. He thinks we are not condemned to moral relativism as scientists but can demonstrate by means of rational criteria that some moral systems are superior to others. See "On the Diversity of Morals," *Journal of the Royal Anthropological Society of Great Britain and Ireland*, 83 (1953), 117–35.

The long quotation on modern social complexity is taken from my book, *The Integration of American Society* (New York: McGraw-Hill, 1941), pp. 13–14. In the present book as in that one I have used the phrase "American society," though I would prefer not to. It is unfortunate that there is no adjective for the noun United States. By using the term American as an adjective for my own society, I run the risk of offending Canadian and Latin-American neighbors. They can claim quite justly that they are Americans too. But the phrase "the society of the United States" is just too awkward.

Chapter 2

"Values" is used throughout rather than "valuations" because the latter has too rational a flavor. "Values" has the disadvantage, however, of being often considered by sociologists as external to the person, in contrast to attitudes which are inside the person. This is not the meaning intended here. Values are things in the act of being desired by someone. As for the rough equivalents of our term common values, Emile Durkheim defines the collective conscience on p. 46 of *On the Division of Labor in Society* (New York: Macmillan, 1933), and William McDougall discusses the collective will on p. 73 of *The Group Mind* (New York: Putnam, 1920). The essence of the notion is touched upon in other terms by Charles Horton Cooley on p. 209 of *Human Nature and the Social Order* (New York: Scribners, 1922), and by Leonard T. Hobhouse on p. 181 (note) in *Social Development* (London: Allen and Unwin, 1924). The quotation on p. 18 is from T. R. Batten "Social Values and Community Development," in *Approaches to Community Development*, Phillipps Ruopp, Ed., pp. 80–86. For a searching discussion of the whole theory of values, see Clyde Kluckhohn, "Values and Value-Orientations in the Theory of Action," in *Toward a General Theory of Action*, Talcott Parsons and Edward A. Shils, Eds. (Cambridge: Harvard University Press, 1951), pp. 388–433.

Some sociologists might even go so far as to question whether there are such phenomena as societal common values. Karl Mannheim's justly famous exposition of the social roots of knowledge, based as it is on a theory of interests, is concerned almost entirely with the common perspectives of the members of particular groups within societies, such as social classes. It is a fair inference that Mannheim would recognize that the societal end of winning freedom from a conquering power would produce a common perspective among all citizens, but it seems doubtful that he would admit the possibility that societal common values could be generated out of the mere experience of living together. Indeed, as my colleague Werner Landecker points out, Mannheim's theory is remarkably devoid of any emphasis on the consequences of communication between those in different social positions. See Karl Mannheim, *Ideology and Utopia* (New York: Harcourt Brace, 1936).

The list of American common values on p. 22 was developed after consulting the following: Robin E. Williams, *American Society* (New York: Knopf, 1951), Chap. 11; Clyde and Florence Kluckhohn, "American Culture: Generalized Orientations and Class Patterns," in *Conflicts of Power in Modern Culture*, Lyman Bryson, *et al.*, Eds. (New York: Harper, 1947), pp. 106–28; Cora Dubois, "The Dominant Value Profile of American Culture," *American Anthropologist*, 57 (December 1955), 1232–39; John R. Beery, *Current Conceptions of Democracy* (New York: Teachers College, Columbia University, 1942), Chap. 6; and John R. Gillin, "National and Regional Cultural Values in the United States," *Social Forces*, 32 (December 1955), 107–13.

The relation between common values and the looseness or tightness of social structure is dealt with by John F. Embree in "Thailand—a Loosely-Structured Social System," *American Anthropologist*, 52 (1950) 181–93, and by Bryce F.

Ryan and Murray A. Straus, "The Integration of Sinhalese Society," *Research Studies of the State College of Washington*, 22 (Dec. 1954), 179–227.

The allusions or quotations concerning the relation between religion and common values come from the following sources: Robert Redfield, *The Primitive World and its Transformations*, pp. 20–21 and 106; John P. Gillin, *The Ways of Men* (New York: Appleton-Century, 1948), p. 527; E. Adamson Hoebel, *The Law of Primitive Man* (Cambridge: Harvard University Press, 1954), p. 266; Edward Sapir, "Culture, Genuine and Spurious," *American Journal of Sociology*, 29 (Jan. 1924), 410; Max Weber, "Politics as a Vocation," *From Max Weber*, H. H. Gerth and C. W. Mills, Eds. (New York: Oxford University Press, 1946), p. 120; T. S. Eliot, "Notes toward a Definition of Culture," *New English Weekly*, (Jan.-Feb. 1943); and Emile Durkheim, *The Elementary Forms of Religious Life* (London: Allen and Unwin, 1926), pp. 375 and 427.

The quotations concerning the role of myth and legend in buttressing common values are from Ruth Benedict, article on Myth in *Encyclopedia of the Social Sciences*, 11 (New York, 1933), p. 180, and Charles Horton Cooley, *Social Process* (New York: Scribners, 1918), p. 116.

The exchange of views between Kenneth E. Boulding and Reinhold Niebuhr on ethical responsibility in modern society is in the former's book *The Organizational Revolution* (New York: Harper, 1953), pp. 228–54.

The classic statement on the subject of legitimate authority is that of Max Weber in *The Theory of Social and Economic Organization* (New York: Oxford University Press, 1947), pp. 324–41.

For a slightly different conceptualization of values and norms from that given, though on the whole a compatible one, see Ralph H. Turner, "Value-conflict in Social Disorganization," *Sociology and Social Research*, 38 (1954), 301–8. The close interdependence of moral norms and common values is emphasized by Macbeath who sees neither as more fundamental than the other: "Rather we find the grounds of the rightness of moral rules in a form of life which is also the realization of a system of ends; and we find the grounds of the goodness of good ends in the same form of life which also involves obedience to certain rules." See A. Macbeath, *Experiments in Living* (London: Macmillan, 1952), p. 33.

George E. G. Catlin points out that whether or not a moral norm exists depends not only on the percentage of the population that shares it but on their relative power. See *A Study of the Principles of Politics* (London: Allen and Unwin, 1930), p. 165. Two writers who have pointed out that the existence of a moral norm implies the necessity of such a standard are: Raymond Firth, *Elements of Social Organization* (London: Watts, 1951), Chap. 6, and Kingsley Davis, *Human Society* (New York: Doubleday Doran, 1945), Chap. 3. The analysis of the components of a norm on p. 36 derives from C. S. Ford, "Society, Culture and the Human Organism," *Journal of General Psychology*, 20 (1939), pp. 135–79.

A penetrating treatment of the relation between subcultures and common values is to be found in David Aberle, "Shared Values in Complex Societies," *American Sociological Review*, 15 (Aug. 1950), 495–502.

Although he uses different terminology, the great jurisprudential scholar, Eugen Ehrlich, is in essential agreement with our position on the relationship between moral norms and law. For him moral norms are termed the living law; what we call law, he calls law created by the state. See his *Fundamental Principles of the*

Sociology of Law (Cambridge: Harvard University Press, 1936). Although it is not directly related to the discussion of moral norms and law in civilized societies, E. Adamson Hoebel's *The Law of Primitive Man* is full of stimulating insights and imaginative interpretations.

Chapter 3

For the degree to which organism is an accurate model for the society, see: A. R. Radcliffe-Brown, "On the Concept of Function in Social Science," *American Anthropologist*, 37 (1935), 394–402; Karl W. Deutsch, "Mechanism, Organism and Society; Some Models in Natural and Social Science," *Philosophy of Science*, 18 (July 1951), 232–52; and Ludwig von Bertalanffy, "The Theory of Open Systems in Physics and Biology," *Science*, 111 (1950), 23–29. The source of the quotation on pp. 46–47 is Lewis Mumford, *Technics and Civilization* (New York: Harcourt Brace, 1934), p. 317.

The quotation from Clyde Kluckhohn on the bipolar character of social life on p. 53 is from "The Limitation of Adaptation and Adjustment as Concepts for Understanding Cultural Behavior," in *Adaptation*, John Romano, Ed. (Ithaca: Cornell University Press, 1949), pp. 112–13. Similarly, Jurgen Reusch and Gregory Bateson have set forth an interesting theoretical model in terms of circular causal chains which can take account of the effect of purpose and value in social life. See "Structure and Process in Social Relations," *Psychiatry*, 12 (May 1949), 105–42. This analysis sees man as a part of nature, and hence an animal who adjusts to conditions, but also capable of foresight and aspiration, and hence a being whose adjustment is in terms of qualities of life that he wants to realize.

It is to be noted that what the sociologists usually call the social structure includes most of what are here called the moral web and the ecological web. These are split in our analysis because we wish to mark off clearly those aspects of social structure that are suffused with normative orientation—particularly institutions—from the rest of the organization of society. For a systematic treatment of the ecological web, see Amos H. Hawley, *Human Ecology* (New York: Ronald, 1950).

The analysis of obstacles to moral integration on pp. 49–50 is drawn from my *The Moral Integration of American Cities*, Pt. 2 of the *American Journal of Sociology*, 57 (July 1951), pp. 16–18.

The Health Inventory project discussed on p. 52 is analyzed by Solon T. Kimball in "An Alabama Town Surveys its Health Needs," *Health, Culture And Community*, Benjamin D. Paul, Ed. (New York: Russell Sage Foundation, 1955) pp. 269–94. The quotation on p. 56 is from Evon Vogt and Thomas F. O'Dea, "A Comparative Study of Values in Social Action in Two Southwestern Communities," *American Sociological Review*, 18 (Dec. 1953), 545–54.

Chapter 4

For the moralization of children, I have drawn most heavily on: Jean Piaget, *The Moral Judgment of the Child* (Glencoe, Ill.: Free Press, 1948), Bernard Lander, *Toward an Understanding of Juvenile Delinquency* (New York: Columbia University, 1954), and Albert K. Cohen, *Delinquent Boys* (Glencoe, Ill.: Free Press, 1955). Duncan McRae, Jr., has supplemented Piaget's theory in a Harvard Ph.D. Dissertation (1950) entitled "The Development of Moral Judgment in Children." He shows that Piaget's change from an ethic of authority to an ethic of co-operation is probably comprised of two related shifts—that from emphasis on consequences to emphasis on intentions, and that from the notion of inevitability of strict punishment to the notion of the imposed character of a possibly flexible punishment.

The long quotation on pp. 63–64 about children's learning of moral standards is from Edward Cahn, *The Moral Decision: Right and Wrong in the Light of American Law* (Bloomington, Ind.: Indiana University Press, 1955), p. 23; the remarks by a municipal judge quoted on pp. 71 and 72 are from Elijah Adlow, "Teen Age Criminals," *Atlantic Monthly*, 196 (July 1955), 47–48; and the quotation on pp. 75–76 concerning delinquency in Chicago is from Southside Community Committee, *Bright Shadows in Bronzetown* (Chicago, 1949), pp. 26–28.

Interesting sidelights on the family in contemporary child rearing are furnished by: William F. Ogburn and Clark Tibbitts, "The Family and its Functions," in *Recent Social Trends in the United States* (New York: McGraw-Hill, 1933), I, 661–708; Hugh Hartshorne and Mark A. May, *Testing the Knowledge of Right and Wrong* (Chicago: Religious Education Association, 1927), p. 43; and James H. S. Bossard and Eleanor S. Boll, *Ritual in Family Living* (Philadelphia: University of Pennsylvania Press, 1950), Chap. 9.

The discussion about community factors on p. 67 draws on Svend Riemer "Villagers in Metropolis," *British Journal of Sociology*, 2 (March 1951), 31–43 and on my own *The Moral Integration of American Cities*, p. 125. The study on middle and lower class children referred to on p. 69 is reported by Rebecca Evans Carroll in *School Review*, 53 (January 1945), 30–38.

It is interesting to compare the analysis of factors in the moralization of children on pp. 76–77 with those discovered by Albert J. Reiss, Jr., in his extensive study of delinquency, reported in "Social Correlates of Psychological Types of Delinquency," *American Sociological Review*, 17 (1952), 710–18. He ordered his data in terms of three psychological types, and then proceeded to look for background factors associated with each. He found that those of the "defective super-ego" type have usually internalized a delinquent subculture carried by their peers. This is the situation that has become well recognized through studies of boys' gangs and is the one that is chiefly emphasized in Cohen's *Delinquent Boys*. Those classified as the "weak ego" type seem to come from conventional neighborhoods but their families tend to be highly mobile and often are marked by marital discord. The children are insecure and manifest hostility to the world. They do not, however, participate strongly in peer groups. The third type, which Reiss calls the "relatively integrated" delinquent, constitutes the great majority. These boys seem to have normal personal controls, and this is reflected in their much lower rate of recidivism. It is not easy to point to any one environmental factor that is deficient. The explanation for their delinquency seems to lie in a combination of several risk factors such as poor residential areas, morally marginal peer associates, and failure to continue schooling through high school. It is an interesting fact that experts are almost unanimous in testifying that mass communication suggestions will not influence a boy who is well adjusted in his primary group relations.

Ideas regarding the absorption of immigrants were drawn from the following sources: S. N. Eisenstadt, *The Absorption of Immigrants* (Glencoe, Ill.: Free Press, 1955); R. Gassain and M. Doré, "Facteurs comparés d'assimilation chez des russes and des arméniens," *Population*, 1 (1946), 99–116; William I. Thomas and Florian Znaniecki, *The Polish Peasant in Europe and America* (New York: Knopf, 1927), Pt. III, Chap. 3; William Lloyd Warner and Leo Srole, *The Social Systems of American Ethnic Groups* (New Haven: Yale University Press, 1945); and Mary Bosworth Truedley, "Formal Organization and the Americanization Process, with Special Reference to the Greeks in Boston," *American Sociological Review*, 14 (Feb. 1949), 44–53. The quotation regarding Spanish-Americans on p. 80 is from Florence Kluckhohn, "Dominant and Variant Culture Value Orientations," *Human Relations*, 1 (1947), 95. For the Molokans, mentioned on p. 80, see Pauline V. Young, *The Pilgrims of Russian Town* (Chicago: University of Chicago Press, 1932).

Robert K. Merton's essay referred to on p. 81 is "Social Structure and Anomie" and is to be found in his *Social Theory and Social Structure* (Glencoe, Ill.: Free Press, 1949) as Chap. 4. The Alfred N. Whitehead reference on professionalization is to his *Adventures of Ideas* (New York: Macmillan, 1933), pp. 71–79.

Chapter 5

It is surprising but true that there is no definitive work on institutions as pillars of the moral order. The references in this chapter are all to studies of special aspects of the subject. The quotation on p. 87 about the Catholic Church in the eleventh century is from the article, "Roman Catholic Church" by Rev. H. Harrington in the 14th edition of the *Encyclopaedia Britannica*. Selznick's doubts about the moral wisdom of "mass man" are expressed in "Institutional Vulnerability in Mass Society," *American Journal of Sociology*, 56 (Jan. 1951), 320–30. The Bales material on types of leadership is to be found in Talcott Parsons, Robert F. Bales and Edward A. Shils, *Working Papers in the Theory of Action* (Glencoe, Ill.: Free Press, 1953), Chap. 4. For Max Weber's point about professional secrecy, see *From Max Weber*, p. 233. Wolpert's discussion of Hitler's leadership is in "Toward a Sociology of Authority," *Studies in Leadership*, Alvin W. Gouldner, Ed. (New York: Harper, 1950), pp. 679–701.

Some of the ideas regarding the effects of disaster and the quotations on p. 103 are drawn from the *Disaster Research Newsletter* put out by the National Academy of Sciences–National Research Council. The cross-pressure between community responsibility and primary group concern is analyzed in Lewis M. Killian, "The Significance of Multiple-Group Membership in Disaster," *American Journal of Sociology*, 57 (Jan. 1952), 309–14. The influence of class membership on reaction to disaster is discussed in Leonard Schatzman and Anselm Strauss, "Social Class and Modes of Communication," *American Journal of Sociology*, 60 (Jan. 1955), 329–38.

Chapter 6

A leading theoretical idea in this chapter—differential association as a factor in deviant behavior—was presented by Edwin H. Sutherland in successive editions of his *Principles of Criminology* (New York, Lippincott). We have also drawn heavily on William F. Whyte's *Street Corner Society* (Chicago: University of Chicago Press, 1943). The quotations about gang boys on p. 107 are from Cohen's

Delinquent Boys. The idea that gangs will use settlement houses and Boys Clubs as "service stations" is brought out in Ethel Shanas, "Recreation and Delinquency," (Chicago Recreation Commission, 1942) and in Frederick Thrasher, "The Boys Club and Juvenile Delinquency," *American Journal of Sociology,* 42 (July 1936), 66–80. Thrasher's famous book, *The Gang* (Chicago: University of Chicago Press, 1927) is full of fascinating research findings.

The Festinger and Kelley study referred to on p. 109 is entitled *Changing Attitudes through Social Contacts* (Ann Arbor: University of Michigan, 1951). The St. Louis program referred to on p. 111 is discussed in Harold S. Keltner, "Crime Prevention Program of the Y.M.C.A., St. Louis," in *Preventing Crime,* Sheldon and Eleanor Glueck, Eds. (New York: McGraw-Hill, 1936). The quotation is from p. 464.

The two quotations concerning the Chicago Area Project are taken from *1953–1954 Data Book: A Program for the Prevention of Delinquency* (Chicago: Institute for Juvenile Research and the Chicago Area Project), pp. 2 and 25. I am indebted to Dr. Henry D. McKay of the Illinois Institute for Juvenile Research for information about the Chicago Area Project.

The long quotation about a crimeless society is from Donald R. Taft's *Criminology* (New York: Macmillan, 1942), p. 681. The Chapin study of dwellers in a new housing project is reported in "An Experiment in the Social Effects of Good Housing," *American Sociological Review,* 5 (Dec. 1940), 868–79. Research evidence on the results of racially desegregated housing is found in Morton Deutsch and May Evans Collins, *Interracial Housing* (Minneapolis: University of Minnesota Press, 1951).

Chapter 7

The chief theoretical works drawn on in this chapter are: Paul Fauconnet, *La responsabilité* (Paris: Alcan, 1920); Bronislaw Malinowski, *Crime and Custom in Savage Society* (New York: Harcourt Brace, 1932); and Edwin H. Sutherland, *White Collar Crime* (New York: Dryden Press, 1949). The outline of the development of criminal law on p. 118 is indebted to the article by George Kirchwey on Criminal Law in the *Encyclopedia of the Social Sciences,* 4 (New York: 1932), 570–71.

The notion that the lower middle class is the one most attached to moral order is supported by the following works: Svend Ranulf, *Moral Indignation and Middle Class Psychology* (Copenhagen: Levin and Murksgaard, 1938); John Dollard, "Drinking Mores of the Social Classes," *Alcohol, Science and Society* (New Haven: Yale University Press, 1943), pp. 95–104; and Martha C. Ericson, "Child Rearing and Social Status," *American Journal of Sociology,* 52 (Nov. 1946), 190–92.

For a pre-World War II discussion of the Borstal Institutions, see William Healy and Benedict S. Alper, *Criminal Youth and the Borstal System* (New York: Commonwealth Fund, 1941). Their status since World War II is briefly discussed in Cicely M. Crave, *Punishment and Reformation* (London: Oxford University Press, 1951). California developments are treated in John B. Ellingston, *Protecting our Children from Criminal Careers* (New York: Prentice-Hall, 1948) and Kenyon J. Scudder, *Prisoners are People* (Garden City: Doubleday, 1952). The study of the Michigan camp mentioned on p. 128 is reported in an unpublished University of Michigan doctoral dissertation: Oscar Grusky, "Treatment Goals and Organizational Behavior," 1957.

The various studies referred to by the investigators' names only are: Raymond Firth, "Authority and Public Opinion in Tikopia," in *Social Structure*, Meyer Fortes, Ed. (Oxford: Clarendon Press, 1949), pp. 168–88; Sheldon and Eleanor Glueck, *500 Criminal Careers* (New York: Knopf, 1939) and *Later Criminal Careers* (New York: Commonwealth Fund, 1937); Lloyd E. Ohlin, *Sociology and the Field of Corrections* (New York: Russell Sage Foundation, 1956); Clarence Schrag, "Leadership among Prison Inmates," *American Sociological Review*, 19 (Feb. 1954), 37–42; Joseph Abrahams and Lloyd McCorkle, "Group Psychotherapy of Military Offenders," *American Journal of Sociology*, (March 1946), 455–64; Marshall B. Clinard, "The Group Approach to Social Reintegration," *American Sociological Review*, 14 (April 1949), 257–62; and Donald R. Cressey, "Changing Criminals: the Application of the Theory of Differential Association," *American Journal of Sociology*, 61 (Sept. 1955), 116–20. Cressey's principle of retroflexive reformation has been known, my colleague Morris Janowitz thinks, to the Salvation Army for decades and to the Roman Catholic Church for centuries.

In addition to the punishments discussed in the text, fines may be imposed for criminal offenses. In order to make fines of equal significance to offenders of differing earning abilities, Sweden has introduced the idea of day-fines. The sentence of the court may specify, for instance, that the culprit must pay the equivalent of thirty days of his work as a fine.

Chapter 8

Although there are excellent works on acculturation, like H. G. Barnett's *Innovation: the Basis of Cultural Change* (New York: McGraw-Hill, 1953), there are no extended discussions of anticipatory rejection. We have used material on this subject from: Lauriston Sharp, "Steel Axes for Stone Age Australians," in *Human Problems in Technological Change*, E. H. Spicer, Ed. (New York: Russell Sage Foundation, 1952), pp. 69–90; E. F. Nadel, *Nupe Religion* (Glencoe, Ill.: Free Press, 1954); Ralph Linton, "Cultural and Personality Factors Affecting Economic Growth," in *The Progress of Underdeveloped Areas*, Bert F. Hoselitz, Ed. (Chicago: University of Chicago Press, 1952), pp. 73–88; Fred Cottrell, *Energy and Society* (New York: McGraw-Hill, 1955), p. 66; and John and Elaine Cumming, "Mental Health Education in a Canadian Community," in *Health, Culture, and Community*, Benjamin D. Paul, Ed. (New York: Russell Sage Foundation, 1955), pp. 43–69.

For the two sources on loosely and tightly structured societies, see Notes to Chap. 2.

Chapter 9

Although the work of many social scientists has contributed to the thought of this chapter, there is no heavy debt to anyone. With respect to the unwillingness of primitive societies to forsake a traditional steady state, I have drawn on: Ralph Pieris, "Ideological Momentum and Social Equilibrium," *American Journal of Sociology*, 57 (Jan. 1952), 339–46; W. H. R. Rivers, *Essays in Depopulation in Melanesia* (Cambridge: University Press, 1922); A. H. Pitt-Rivers, *The Clash of Cultures and the Contact of Races* (London: Routledge, 1927), Chap. 12. The Thomas and Znaniecki quotation at the beginning of the chapter is from *The Polish Peasant in Europe and America* (New York: Knopf, 1927), II, 1130. In addition to the Deutsch article mentioned in the notes to Chap. 3, W. Ross Ashby's *Design for a Brain* (New York: Wiley, 1952) is suggestive for a theory of problem-solving. The necessity for factual cohesion as a foundation for problem-working is well established for small groups. See Robert C. Angell, *The Family Encounters the Depression* (New York: Scribners, 1935), p. 26. Festinger has performed experiments that show that the less cohesion in a group the less it can develop modes of facing problems. See Leon Festinger, Stanley Schacter, and Kurt Back, *Social Pressures in Informal Groups*, (New York: Harper, 1950), p. 100. A different, but related idea is that factual cohesion may actually consist in a multiplicity of conflicts within a society which offset one another. A recent book, drawing heavily upon the social theory of Simmel, states the matter thus: "Loosely structured groups and open societies, by allowing conflicts, institute safeguards against the type of conflict which would endanger basic consensus and thereby minimize the danger of divergences touching core values. The interdependence of antagonistic groups and the crisscrossing within such societies of conflicts, which serve to 'sew the social system together' by cancelling each other out, thus prevent disintegration along one primary line of cleavage." See Lewis A. Coser, *The Functions of Social Conflict* (Glencoe, Ill.: Free Press, 1956), p. 80.

The question whether modern societies can learn anything about problem-solving from primitive ones is moot. For the negative view, see Carroll D. Clark "The Concept of the Public," *Southwestern Social Science Quarterly*, 13 (March 1933), 312–20. Dr. Clark believes that what we know as public opinion has been produced by the impersonality of the market, and that primitive groups would only have what he calls social opinion, which reinforces the mores but does not lead to normative reorientation. I take it he believes that the process of normative reorientation in primitive tribes would be solely one of a moving equilibrium.

One of the earliest formulations of a process-sequence in problem-solving is contained in Richard C. Fuller and Richard R. Myers, "The Natural History of a Social Problem," *American Sociological Review*, 6 (June 1941), 320–29. In his comment appended to this article James H. S. Bossard gives another series of historical stages. A more recent formulation is that of Nelson N. Foote and Clyde W. Hart in "Public Opinion and Collective Behavior," in *Group Relations at the Crossroads*, Muzafer Sherif and M. O. Wilson, Eds. (New York: Harper, 1953).

Bogardus' discussion of the reformer, mentioned on p. 158 is in *The Making of Public Opinion* (New York: Association Press, 1951) on p. 127. The traditionalism in institutions which reformers so often attack should be distinguished from formalism, discussed in Chap. 5. Traditionalism refers to a substantive maladjustment among the elements of moral order, whereas formalism refers to a procedural maladjustment. For a fascinating analysis of a reform movement, see Peter Odegard, *Pressure Politics: The Story of the Anti-Saloon League* (New York: Columbia University Press, 1926).

The discussion phases of the public opinion process are treated searchingly by Cooley in *Human Nature and the Social Order*, Chap. 9, and *Social Organization*, Chaps. 12 and 13. (Both of these books have been reprinted in a single volume by The Free Press under the title *The Two Major Works of Charles H. Cooley*.) The concept of opinion-leaders comes from Paul F. Lazarsfeld, Bernard Berelson and Hazel Gaudet, *The People's Choice* (New York: Columbia University Press, 1948), Chap. 16. The Wirth article referred to on p. 164 is "Consensus and Mass Communication," *American Sociological Review*, 13 (Feb. 1948), 1–15. For an analysis of the controversy over President Roosevelt's move to enlarge the Supreme Court, see Frank Cantwell, "Public Opinion and the Legislative Process," *American Political Science Review*, 55 (1946), 121–31. Selznick's fear of stereotyped thinking in the masses is voiced in "Institutional Vulnerability in Mass Society," *American Journal of Sociology*, 56 (Jan. 1951), 320–31. The Stouffer study which was cited on p. 165 is *Communism, Conformity and Civil Liberties* (New York: Doubleday, 1955). For an interesting discussion of the need for a vital democracy of so-called people's organizations see Saul D. Alinsky, *Reveille for Radicals* (Chicago: University of Chicago Press, 1946). The effect of the passage of law on public opinion is dealt with in Hadley Cantril, *Gauging Public Opinion* (Princeton: Princeton University Press, 1944) on p. 228. For a balanced discussion of the factors involved in such cases, see John P. Roche and Milton M. Gordon, "Can Morality be Legislated?" *New York Times Magazine*, May 22, 1955, pp. 10, 42–9.

Chapter 10

William F. Ogburn's theory of cultural lag is developed in his *Social Change* (2nd ed.; New York: Viking, 1950). The discussion of change in Tanala society is drawn from two chapters—"The Tanala of Madagascar," and "The Analysis of Tanala Culture"—by Ralph Linton in Abram Kardiner, *The Individual and his Society* (New York, Columbia University Press, 1944). For a systematic development of the thought that the ecological web has its own momentum and limits the directions of societal change, see Peter Murdock, *Social Structure* (New York: Macmillan, 1949). The example of social change among the Navajo on p. 173 was contributed by my colleague, David Aberle.

Joseph W. Eaton's "Controlled Acculturation: A Survival Technique of the Hutterites," *American Sociological Review*, 17 (June 1952), 331–39 is the source of the analysis on p. 177. The discussion of the selective use of the gun on the next page is from D. B. Stout, *San Blas Cuna Acculturation: An Introduction*, Viking Fund Publications in Anthropology, No. 9, (New York, 1947), p. 110. The story about the three little vitamins is from Robert Redfield, *The Folk Culture of Yucatan* (Chicago: University of Chicago, 1941), p. 144.

The planning process in the Tennessee Valley Authority is discussed by Philip Selznick in *TVA and the Grass Roots*, University of California Publications in Culture and Society, Vol. 3 (Berkeley and Los Angeles: University of California Press, 1949), pp. 37–41. The author does not believe that the plan worked well in practice. Others disagree sharply with his conclusion. The Fuller and Myers paper referred to on p. 187 is discussed in Notes to Chap. 9. The comparison of the attitudes of Latin-American and Anglo-Saxon law to slavery is derived from Frank Tannenbaum, *Slave and Citizen: The Negro in America* (New York: Knopf, 1947), p. 54.

For nativistic movements, see Raymond Firth, *Primitive Economics of the New Zealand Maori* (London: Routledge, 1929), Chap. 14; Ralph Linton, "Nativistic Movements," *American Anthropologist*, 45 (1943), 230–40; and W. E. H. Stanner, *The South Seas in Transition* (Sydney: Australian Publishing Company, 1953), Chap. 5. For a remarkable case of the adoption of Western technology with few serious repercussions, see Margaret Mead, *New Lives for Old* (New York: Morrow, 1956). The people of Manus (Admiralty Islands) seem to have become very dissatisfied with their old way of life before the American Navy descended upon them in World War II and hence were wide open to new suggestions. Something very similar seems to have happened to the ancient Hawaiians. See A. L. Kroeber, *Anthropology* (New York: Harcourt Brace, 1948), pp. 403–5.

Chapter 11

While many sociologists would agree that social system analysis has often been overly static, some would go further than I do and would claim a scientific criterion for preferring one set of common values to another in situations of conflict. See Morris Ginsberg (mentioned in Notes to Chap. 1); Robert Lynd, *Knowledge for What?* (Princeton: Princeton University Press, 1939); Gunnar Myrdal, *An American Dilemma* (New York: Harper, 1944), Appendix 2; and Wayne Hield, "The Study of Change in Social Science," *British Journal of Sociology*, 5 (March 1954), 1–11.

The interpretation on page 195 of what is happening in Southeast Asia is from Eric Hoffer, "The Awakening of Asia," *The Reporter*, 10 (June 22, 1954), 16–17. The accommodation process between immigrants and the host society has been studied by Eisenstadt. See his "Institutionalization of Immigrant Behavior," *Human Relations*, 5 (1952), 373–95. For the effects of isolation in allowing distinctive normative subcultures, see David Aberle's article cited in Notes to Chap. 2.

The discussion of the breakdown of a steady state and the development of social movements is greatly indebted to Herbert Blumer, "Collective Behavior," in *An Outline of the Principles of Sociology*, Robert E. Park, Ed. (New York: Barnes and Noble, 1939), pp. 221–80. Another important source, referred to on p. 205 is Rudolf Heberle, *Social Movements: An Introduction to Political Sociology* (New York: Appleton-Century-Crofts, 1952). Material on the Anti-Saloon League comes from Odegard's book cited in Notes to Chap. 9.

The research on a small town referred to on p. 210 is reported in A. Alexander Fanelli, "Extensiveness of Communication Contacts and Perceptions of Community," *American Sociological Review*, 21 (Aug. 1956), 439–45. Park's distinction with respect to knowledge and acquaintance is made in his "News as a Form of Knowledge," *American Journal of Sociology*, 45 (March 1940), 669–86.

For an interesting discussion of what a developed sociology of law would encompass, see Morris Ginsberg, "The Problems and Methods of Sociology," Chap. 19 in *The Study of Society*, Ed. by F. C. Bartlett, *et al.* (New York: Macmillan, 1939).

The importance of the intelligentsia in societal problem-solving is brought out by Karl Mannheim in *Ideology and Utopia*, pp. 136–46. Sociological students may wonder why there has not been discussion of the sociology of knowledge as developed by Mannheim in relation to the problem of overcoming incompatibility in the moral order. The reason is that the sort of dialectic process which he discusses involves a much longer time span and much broader issues than the problem-solving we have been discussing. Mannheim is mainly concerned with the differentiation of *knowledge* because of different social perspectives, knowledge which is relevant to all important societal issues. The achievement of a synthesis of perspectives in his sense is so difficult and long-term a process—if it is possible at all—that it is of little practical significance for the short-run transition to a new steady state. The consensus on specific moral incompatibilities that concerns us here is achieved in the face of the differing perspectives he posits because of the urgent practical need to find workable solutions and because of the under-lying acceptance by all of societal common values.

Chapter 12

The central position of the moral web in the integration of society would be disputed by many others besides Marxists. An interpretation in terms of power is forcefully if somewhat wildly expressed by C. Wright Mills in *The Power Elite* (New York: Oxford University Press, 1956).

I have discussed problems of the world moral order in the following: "Sociology and the World Crisis," *American Sociological Review*, 16 (Dec. 1951), 749–57; and "Discovering Paths to Peace," in International Sociological Association, *The Nature of Conflict* (Paris: UNESCO, 1957), 204–33.

The Merton quotation about theories of the middle range is from his *Social Theory and Social Structure* (Glencoe, Ill.: Free Press, 1949), p. 5.

Author's Note

The reader may be interested in knowing how this book came to be written. In the fall of 1951, having just published a monograph on *The Moral Integration of American Cities*, I took stock of matters in my field of interest—the sociology of the moral order—in order to decide what to do next. My conclusion was that further empirical research was less needed than the clarification of sociological theory. There were many studies by sociologists, anthropologists, and social psychologists that were pertinent to the development of theory in this field, and a number of scholars had made limited theoretical contributions, but no one had taken it as his task to digest and "codify" these materials. Until this was done, it seemed to me, empirical studies would be handicapped. I determined therefore to try my hand at the task. Now that I have made the attempt, I realize that my ambition was excessive. My solace is that Rome was not built in a day.

To an even greater degree than is usual with a study like this, I am indebted to colleagues for their stimulating suggestions and helpful criticisms. Dr. Werner S. Landecker has been most generous of his time. He and I discussed together almost every paragraph of every chapter, and many of them bear the imprint of his searching mind. Dr. Morris Janowitz, another colleague in the Sociology Department of the University of Michigan, gave the manuscript a careful reading. His comments were particularly valuable in making me appreciate more fully the relationship of my system of thought to other systems, and thus in helping me present it clearly. To those whom I have called on less demandingly I wish to express general thanks for assistance at particular points. For the use that I have made of my friends' ideas, however, I am of course wholly responsible.

During the summer of 1952 I had the privilege of participating in an Inter-University Summer Seminar on Social Integration sponsored by the Social Science Research Council. In addition to Dr. Landecker, the members of the group were Dr. Albert K. Cohen of Indiana University, Dr. Walter Firey of the University of Texas, Dr. William L. Kolb of Tulane University, and Dr. Albert J. Reiss, Jr., of Vanderbilt University. The vigorous intellectual interchange which took place that summer gave my young project the sort of shakedown it needed. For the pleasant hours together as well as for the analysis of theoretical questions, I am grateful.

R. C. A.

Index

Aberle, David, 235, 242, 243
Abrahams, Joseph, 240
Adherence, expedient, 44, 61, 81; genuine, 43–44, 61, 81
Adlow, Elijah, 237
Alinsky, Saul D., 242
Alper, Bernard S., 239
American society, 13–14, 20, 21–22, 24, 73–74, 81, 113–16, 135–36, 181–82, 187, 188
Analysis (of a social problem), 159–60, 183–85, 208–9
Angell, Robert C., 13–14, 29, 49–50, 67, 87, 233, 236, 237, 241, 244
Anomie, 74, 105
Ashby, W. Ross, 241
Atomic bomb, 184
Atomic energy, 188–89

Back, Kurt, 241
Bales, Robert F., 93, 168, 238
Baltimore, delinquency in, 66
Barnett, H. G., 188, 240
Bateson, Gregory, 236
Batten, T. R., 18, 234
Beery, John R., 234
Benedict, Ruth, 23, 27, 235
Bentham, Jeremy, 69, 119, 213–14
Berelson, Bernard, 242
Berle, Adolf, 135
Bertalanffy, Ludwig von, 48, 236
Blumer, Herbert, 203–5
Bogardus, Emory S., 158, 241
Boll, Eleanor S., 237

Borstal institutions, 127–28, 131, 213
Bossard, James H. S., 237, 241
Boulding, Kenneth E., 29, 235
Boys Clubs, 109–10
Brinton, Crane, 200
British society, 42, 65, 179, 185, 213–14
Bryan, William Jennings, 194
Buck, Paul H., 218
Bureaucracy, 91, 96, 97

Cahn, Edward, 63, 327
California penal system, 128–30
Cantril, Hadley, 167, 242
Cantwell, Frank, 242
Caroll, Rebecca Evans, 237
Carr, Lowell J., 74–75
Cartwright, Dorwin, 233
Caste system of India, 200
Catholic church, 87, 146, 212, 229
Catlin, George E. G., 235
Change, ecological, 101–4. *See also* Social change; and Technological change.
Chapin, F. Stuart, 114, 239
Character-building groups, 109, 122–24
Chicago Area Project, 111–14, 116, 228
Child guidance clinics, 123
Christianity, 193
Churches, 76, 109, 212, 229
Churchill, Winston, 97
Civil liberties, 37, 43, 147
Clark, Carroll D., 241

Clinard, Marshall, 131, 240
Cohen, Albert K., 66, 68–69, 106–7, 236, 237, 238
Collective bargaining, 201, 214, 215
Collins, May Evans, 239
Common ends, 18
Common values, societal, 8, 16–26, 53–57, 121, 221–22
Communication, 158–59, 183, 188, 210–13, 216, 230–31. See also Mass communication.
Communism, 146
Community councils, 214–15
Compulsory military service, 212, 229–30
Comte, Auguste, 88
Concepts, scientific, 6–9
Conditions, habitat, 16–17, 53–57, 222; changes in, 171–91
Conduct norms, 36–37
Conscience, collective, 20, 122; personal, 29, 36, 40, 43, 61, 63, 210–11
Consensus, 18–19, 24, 36, 40, 148, 163–70, 189–90, 212–19
Cooley, Charles Horton, 10, 20, 21, 22, 28, 91, 92, 151, 155, 164–65, 233, 234, 235, 241
Coser, Lewis A., 241
Cottrell, Fred, 144, 240
Courts, 215–18, 232
Crave, Cicely M., 239
Cressey, Donald R., 132, 240
Crime, 113–14, 117–18, 125, 224; white-collar crime, 133–35
Criminal law, 118
Crisis, moral, 3–5
Cultural lag, 176–77
Cumming, John and Elaine, 240

Darrow, Clarence, 194
Davis, Kingsley, 235
De Jouvenel, Bertrand, 42
Delinquency, juvenile, 66–67, 105–16, 123
Democracy. See Societies, democratic
Depression, economic, 24, 159, 182, 201, 208, 217–18, 229
Desegregation, racial, in schools, 24, 148, 161, 167, 196, 216

Detection (of a problem), 156–58, 182–83, 203
Deterrence, 82, 123, 124
Deutsch, Karl W., 236
Deutsch, Morton, 239
Deviant groups, 39, 74–76; reorienting of, 105–16, 125
Deviation, from moral norms, 8, 17, 43–44, 120
Dicey, Edward, 202, 213
Differentiated areas of residence, 59–60
Diffusion, cultural, 175 ff.
Disaster, 102–4
Disaster Research News Letter, 238
Discovery, 175 ff.
Disloyalty, to institutions, 8, 17
Disorganization, 4, 92, 125, 151
Dollard, John, 239
Doré, M., 237
Dubois, Cora, 234
Durkheim, Émile, 20, 26, 30, 65, 67, 234, 235

Eaton, Joseph W., 177, 242
Ecological interdependence, 154
Ecological web, 17, 55–57, 175, 181, 184, 222
Economic organizations, 98, 110
Education of Henry Adams, The, 73
Egyptian society, 144, 188
Ehrlich, Eugen, 235
Eisenstadt, S. N., 77, 78, 237, 243
Eliot, T. S., 26, 235
Elites, 82–83, 90–91, 143–48. See also Leadership
Ellingston, John B., 239
Embree, John F., 140, 234
Employment of ex-convicts, 132–33
Ericson, Martha C., 239
Ethic of responsibility, 23, 142–43, 162
Ethic of ultimate ends, 23, 142, 162
Evaluation, of proposals and essays, 161–63, 186–89

Family, 69–75, 90, 95, 97, 101
Fanelli, A. Alexander, 243
Fauconnet, Paul, 117–18, 239
Feedback. See monitoring
Festinger, Leon, 109, 239–41
Feudal system, 199

Firth, Raymond, 121, 235, 240, 242
Folklore, 27–28
Foote, Nelson N., 241
Ford, C. S., 36, 235
Formalism, 91–95, 153
Frankel, S. Herbert, 177
Free will, 5–6
French society, 146
Fromm, Erich, 54
Fuller, Richard C., 187, 241, 242
Functional co-ordination, 58–60, 166

Gangs, boys'. *See* Deviant groups
Gassain, R., 237
Gaudet, Hazel, 242
German society, 14, 37, 145, 200–201, 231
Gewirth, Alan, 233
Gillin, John R., 24, 234, 235
Ginsberg, Morris, 233, 243
Glueck, Sheldon and Eleanor, 127, 240
Greek-Americans, 79–80
Grodzins, Morton, 65
Group dynamics, 9, 55
Grusky, Oscar, 240

Halifax, disaster at, 102–3
Harrington, H., 238
Hart, Clyde, 241
Hartshorne, Hugh, 237
Hawaiians, 195, 243
Hawley, Amos H., 236
Healy, William, 239
Heberle, Rudolf, 205, 243
Heroic figures, 28
Heterogeneity, of population, 49–50, 101
Hield, Wayne, 243
Hitler, Adolf, 97, 101, 164–65
Hobbes, Thomas, 47
Hobhouse, Leonard T., 20, 234
Hoebel, E. Adamson, 24, 122, 235, 236
Hoffer, Eric, 243
Homans, George, 48, 67

Ideals, 34–35
Immigrants, 56, 62, 77–80, 196–98
Inadequacy, in the moral order, 8, 44, 157–58, 171–91, 224
Incompatibility, in the moral order, 8, 141–46, 179, 191–219, 225

Industrial revolution, 68, 200, 202
Industrial Workers of the World, 206–7
Inkeles, Alex, 233
Instability, social, 66–68, 227
Institutions, 8, 16–17, 29–33, 43, 74, 81, 85–104, 106, 125, 165, 223, 231–32
Integration, interpersonal, 9, 93. *See also* Moral integration
Intelligentsia, 163, 219
Internalization, of common values and moral norms, 31, 61–84, 125, 223
Invention, 175 ff.

Janowitz, Morris, 240
Japanese society, 175
Jefferson, Thomas, 28, 99, 207

Kaplan, Abraham, 39
Kardiner, Abram, 23
Kelley, Harold H., 109, 239
Keltner, Harold S., 239
Keynes, John M., 186
Killian, Lewis M., 238
Kimball, Solon T., 52, 236
Kinsey reports, 34
Kirchwey, George, 239
Kluckhohn, Clyde, 53, 234, 236
Kluckhohn, Florence, 80, 234, 238
Kroeber, A. L., 195, 243

Landecker, Werner, 78, 234
Lander, Bernard, 66–68, 73, 236
Lasswell, Harold, 39
Law, 16–17, 29–30, 40–43, 45, 100, 121–22, 160–61, 167–68, 189–90, 216–18
Lazarsfeld, Paul F., 242
Leadership, 93–94, 101, 162–63, 164–70, 187, 205, 227, 231. *See also* Elites; and Legitimate authority
Legislatures, 215–18, 232
Legitimate authority, 32–33, 96–99
Lewin, Kurt, 55
Like values, 18–19, 81, 223
Lincoln, Abraham, 28
Linton, Ralph, 140, 141, 240, 242
Lippmann, Walter, 163
Literature, 213
Llewellyn, Karl, 122

Loeb, Edwin M., 144
Long, Huey, 99
Lowell, A. Lawrence, 210
Lynd, Helen M., 206
Lynd, Robert S., 206, 243

Macbeath, A., 235
"McCarthyism," 119, 147, 165
McCorkle, Lloyd, 240
McDougall, William, 20, 234
MacIver, Robert M., 18
McKay, Henry D., 239
McRae, Duncan, Jr., 236
Madison, James, 186
Malinowski, Bronislaw, 122, 239
Mannheim, Karl, 23, 234, 243–44
Manus society, 243
Marx, Karl, 54
Marxism, 26, 55, 172, 200, 208, 221
Masaryk, Thomas G., 56
Mass communication, 95, 211, 215, 229
Masses, 90–91, 143–48, 164–66
May, Mark A., 237
Mead, Margaret, 243
Merton, Robert K., 81, 227, 238, 244
Mills, C. Wright, 243
Mobility, horizontal, 50, 101; vertical, 209
Modal behavior, 34
Molokans, 80
Monitoring, 90, 93–94, 224, 228
Moore, Barrington, 233
Moral action, 14
Moral integration, 8–9, 12, 14-15, 45, 65–66, 226, 232
Moralization. See Internalization of common values and moral norms
Moral norms, 8, 16–17, 29, 33–44
Moral order, 8–12, 15, 16–45, 220–21
Moral web, 16–17, 29–43, 46–60, 118–19, 185, 222
Mores. See moral norms
Morley, John, 42
Moving equilibrium, 151–53, 173, 174, 224
Mumford, Lewis, 46, 115, 236
Murdock, Peter, 242
Myers, Richard R., 187, 241, 242
Myrdal, Gunnar, 168, 243

Myth, 27–28

Nadel, E. F., 140, 240
Nativistic movements, 190–91
Navajo Indians, 173–74
Neighborhood, 68–69, 72–73, 74, 90, 97, 110, 227, 231
New Deal, The, 164, 165, 182, 217–18
Niebuhr, Reinhold, 29, 235
Nisbet, Robert A., 88
Norms, moral. See Moral norms; Conduct norms; and Situation norms
Nucleation of social structure, 59–60, 134, 166

O'Dea, Thomas F., 56, 236
Odegard, Peter, 241, 243
Ogburn, William F., 176–77, 237, 242
Ohlin, Lloyd E., 130, 240
Order. See Moral order; and Political order
Ortega y Gasset, J., 26, 91

Park, Robert E., 211, 243
Parole, of prisoners, 133
Parsons, Talcott, 238
Patterned evasion, 167–68
Philosophers, 213–14
Piaget, Jean, 64, 74, 236, 237
Pieris, Ralph, 150, 240
Pilgrims, 54
Pitt-Rivers, A. H., 150, 240
Polak, Frederick L., 162
Police, 125
Polish society, 198
Political institutions, 96, 97, 100–101, 110
Political order, 16
Political parties, 205
Population change, 174–75
Power, crude or nonmoral, 42–43, 44–45, 59–60, 96–102, 167, 217
Pressure groups, 205
Primary groups, 10, 22, 83, 102, 166
Prince, Samuel H., 102
Prisons, 128–32, 224
Probation, 126
Problem-solving, societal, 151, 154–70, 224, 230–32
Professionalization, 31–32, 82–84, 135, 223–24

Professional men, 89, 93, 95, 153, 160, 228, 231
Prohibition, 205, 218
Proposal (or essay), in problem-solving, 58, 160–61, 185–86
Psychotherapy, 131
Punishment, 117–32

Radcliffe-Brown, A. R., 47, 236
Ranulf, Svend, 239
Readjustment, of the moral web, 51–. 58, 149–70, 230–32
Redfield, Robert, 24, 25, 179, 233, 235, 242
Reformation (of deviants), 123, 125–33, 135–36, 229
Reformatories, 126–27, 129
Reiss, Albert J., Jr., 237
Rejection, anticipatory (of culture traits), 51, 139–48, 224
Religion, 14, 82
Reusch, Jurgen, 236
Revolution, 200
Riemer, Svend, 67, 237
Riesman, David, 67, 174–75
Ritual, 26–27
Rivers, W. H. R., 150, 240
Roche, John P., 242
Roosevelt, Franklin D., 97, 165, 184, 217, 242
Rostow, A. A., 33
Rural-urban differences, 190, 201, 207–8
Russell, Bertrand, 28
Ryan, Bruce F., 140, 234–35

St. Louis, reorientation of delinquents in, 111
Sanctions, 35–36, 38–39, 81, 101. *See also* Punishment
Sapir, Edward, 25, 235
Schacter, Stanley, 241
Schatzman, Leonard, 238
Schools, 76, 91, 102, 212. *See also* Desegregation
Schrag, Clarence, 130, 240
Scudder, Kenyon J., 239
Selznick, Philip, 90, 147, 165, 238, 242
Shanas, Ethel, 239
Sharp, Lauriston, 139, 143–44, 240

Shils, Edward A., 238
Simmel, Georg, 241
Situation norms, 37–38
Social change, 12. *See also* Change, ecological; Technological change; and Readjustment
Social classes, 40, 59–60, 68–69, 103, 106–7, 119, 135, 157, 186, 187, 199–219, 229–31
Social movements, 204–6
Social planning, 32, 52, 169–70, 232
Social sciences, 5, 46, 186–87, 222, 226
Social settlements, 77, 110
Societies, democratic, 11–13, 45, 47, 147, 220, 226; loosely and tightly structured, 21, 140–41, 152, 168, 176; totalitarian and authoritarian, 11, 146–47, 158–59
Society as a system, 46–48
Sociologists, 6, 14, 193–94, 222–23, 243
Sorokin, Pitirim, 53
South Asian societies, 195
Southside Community Committee, 237
Spanish-Americans, 80
Spengler, Oswald, 23
Srole, Leo, 79, 238
Stanner, W. E., 243
Steady state, 48–51, 87–89, 102, 115–16, 120, 135–36, 137–38, 149–50, 202, 222–23
Steinbeck, John, 213
Stouffer, Samuel A., 165, 242
Stout, D. B., 178, 242
Strain for consistency (in culture), 61, 151–52
Straus, Murray A., 140, 235
Strauss, Anselm, 238
Structural drift, 151–52
Subcultures, 38, 58, 68–69, 74, 82, 86, 103, 107, 187, 198, 232
Sumner, William Graham, 23, 62, 151, 233
Sutherland, Edwin H., 105, 133–34, 238, 239

Taft, Donald R., 113, 239
Tanala society, 54, 181–82
Tannenbaum, Frank, 242

[